Collins

Key Stage 3
Science

Student Book 3

Series editor: Ed Walsh
Authors: Tracey Baxter
Sunetra Berry
Pat Dower
Ken Gadd
Anne Pilling

William Collins' dream of knowledge for all began with the publication of his first book in 1819. A self-educated mill worker, he not only enriched millions of lives, but also founded a flourishing publishing house. Today, staying true to this spirit, Collins books are packed with inspiration, innovation and practical expertise. They place you at the centre of a world of possibility and give you exactly what you need to explore it.

Collins. Freedom to teach.

Published by Collins
An imprint of HarperCollins*Publishers*
77 – 85 Fulham Palace Road
Hammersmith
London
W6 8JB

Browse the complete Collins catalogue at www.collins.co.uk

10 9 8 7 6 5 4 3

ISBN 978-0-00-754023-5

Tracey Baxter, Sunetra Berry, Pat Dower, Ken Gadd and Anne Pilling assert their moral rights to be identified as the authors of this work.

British Library Cataloguing in Publication Data
A Catalogue record for this publication is available from the British Library

Commissioned by Letitia Luff
Project managed by Jane Roth
Series editor Ed Walsh
Managing editor Caroline Green
Project editor Amanda Redstone
Editorial assistant Lucy Roth
Edited by Phillipa Allum, Elizabeth Barker, Hugh Hillyard-Parker, John Ormiston, Kate Redmond, Ros Woodward
Proofread by Tony Clappison
Illustrations by Ken Vail Graphic Design
Typesetting by Ken Vail Graphic Design
Cover design by Angela English
Cover photograph by Riyazi/Shutterstock
Picture research by Amanda Redstone and Hayley Shortt
Production by Rachel Weaver
Printed in Italy by Grafica Veneta S.p.A.

Contents

How to use this book

These tell you what you will be learning about in the lesson.

This introduces the topic and puts the science into an interesting context.

Each topic is divided into three parts. You will probably find the section with the blue heading easiest, and the section with the purple heading the most challenging.

Try these questions to check your understanding of each section.

Chemistry

Exploring ceramics and their properties

We are learning how to:
- Describe what is meant by the term ceramic.
- Describe the properties of ceramics.

We think of a 'ceramic' as clay or pottery. This group of materials has greatly changed over the centuries, with the development of a wide set of very useful properties.

What is a ceramic?

Archaeologists have uncovered human-made **ceramics** dating back to 24000 BCE. Animal and human figurines were made from animal fat, bones, bone ash and fine clay and fired in a kiln. Ceramic pottery vessels have been used since 9000 BCE to store grain and other foods. In 4000 BCE, glass was first discovered and in 1600 BCE the first porcelain ('china') was made in China.

A ceramic is an inorganic (not carbon-based), non-metallic solid. It is prepared by the action of heat followed by cooling. Ceramics are used for making tiles, glass, bricks, plates and vases and ornamental objects.

1. List three items made from ceramics in your home.
2. Ceramic materials have been uncovered since earliest human history. What does this tell you about the nature of ceramics?

General properties of ceramics

Ceramics are very useful because of their properties. Most are:

- hard and resistant to wear
- relatively light
- brittle – they can break easily if a force is applied
- thermal insulators – they keep heat in
- electrical insulators – they do not allow electric current to pass through
- non-magnetic
- chemically stable – they do not break down in air
- non-toxic – they can be used for food and drink
- non-ductile – they cannot be drawn out into wire.

FIGURE 3.3.12a: A Bronze Age ceramic pot

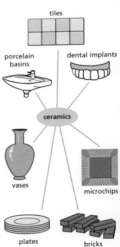

FIGURE 3.3.12b: Some of the uses of ceramics

3. Draw a table to compare the properties of ceramics with metals.

4. Suggest why ceramics may be used for some purposes instead of metals.

The chemistry of ceramics >>>

Clay, sand and other natural materials were important ingredients in early ceramics. Nowadays, advanced ceramics are based on oxides like aluminium oxide – nitrides, silicides and carbides, for example boron carbide (B_4C), are also used. Hardly any natural materials are used now. The ingredients are carefully manufactured to produce exact properties.

There are two main types of ceramic, although with modern materials the classification is less simple:

- **crystalline** – usually made from one or more varieties of a metal oxide
- **amorphous** (which means without shape) – glass based ceramics come into this category.

The atoms are bonded in a regular 3D pattern. Powdered raw materials are used, and additives and water added to form specific shapes. The mixture is then heated to a high temperature, which expels water and causes the particles to take up a permanent regular structure.

When molten glass mixtures are thrust in very cold conditions quickly, they cannot form a regular structure and as a result they can be 'blown' or moulded into very specific shapes. Once they are cooled they form permanent irregular structures.

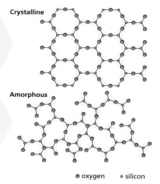

Crystalline

Amorphous

● oxygen   ○ silicon

FIGURE 3.3.12c: Some ceramic materials, like silicon dioxide (SiO_2), can exist in either amorphous or crystalline form.

5. Summarise the key differences between crystalline ceramics and amorphous ceramics.

6. Why are ingredients that are taken directly from nature no longer used in making ceramics?

Did you know...?

The world's most expensive 18th century Chinese vase sold for £53 million in 2010.

FIGURE 3.3.12d: The world's most expensive Chinese vase

Key vocabulary

ceramic

crystalline

amorphous

Each topic has some fascinating extra facts.

These are the most important new science words in the topic. You can check their meanings in the Glossary at the end of the book.

Key this phrase into an internet search box to find out more.

The first page of a chapter has links to ideas you have met before, which you can now build on.

This page gives a summary of the exciting new ideas you will be learning about in the chapter.

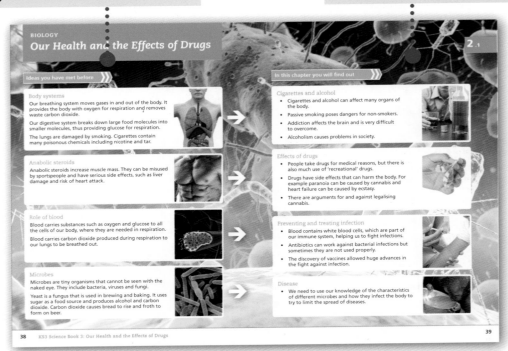

When you are about halfway through a chapter, these pages give you the chance to find out about a real-life application of the science you have been learning about.

The tasks – which get a bit more difficult as you go through – challenge you to apply your science skills and knowledge to the new context.

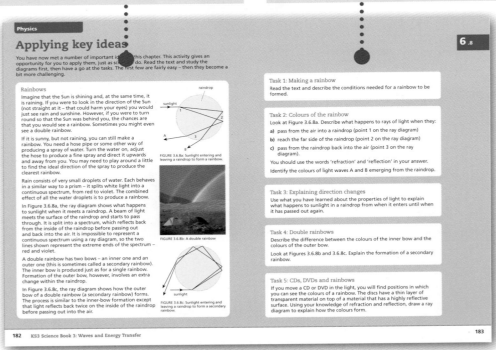

These lists at the end of a chapter act as a checklist of the key ideas of the chapter. In each row, the blue box gives the ideas or skills that you should master first. Then you can aim to master the ideas and skills in the orange box. Once you have achieved those you can move on to those in the purple box.

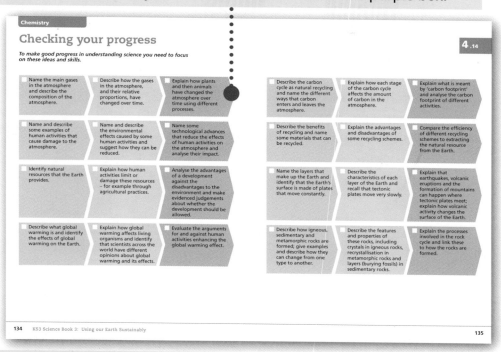

These end-of-chapter questions allow you and your teacher to check that you have understood the ideas in the chapter, can apply these to new situations, and can explain new science using the skills and knowledge you have gained.

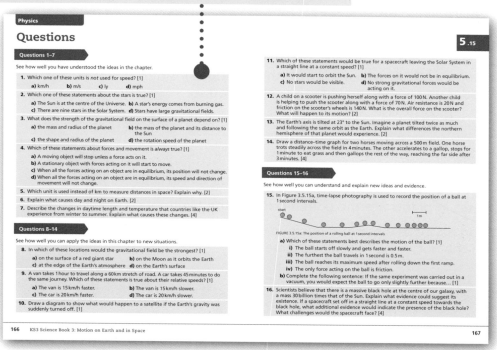

BIOLOGY
Variation for Survival

Variation and classification

Living things are classified into broad groups according to observable characteristics, similarities and differences.

Adaptations

Animals and plants are adapted to the conditions of the habitats in which they live. An adaptation is a way an animal's body helps it survive in its environment – for example meerkats have dark circles around their eyes, which act like sunglasses, helping them see even when the Sun is shining very brightly.

Cells

Cells are the building blocks of life. They contain structures called organelles, which all have specific jobs.

Every cell, except red blood cells, contains a nucleus. The nucleus contains DNA, which controls the reactions inside the cell and is involved in making the cell reproduce.

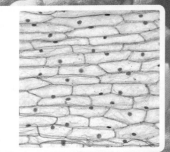

Reproduction

The gametes in animals are the egg cell and the sperm cell.

The gametes in plants are the pollen cell and the ovule.

Fertilisation happens when the nucleus of a male gamete fuses with the nucleus of a female gamete.

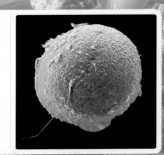

Variation and classification

- Variation within a species can be measured.
- Humans value some variations in plants and animals more than others. Organisms with desirable features are used to breed the next generation to replicate these features.
- There is a common method for naming organisms.
- Carl Linnaeus was a pioneer in the field of classification.

Survival of the fittest

- Variation between organisms ensures that some organisms survive.
- Variation between animals causes competition.
- Organisms that have too little variation may die out.

Inside the nucleus

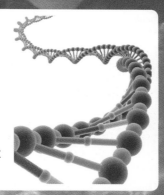

- DNA has a very complex structure. Understanding the structure of DNA allows us to understand how it determines our features.
- Chromosomes and genes are portions of DNA that carry inherited information.
- Wilkins, Franklin, Watson and Crick played important roles in discovering the structure of DNA.

Inheritance

- Chromosomes from each parent are passed on during reproduction.
- The features that you have are determined by the form of the genes you inherited from your parents.
- Some genes can mask the effects of others.
- A small change in a chromosome can cause a genetic defect.

Exploring differences

We are learning how to:

- Identify the differences between different species.
- Explain the importance of diversity.

Our knowledge of the diversity of life is greater now than it has been at any other time in the Earth's history. Some 1.7 million species have been named and classified by scientists. Why do we have such a variety of life? How are species different from each other?

Variety of life

A **species** is a group of organisms with similar features that distinguish them from all other organisms. Individuals from the same species breed to produce fertile offspring. Scientists estimate that there could be 8.7 million different species on Earth.

Although species can be very different from each other, many of them have similar features. The **variation** between different species is used to classify them into groups. Variation *between* different species is always greater than the variation *within* a species. Look at Figure 3.1.2a. These animals all belong to the cat family, but they look very different from each other.

1. What is a species?

2. Look at Figure 3.1.2a. How are the lion, cheetah and tiger similar to each other? How are they different?

3. Which two cats are the same species? How do you know?

Why is biodiversity important?

Biodiversity is the variety of living things (plants, animals and microorganisms), their relationships and the **ecosystems** they form.

Biodiversity is vital for supporting all life on Earth. It ensures clean air and water, as well as fertile soils. Every organism, no matter how small, has a part to play in what we call the 'balance of nature'.

FIGURE 3.1.2a: What are the similarities and differences between small and big cats?

Living organisms, rocks and soils, water and the atmosphere all interact to provide the conditions needed to sustain life on Earth. If these ecological systems break down or change dramatically, life on our planet will be threatened. For example the oceans play a major role in absorbing carbon dioxide from the atmosphere. Phytoplankton (microscopic aquatic plant life) absorb carbon dioxide and release oxygen. Loss of phytoplankton would mean a reduction in levels of oxygen, which is needed by other organisms.

An ecosystem with a high level of biodiversity is more able to survive changes, because there is a greater chance of one of the species having features that enable it to adapt to change. This safeguards the system against the loss of other species, because the food webs are not affected.

Tropical rainforests and coral reefs are the ecosystems with the greatest biodiversity on the planet.

4. What is biodiversity?

5. Why is it important for ecosystems to have high levels of biodiversity?

Classification)))

Some organisms are known by many different names. For example cougar, puma and mountain lion are different names for the same animal. In the 18th century, the Swedish scientist Carl Linnaeus started the modern system of **classification** that is now recognised internationally. Each species is given a scientific name using Latin words – for example *Panthera tigris* is the Bengal tiger.

Classification systems help us to:

* clarify relationships among organisms

* remember organisms and their typical features

* communicate the identity of organisms being studied.

6. Why is it important to have a universal classification system?

7. Explain how scientists would use classification to improve their knowledge of a newly discovered organism.

Did you know...?

Various animals worldwide are called 'badgers'. The European badger and the honey badger (found in Africa and parts of Asia) are members of the same mammalian family, but they are not each other's closest relatives.

FIGURE 3.1.2b: A European badger and a honey badger are not closely related.

Key vocabulary

species

variation

biodiversity

ecosystems

classification

Looking more closely at variation

We are learning how to:
- Explain the difference between continuous and discontinuous variation.
- Investigate variation within a species.
- Evaluate the importance of variation in organisms.

Variation in characteristics can be classified in different ways depending on whether it can be measured or not. Is there a link between some characteristics? Why is variation important?

Types of variation

The height of a human population ranges from the shortest to the tallest individuals (called the range) – any height is possible between these values. Any feature that changes gradually over a range of values is said to have **continuous variation**. Examples of such features are height and wing span.

The bell-shaped graph showing height values (Figure 3.1.3a) is called a 'normal distribution'. This what you would expect to find in any feature with continuous variation. The most frequently occurring value is called the mode.

Some features have only a limited number of values. An individual has one type of the feature or another. This is called **discontinuous variation** – examples of this are gender, blood group and vein patterning in leaves.

> 1. List five features that differ in dogs and five that differ in humans. For each feature, identify whether it is an example of continuous variation or discontinuous variation.
>
> 2. Explain the difference between continuous and discontinuous variation.

Investigating variation

Scientists can investigate variation to find out if features are linked, such as students' height and shoe size.

To make this a fair test, both of the measurements for each student should be taken at the same time. Each height or foot size should be measured in the same way using the same measuring device. This ensures that the same units are

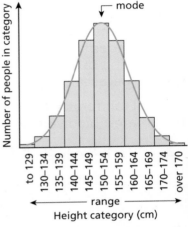

FIGURE 3.1.3a: Height shows normal distribution.

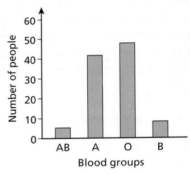

FIGURE 3.1.3b: Blood groups show discontinuous variation.

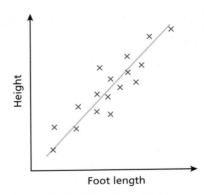

FIGURE 3.1.3c: There is a positive correlation between height and foot length in humans.

used for the measurements and the same level of accuracy is achieved. The larger the sample size used, the more reliable the data.

Scattergraphs are used to show whether or not there is a relationship between two sets of data. The relationship can be described as either:

- a positive **correlation** – one quantity increases as the other does (as in Figure 3.1.3c)

- a negative correlation – one quantity increases as the other decreases

- no correlation – there is no clear relationship.

3. Describe an investigation to see if there is a link between the length of a holly leaf and the number of spikes on the leaf.

4. Explain why sample size is important.

The importance of variation

Variation is important for the survival of a species. If all organisms were identical and an adverse change in the environment occurred that none of the organisms were adapted to survive, they would die out. Variation in a population gives certain organisms with more favourable features a survival advantage. When these organisms reproduce, the feature is passed on to offspring.

Some variation benefits a species, for example:

- Not all rabbits are killed by the viral disease myxomatosis. Some are resistant and can survive an outbreak.

- Peacocks with the best display of feathers are most likely to attract a mate.

Some differences are not beneficial, for example:

- Albino (pure white) giraffes do not survive long in the wild.

- Antelopes that run slower than the herd do not survive.

5. Evaluate the importance of variation to living organisms.

6. Look at Figure 3.1.3d. Which squirrel has the survival advantage? Explain your answer.

FIGURE 3.1.3d: Some animals are born with no pigment. They are called albinos.

Key vocabulary

continuous variation

discontinuous variation

correlation

inbreeding

Exploring the causes of variation

We are learning how to:

- Identify some features of organisms that are inherited and some that are determined by their environment.
- Understand that offspring from the same parents may show considerable variation.
- Evaluate the importance of genetic and environmental variation to the survival of the organism.

There are millions of plants and animals on Earth. They are all different from one another. What causes these differences? Why are some organisms almost identical?

What causes variation?

One cause of variation in organisms is their environment. For example your diet, health and the amount of exercise you do affect your growth. Climate and food supply influence all living things. When animals fight (for example over available resources), they may lose teeth or develop scars from deep wounds. A person's country and culture can also be a source of variation – for example Buddhist monks shave their heads.

FIGURE 3.1.4a: The foal inherits the length of its legs from its parents.

The other major cause of variation in organisms is the passing on of features from parents to offspring, and from their parents before them, and so on. **Inherited** variations are **genetic** and cannot be altered. For example you may dye your hair purple, but it will always grow back in your natural colour. Sometimes there are clear traits that run in families, such as the shape of your nose or the presence of a dimple or freckles.

1. Name one characteristic that you have inherited from your parents, and one caused by the environment.

2. Apart from leg length, name three other features that a foal inherits from its parents.

Why are offspring different?

Brothers and sisters from the same parents can look very different from each other. Parents pass on genetic information to their offspring in the nucleus of their

Did you know...?

In the 1980s the Florida panther came close to extinction. Eight female pumas were introduced to the population, bringing genetic variation and improving their chances of survival.

sex cells. The offspring inherit one set of information from the mother's egg cell nucleus and one set from the father's sperm cell nucleus. Every egg cell and every sperm cell contains different hereditary information from the respective parent. Each fertilised egg cell will therefore contain a different, random and unique combination of characteristics inherited from the parents. Offspring may have some similarities to their siblings, but may also look very different.

3. Why can children from the same parents be very different from each other?

4. Look carefully at Figure 3.1.4b.

   a) How are the children similar to each other?

   b) How are they different from each other?

FIGURE 3.1.4b: What variation can you see in this family?

Genetic or environmental? >>>

Scientists have debated whether certain characteristics are inherited or are caused by the environment in which people live. They now generally agree that only four human features are entirely inherited and are not in any way affected by the environment. These features are:

- natural eye colour
- natural hair colour
- blood group
- some inherited diseases.

Genetic variation is needed for the process of natural selection to produce evolutionary change that enables a species to change gradually and survive. Sometimes this results in the development of a new species. This is explored further in Topic 1.6.

Some features have a well-established genetic basis; others are mostly due to the environment. However, most features are caused by the interaction of genetic and environmental factors. For example a person's skin may have birthmarks and moles, but during their lifetime scars may form and tattoos may be added.

FIGURE 3.1.4c: Tattoos are important in many cultures.

5. Give three other examples of inherited human features that can be affected by the environment in which a person lives.

6. Evaluate the importance of genetic and environmental variation in the survival of an organism.

Key vocabulary

inherited

genetic

Learning about selective breeding

We are learning how to:

- Describe how selective breeding can produce organisms with desirable characteristics.
- Explain the process of selective breeding.
- Evaluate the importance of selective breeding, and explore the ethical issues involved.

Many animals and plants that provide us with food look very different from their ancestors. How has this happened? What are the advantages and disadvantages of this process?

FIGURE 3.1.5a: Selective breeding means that there is more food for people.

Why do we use selective breeding?

Farmers and horticulturists (plant growers) have used **selective breeding** for centuries. They select organisms with desirable features – such as cows that produce large amounts of milk – and use these to breed from. Using selective breeding in this way helps us to produce, for example:

- better beef – bred for low fat content and appearance
- higher-quality wool/leather – higher quality means more profit
- chickens that produce bigger eggs – again meaning more profit
- better wheat that is more disease resistant
- bigger and more colourful flowers.

The farm pig is the product of selective breeding over many years starting from a wild pig. The features that were selected for included less hair, more fat and a gentler manner. This continued until the new breed resulted.

FIGURE 3.1.5b: How is a modern farm pig different from its ancestor, the wild pig?

1. Describe what is meant by 'selective breeding'.
2. Why do farmers and horticulturists use selective breeding?

The process

In selective breeding, males and females showing desired features are bred together. From their offspring, those that show the most desired characteristic the most are then bred together. This process is repeated over many generations.

> **Did you know...?**
>
> Selective breeding of endangered animals in zoos and wildlife parks is protecting them from extinction. Zookeepers need to make sure that siblings (brothers and sisters) do not breed together because this can reduce variation and make the animals vulnerable.

For example, Jersey cows produce very creamy milk in small amounts; Friesian cows produce large quantities of milk. Jersey cows producing the creamiest milk are bred with the male offspring of Friesian cows producing the most milk. The offspring cows produce large amounts of creamy milk. These are then bred together and the process repeated until there is a herd of cows producing large amounts of very creamy milk.

Plant growers also use selective breeding. They transfer pollen from one flower to another to breed plants with specific characteristics.

FIGURE 3.1.5c: Why would a farmer breed a Jersey bull with a Friesian cow?

3. What characteristics may be desirable in breeding roses and tomatoes?

4. Explain how a tomato grower would selectively breed tomatoes for a characteristic you identified in question 3.

Why is selective breeding important? 》》》

Selective breeding plays a major role in supplying the Earth's population with food. The development of plant and animal breeds has allowed plant growing and animal farming to become an industry, for example producing:

- short-stemmed varieties of grain crops suitable for combine harvesting

- vegetable varieties suitable for cultivation in greenhouses

- grapes and tomatoes suitable for machine harvesting

- cattle adapted to maintenance in large livestock buildings.

There are drawbacks to selective breeding. The genetic variation in the population is reduced. If there is a change in the environment, such as a new disease, the population may not be able to survive. Also, many animals produced using selective breeding suffer from deformities. The selectively bred Belgian Blue cattle have a number of problems:

- difficulty with calving (Caesarean births are common)

- jaw deformities and over-enlarged tongues, which mean that calves cannot suckle and may die

- heart and respiratory (breathing) problems.

FIGURE 3.1.5d: Belgian Blue cattle have been selectively bred for meat production.

5. How has selective breeding of plants impacted on farming?

6. Do the advantages of selectively breeding animals outweigh the drawbacks?

Key vocabulary

selective breeding

Finding out how organisms survive

We are learning how to:

- Describe how variation causes competition for resources, and drives natural selection.
- Explain the theories of Lamarck, Wallace and Darwin.
- Evaluate the importance of Darwin's work.

Many organisms that once existed on Earth did not survive changes to their environment and became extinct. How have other organisms survived?

What can cause a population to change?

All giraffes compete for food and other resources. One feature showing variation in giraffes is neck length. There were ancestors of the giraffe with both long and short necks. When food became scarce, the giraffes with longer necks were better able to reach leaves of the taller trees. Longer necks meant they were more likely to survive and breed. Over many generations, more and more giraffes with long necks were born. This is called **natural selection**.

After many generations the differences caused by natural selection may be so great that a new species is formed.

1. What is 'natural selection'?

2. Explain why having a longer neck might make the giraffe more successful at spotting predators such as lions.

FIGURE 3.1.6a: What might happen to the shorter giraffe?

Which theory?

Living organisms compete for resources and try to avoid being eaten. They try to ensure that their offspring have a survival advantage. How do they do this?

Jean-Baptiste de Lamarck (1744–1829) was the first scientist to put forward a worked-out theory of **evolution**. He thought that organisms acquired characteristics they needed during their struggle for survival and passed these on to their offspring. For example, giraffes needed longer necks to reach the leaves of the trees on which they fed. By stretching their necks, they were able to eat and survive. The longer necks were then passed on to offspring.

> **Did you know...?**
>
> Evolution of living organisms began 3.7 billion years ago. The earliest 'species' were bacteria. Human beings are direct descendants of these bacteria, showing the massive changes that evolution can drive.

Charles Darwin (1809–82) had a different idea. He thought that organisms struggle for survival and have to produce many offspring to ensure that some survive. He decided that for a species to survive, the best ('fittest') had to survive long enough to reproduce and pass on the feature.

Alfred Russel Wallace (1823–1913) also came up with the idea of natural selection, but after Darwin had. Darwin had not published his work, so the two scientists wrote a scientific article together to propose the theory of natural selection in 1858.

3. Explain the theory of acquired characteristics and natural selection.

4. If you always put your hand up to answer questions in class, does your arm get longer? Does this support or refute the theory of acquired characteristics?

FIGURE 3.1.6b: Charles Darwin is well remembered for his work, but Alfred Russel Wallace also made a great contribution to the development of the science of evolution.

Charles Darwin's conclusions

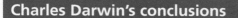

Darwin collected many thousands of specimens and made many observations on his travels. He wrote extensively about the finches living on the Galapagos islands in the Pacific Ocean. He observed that variation in beak structure gave certain advantages to some finches in their search for food. For example, some beaks were designed for crushing seed shells, but others for catching insects.

Darwin drew these conclusions:

- All organisms produce more offspring than is needed.

- Organisms have a fairly constant population size.

- There is a wide range of features within a species.

- Some variations are inherited by the offspring.

Scientists have tested Darwin's hypothesis over the years, and it has continued to give information that has informed contemporary biology.

5. What two things did Darwin link together to work out his explanation of natural selection?

6. Why is the work of Charles Darwin so important?

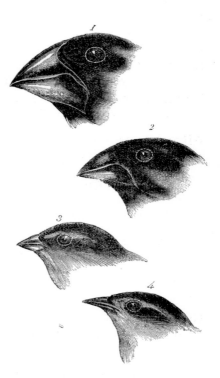

FIGURE 3.1.6c: Why do these finches have differently shaped beaks?

Key vocabulary

natural selection

evolution

Applying key ideas

You have now met a number of important ideas in this chapter. This activity gives an opportunity for you to apply them, just as scientists do. Read the text first, then have a go at the tasks. The first few are fairly easy – then they get a bit more challenging.

The problem with dogs

Most breeds of dogs were originally selected to do a certain job for humans – for example to hunt or guard property or livestock. When dogs were selected to breed, those best suited for the roles the breeders wanted them to do were selected. The desirable traits (relating to fitness, ability and effectiveness to do the job required) were the priorities.

Some dogs were also selected to emphasise their different physical features, such as long floppy ears, short legs or flattened faces.

Breeding dogs for their physical features has resulted in two distinct, but related, issues:

FIGURE 3.1.7a: Different dogs such as the saluki, red setter and labradoodle (bred from a Labrador crossed with a poodle) have different features.

- Exaggerated physical features can directly reduce a dog's quality of life.
- The lack of inherited variation can lead to an increase in inherited disorders.

Over the years, some physical features have been exaggerated to such an extent that they may cause pain and suffering. In some dog breeds, these features are seen as normal, but that does not mean they are not a problem. A recent study showed that the 50 most popular breeds all have some feature(s) that can cause suffering because of selective breeding. The problems range from those that are merely irritating to the dog, to others that are life-threatening or require risky surgery.

There are many examples of exaggerated physical features that can result directly in reduced quality of life:

- Dogs with short, flat faces (such as the pug in Figure 3.1.7b) often have narrow nostrils and abnormal windpipes. They can have breathing difficulties and difficulty walking.

- Very large and heavy dogs are more likely to suffer heart, digestion, muscle or joint problems, and have shorter lives. The life expectancy of a Bernese mountain dog has shortened to only seven years.

- Dogs with folded or wrinkled skin (such as the Shar-Pei in Figure 3.1.7b) are prone to itchy and painful skin complaints, and infolding eyelids that can scratch the eyeball.

FIGURE 3.1.7b: Many people believe the practices in pedigree breeding are wrong and they campaign to stop them. What do you think?

Task 1: Identifying variation in dogs

Describe five ways in which the dogs pictured are different from each other.

Task 2: Exploring types of variation

Give two examples of continuous variation and two examples of discontinuous variation in these dogs.

Task 3: Exploring breeds of dog

Explain how new breeds of dog have been produced.

Task 4: Exploring the importance of variation

Explain why variation in dogs is important.

Task 5: Analysing the importance of selective breeding

Analyse the importance of selective breeding in dogs. Do you think selective breeding of dogs is being taken too far? Justify your view.

Task 6: Evaluating dog breeding practices

Evaluate the importance of variation in dog breeding and the ethics around the use of selective breeding.

Understanding why siblings are different

We are learning how to:

- Identify inherited features in plants and animals that vary between offspring.
- Explain how inherited differences arise by genetic material from both parents combining.
- Describe how identical twins occur and analyse data about their features.

Brothers and sisters with the same parents are often not alike. How do these differences occur? In the case of twins, however, siblings can sometimes be identical. How do identical twins develop?

Inherited features

The variation in shape, size and colour of living things is caused by parents passing on their features to their offspring. Animal and plant features that are **inherited** by offspring from their parents are called genetic **traits**.

There is a huge number of these traits. In humans, they include eye colour, blood types and having freckles. With the exception of identical twins, it is highly unlikely that any two people will have the same combination of genetic traits.

1. What is a genetic trait?

2. List ten inherited features in humans.

Why are siblings different?

During fertilisation, animal and plant cells pass on genetic information in the nucleus from one generation to the next. Genetic information is contained in **chromosomes**. These are normally found in pairs in the nuclei of cells.

Every cell in the father contains a set of chromosome pairs. These came from his father and mother. The mother's cells also have a set of chromosome pairs, which came from her parents.

To make a sperm cell, only half of the chromosomes are used – one from each pair of the father's chromosomes. Every sperm cell therefore contains a random mix of the father's genetic information. The same thing happens when eggs are formed in the mother.

This means that each child with the same two parents has a random mix of their parents' genetic information.

A rose with large flowers and large thorns...

+

...can be bred with a rose that has small flowers and small thorns...

...to produce rose plants with large flowers and small thorns.

FIGURE 3.1.8a: How did the new rose bush get large flowers and small thorns?

each chromosome in a pair contains different genetic information

only one of the pair is passed on from parent to offspring

FIGURE 3.1.8b: The nuclei of cells contain pairs of chromosomes.

Each parent has a random mix of *their* parents' genetic information. Therefore, each child has a random mix of genetic information from their four grandparents.

FIGURE 3.1.8c: What features has the child inherited from his grandparents?

3. Explain why brothers and sisters with the same parents inherit different features.

4. Where in the nucleus is genetic information found?

Identical twins

Identical twins happen when one egg is fertilised by one sperm. The egg then divides into two halves. There is no reason why or when the egg splits – it is a random occurrence. The split usually occurs within the first twelve days of growth. After twelve days, the egg may not split entirely and this results in **conjoined twins**.

FIGURE 3.1.8d: Are these twins exactly the same?

Because the two embryos are the result of a single egg–sperm combination, they have the same genetic origins. Identical twins are not always exactly the same. Sometimes there are very slight differences that occur when the cells start dividing to form the embryo.

There is no hereditary trait that influences a tendency towards having identical twins. Identical twins do not run in families. Although there are families with a high incidence of identical twins, it is due to chance.

5. How do identical twins occur?

6. List five things that could happen to identical twins to make them look different.

Did you know...?

Historically, the most famous conjoined twins were Chang and Eng, born in Siam in 1811. This is where the term 'Siamese twins' come from. Chang and Eng died on the same day in 1874.

FIGURE 3.1.8e: Chang and Eng. How are conjoined twins formed?

Key vocabulary

inherit

trait

chromosome

identical twins

conjoined twins

Looking inside a cell's nucleus

We are learning how to:

- Identify that the nucleus contains chromosomes which carry inherited genetic information.
- Explain that chromosomes are made of genes containing DNA, and describe the structure of DNA.
- Assess the work of Watson, Crick, Wilkins and Franklin on DNA structure.

Inside the nucleus is a very special molecule, which is often called the 'miracle of life'. What is this molecule? Why is it so special?

Inside the nucleus

The nucleus of every cell contains genetic information, which is arranged into chromosomes. These are thread-like strands made of a chemical called **DNA** – this is short for deoxyribonucleic acid.

This chemical is divided into regions called **genes**. Different genes control the development of different characteristics. Genes can be passed down from generation to generation. You therefore inherited your genes from your parents. Organisms differ because they have different genes.

Chromosomes come in pairs. Humans have 23 pairs of chromosomes. Fruit flies have four pairs, whereas the adder's tongue fern has over 1000 chromosome pairs!

1. Explain what the difference is between a gene and a chromosome.

2. What is the role of a gene?

3. How many chromosomes do humans have?

genes are parts of chromosomes carrying specific genetic information

FIGURE 3.1.9a: The nucleus of every cell in a fruit fly contains four pairs of chromosomes.

DNA

A DNA molecule is made up of four chemicals called **bases**. Each gene is made up of a different pattern of these four bases.

A DNA molecule consists of two strands that wind around each other like a twisted ladder. This shape is called a **double helix**. The sides of the ladder are held together by 'rungs', each made from two of the bases. The four bases are called A, T, C and G for short. They work in two pairs: A always pairs with T, and C always pairs with G.

Did you know...?

You have about 9 million kilometres of DNA in your body, and about 50 per cent of human DNA is the same as the DNA found in bananas.

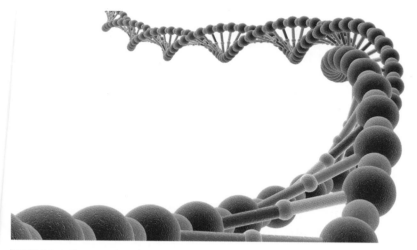

FIGURE 3.1.9b: A model of part of the DNA molecule

4. Describe what a DNA molecule looks like.

5. Name the base pairs that make up a DNA molecule.

Finding the structure

Scientist Maurice Wilkins had the idea of studying DNA using the technique of X-ray crystallography, which involves firing X-rays at the DNA. The X-rays scatter, forming a pattern that shows the structure. Rosalind Franklin was appointed to work with Wilkins, and she produced the clearest picture of DNA using this method. This demonstrated that DNA had a helical structure.

Wilkins shared this information with James Watson and Francis Crick, who were also working on the structure of DNA. They used a molecular insert modelling technique devised by Linus Pauling to create a large-scale model of DNA in their laboratory.

Meanwhile Erwin Chargaff in the USA investigated the composition of DNA. He met with Watson and Crick in 1952 and shared his findings that A always paired with T, and C always paired with G. Watson and Crick used the work done by Franklin, Wilkins and Chargaff to determine the double helix shape.

Watson, Crick and Wilkins were awarded a Nobel Prize in 1962 for their work (unfortunately Rosalind Franklin died in 1958).

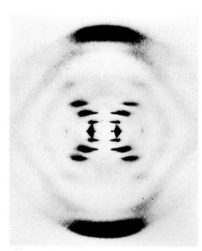

FIGURE 3.1.9c: One of Rosalind Franklin's X-ray diffraction images of DNA. The cross of bands indicates the helical structure.

6. What was Franklin's contribution to the discovery of DNA structure?

7. Explain how the work of Watson and Crick was made possible by other scientists.

Key vocabulary

DNA

gene

base

double helix

Learning about DNA

We are learning how to:

- Identify that all plant and animal cells contain DNA.
- Explain why it is important for scientists to be able to extract DNA from cells.
- Analyse and evaluate the use of extracted DNA.

DNA is the 'instruction manual' for an organism. Scientists are finding out more and more about the DNA molecule. How do scientists find and extract the DNA? What do they do with DNA they have extracted?

DNA everywhere!

Did you know that you eat plant and animal DNA every day? You cannot eat anything without eating DNA. When you eat an apple, you eat the DNA and genes in the apple cells. The apple genes do not affect you because they are mostly digested. When an organism dies or DNA is heated, it denatures (falls apart). The DNA is broken up by the enzymes and acid in the gut, but it is still there. Some DNA passes out of the digestive system in faeces.

It is estimated that every day the average person eats more than 100 trillion genes (approximately 0.1 to 1.0g of DNA).

A whole industry has been set up around testing the DNA of our food sources. These tests ensure that a product is actually made from the plant(s) and animal(s) that it claims to be made of and that the DNA has not been changed in any way.

FIGURE 3.1.10a: Sheep eat grass. Do you think the grass DNA affects them?

1. Explain why DNA is in the food we eat.
2. What happens to DNA in the food an animal eats?

Extracting DNA

DNA extraction allows scientists to study the structure of DNA. This is very important in the development of **biotechnology** and **forensic science**. DNA extraction allows scientists to analyse and manipulate the DNA. This enables them:

- to detect **genetic disorders**
- to produce DNA fingerprints of individuals
- even to create genetically altered organisms that can make beneficial products such as insulin, antibiotics and hormones.

Did you know...?

If the DNA from all the cells in your body was stretched out, it could reach to the Sun and back 700 times!

In forensics, DNA (from blood, saliva hair or skin for example) can help to solve crimes or find missing or unknown family members.

DNA can be extracted from many types of cells. The cells are broken up by grinding some tissue. Then a salt solution and a cleaning agent are added to break down the fat and proteins in the cell membranes. Finally, ethanol is added (because DNA is soluble in water) to solidify the DNA.

FIGURE 3.1.10b: Why are blood samples taken from a crime scene?

3. How is DNA used in medicine?

4. Name three sources of DNA found at crime scenes.

How should we use DNA? >>>

The use of DNA in forensics is a powerful tool in the fight against crime. It has also been used to disprove wrongful convictions, so that convicted people have been proved innocent and freed from prison. Forensic **DNA profiles** are stored on a database, but profiles of innocent people are usually removed.

The use of DNA in medical genetics raises many ethical issues. For example, it could be very damaging if data were used to predict if a person is likely to develop illnesses such as cancer or HIV.

If DNA profiling shows there is a high risk of serious harm to other family members, should patient confidentiality be kept or should the family be told? This issue becomes more complex if there are adopted family members. For example, if an adopted child has a life-threatening condition, should the child's natural siblings be found and told? There are also concerns over the use of stored DNA for further medical research.

5. What are the advantages of DNA profiling?

6. Evaluate the use of a national DNA database. What are the pros and cons?

FIGURE 3.1.10c: Forensic scientists looking at evidence.

Key vocabulary

biotechnology

forensic science

genetic disorders

DNA profile

Exploring human chromosomes

We are learning how to:

- Identify that, at fertilisation, one chromosome in each pair comes from each parent.
- Explain how fertilisation results in each new individual being genetically unique.
- Explain how some genetic disorders arise.

People have always wondered how traits are inherited from one generation to the next. Most offspring seem to be a blend of the features of both parents. How does this happen? Can it go wrong?

Making a new individual

All human body cells have a full set of chromosomes, consisting of 23 pairs. The two chromosomes in each pair carry the same genes in the same places.

Parents pass on their genes to their offspring in their sex cells (eggs or sperm). Each sex cell contains half the full set of chromosomes – 23 single chromosomes. There is one from each pair of chromosomes found in the body cells.

When an egg is fertilised, the nucleus of the male sperm joins with the nucleus of the female egg. The cells of the baby then have a complete set of chromosome pairs. One chromosome in each pair comes from the mother and the other comes from the father.

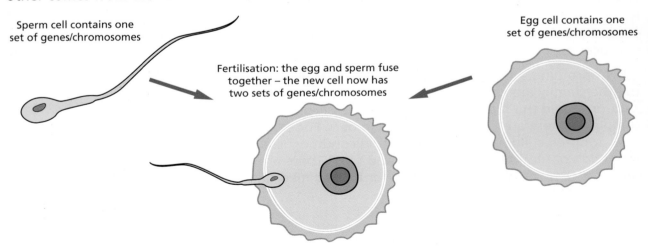

Sperm cell contains one set of genes/chromosomes

Egg cell contains one set of genes/chromosomes

Fertilisation: the egg and sperm fuse together – the new cell now has two sets of genes/chromosomes

FIGURE 3.1.11a: Genes and DNA are passed on in the nucleus of the sperm and egg.

1. Which parts of the egg cell and sperm cell fuse at fertilisation?

2. Why do the sex cells have half the number of chromosomes?

Different and unique »»

Just which of the two chromosomes a person gets from each pair in the mother and each pair in the father is completely random. This means different children in the same family will each get a different combination. This is why children in the same family look a little like each other and a little like each parent, but are not identical to them. They are unique.

A set of chromosomes is called a **karyotype**. A karyotype can be separated from its cell, spread out on a microscope slide and magnified many thousands of times.

There is one pair of chromosomes where the two chromosomes are slightly different from each other. They are called the sex chromosomes, X and Y. They determine the gender of the new individual.

3. What makes every new individual unique?

4. What is a karyotype?

When things go wrong »»»

A genetic disorder is caused by abnormalities in an individual's genetic material. During the creation of sex cells and embryos, errors sometimes happen and individuals are born with additional or missing chromosomes. **Trisomy** means that there are three chromosomes instead of a pair.

The most common chromosomal disorder is trisomy 21 – this is also known as Down's syndrome. Symptoms of trisomy 21 include a broad, flat face, a thick tongue and a small nose.

Sometimes one or more chromosomes have irregular structures. For example, parts of an individual chromosome may be either duplicated or deleted. The effects of this vary greatly depending on the gene.

Children can inherit a gene type that gives them an inherited condition, such as cystic fibrosis. Sometimes genetic defects occur and scientists are unsure of the exact cause. An example is polydactyly, when a person has extra fingers or toes.

5. Explain how genetic disorders occur.

6. Explain, with an example, what trisomy is.

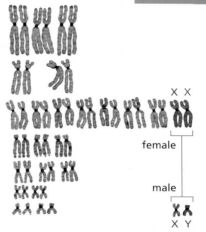

FIGURE 3.1.11b: A female karyotype – a full set of human female chromosomes. In a male, one of the X chromosomes is replaced by a Y chromosome.

Did you know...?

Stalin had webbed toes. This is another genetic defect with an unknown cause, called syndactyly.

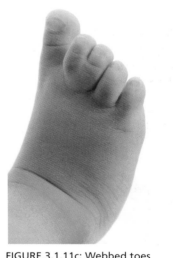

FIGURE 3.1.11c: Webbed toes

Key vocabulary

karyotype

trisomy

Understanding cloning

We are learning how to:

- Define cloning and describe some natural cloning processes.
- Explain how organisms may be artificially cloned.
- Explore ethical issues around artificial cloning.
- Compare and contrast asexual and sexual reproduction.

Many organisms can reproduce without a female sex cell fusing with a male sex cell to produce offspring. How do they do this? Why do they do this? Why do we need sexual reproduction?

Natural clones

A **clone** is an identical copy that has been created of an organism. Some organisms can produce new individuals without using sex cells – this is called **asexual reproduction**. This means that every cell in every organism has exactly the same set of genes. The new individual is called a natural clone.

An example of cloning in plants is when a spider plant has small plants dangling from the end of 'runners' coming from the parent plant. All the small plants look the same. Strawberry plants also spread by using runners. The new plants rely on the parent plant until their own root system is fully formed. Plant clones are also formed by bulbs, corms, tubers and rhizomes.

Asexual reproduction in animals happens less often. It occurs in sea anemone, hydra and starfish, for example.

Identical twins are are natural clones because they are formed after one fertilised egg cell splits into two cells. As a result they are genetically identical.

FIGURE 3.1.12a: The dandelion can re-grow from small sections of root – each new plant is a replica of the original plant.

1. What is a clone?

2. Why are clones identical?

Artificial clones

Clones can also be made artificially. The simplest way to clone a plant artificially involves taking a cutting. A branch from the parent plant is cut off, its lower leaves removed and the stem planted in damp compost to allow roots to develop. Plant clones can also be produced by tissue culture.

Did you know...?

The first artificial cloning of an animal was done in the 1890s by Hans Driesch who cloned a sea urchin from a single sea urchin embryo cell.

In animals, cloning is much more complex. One method is to take an egg cell, remove its nucleus and replace it with the nucleus from a normal body cell of the animal they want to clone. This process is called **nuclear transfer**. 'Dolly the sheep' was the first mammal to be cloned using adult cell cloning. She was born in the UK in 1996 and died in 2003.

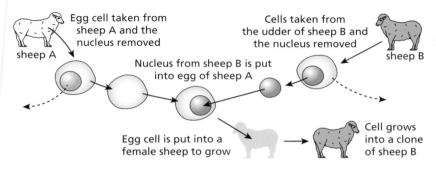

FIGURE 3.1.12b: Dolly the sheep was created using a nucleus from her sister's udder.

The cloning of animals has many important commercial implications. It allows an individual animal that has desirable features, such as a cow that produces a lot of milk, to be duplicated several times. It is illegal to try to clone humans in the UK.

FIGURE 3.1.12c: Would Dolly have looked the same if a nucleus from another part of her sister's body had been used?

3. What is the difference between natural cloning and artificial cloning?

4. Explain how Dolly the sheep was created.

Cloning: good or bad? >>>

Asexual reproduction differs from sexual reproduction in several ways:

- Only one parent is needed.
- Large numbers of offspring can be produced very quickly.
- Favoured features can be passed on.
- No fusion of sex cells occurs.

However, some people believe that artificial cloning is unethical and should be banned. Others are concerned about what might happen in the future. Most clones die during development, are poorly developed when they are born, or age prematurely and have a shorter life. Also, if too many organisms are cloned this will result in less variation and a smaller gene pool. This can make a species vulnerable to disease and defects.

5. Why is there no variation in clones?

6. Give one advantage and one disadvantage of cloning.

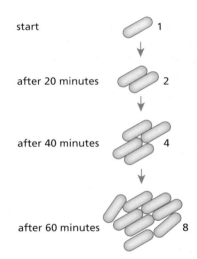

FIGURE 3.1.12d: Bacteria reproduce every 20 minutes. Starting with just one, how many will there be after 3 hours?

Key vocabulary

clone

asexual reproduction

nuclear transfer

Explaining extinction

We are learning how to:

- Identify changes that can cause a species to become extinct.
- Explain the use of gene banks to preserve hereditary material before a species becomes extinct.
- Analyse and evaluate theories of what caused the extinction of the dinosaurs.

Throughout history animals have become extinct as the world changed. Today, about one quarter of the world's mammals are in danger of being wiped out. What are the causes of extinction? What can humans do to help prevent them?

Causes of extinction

Extinction of a species occurs when there are no more individuals of that species alive in the world. This is a natural part of evolution, but sometimes extinctions happen at a much faster rate than usual. For example, at the end of the Cretaceous period 65 million years ago, a mass extinction called the 'K/T event' caused the death of many different species. Natural causes of extinction include climatic heating and cooling, changes in sea level, asteroid impacts and disease.

Today human intervention is causing rapid extinction, which in turn is causing a rapid decline in global biodiversity. Hunting, habitat destruction, the introduction of invasive species and the over-exploitation of wildlife mean that many different types of plants and animals are being pushed to the edge of extinction.

FIGURE 3.1.13a: The quagga was a variety of zebra with stripes only at the front of its body. Large herds lived in South Africa until Boer settlers began hunting them. Quaggas became extinct in 1878.

1. When is a species extinct?
2. What are the causes of extinction?

Preventing more extinctions

Endangered species are those at risk of becoming extinct. A species can become endangered when:

- the number of available habitats falls rapidly
- the population of the species is very small
- there is too little genetic variation in the population (even if the population is still quite large).

FIGURE 3.1.13b: The Pyrenean ibex became extinct in 2000. It was cloned and brought back to life in 2009, but unfortunately the kid did not survive.

The creation of **gene banks** is a new strategy being used to protect species. An organism's genes give the details of what the organism looks like. By freezing genetic material, the details are preserved. Scientists hope we will be able to reintroduce species through cloning in the future.

3. Explain what a 'gene bank' is.

4. Why is it easier to store plant genes than animal genes?

Mass extinctions

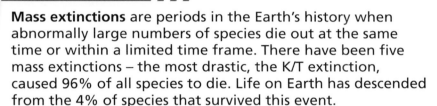

Mass extinctions are periods in the Earth's history when abnormally large numbers of species die out at the same time or within a limited time frame. There have been five mass extinctions – the most drastic, the K/T extinction, caused 96% of all species to die. Life on Earth has descended from the 4% of species that survived this event.

The K/T mass extinction is the most famous because it caused the death of the dinosaurs. Many other organisms became extinct at this time, although some species had been declining for several million years before this final event. Scientists have researched the causes of the K/T event and have proposed a number of theories about what happened. These include supervolcano eruptions, falls in sea level and the impact of a giant asteroid.

FIGURE 3.1.13c: Seed banks like this one at Kew Gardens, London, are a conservation measure for plants. Seeds are carefully stored so that new plants can be grown in the future.

FIGURE 3.1.13d: Why did the dinosaurs die out at the end of the Cretaceous period?

> **Did you know...?**
>
> Some scientists think that Earth is currently faced with a mounting loss of species that threatens to rival the five great mass extinctions of the past.

5. Explain the effect of a mass extinction.

6. Suggest how some organisms were able to survive mass extinctions.

Key vocabulary

extinction

endangered species

gene bank

mass extinction

Checking your progress

To make good progress in understanding science you need to focus on these ideas and skills.

- Give some examples of differences between similar species and explain how these are used to classify organisms.

- Explain the importance of the diversity of living organisms to life on Earth and why we have a common system for naming organisms.

- Explain how scientists can use the universal system of classification to research or discuss an organism and to understand ecological relationships between organisms.

- Identify some features of different organisms that are inherited and some that are determined by the environment in which the organism lives.

- Explain the difference between continuous and discontinuous variation; explain why offspring from the same parents can be very different.

- Use ideas and evidence to evaluate the importance of genetic and environmental variation.

- Describe what selective breeding is and explain that it has produced new breeds of an organism.

- Explain the process of selective breeding and why new breeds have been produced.

- Explore and evaluate the advantages and disadvantages of selective breeding.

- Identify examples of how variation causes competition for resources and causes natural selection.

- Explore how the theories of Lamarck, Wallace and Darwin explained why some organisms are better able to survive than others.

- Evaluate Darwin's theories and their impact on contemporary science.

Describe chromosomes and their role in transferring heredity information to offspring.

Explain the relationship between chromosomes, genes and DNA; explain why offspring of the same parents may look very different.

Explore the role of scientists in the discovery of DNA and evaluate the relative importance of their contributions.

Describe how fertilised egg cells contain half of the chromosomes from each parent with a random mix of genetic information from each parent.

Explain how every new individual produced by sexual reproduction is genetically unique.

Explain the impact of slight 'changes' to DNA passed on from parents to offspring.

Describe cloning as one parent producing new individuals and identify examples of cloning that occur naturally; describe natural cloning as asexual reproduction.

Explain how artificial cloning is performed – for example in the creation of Dolly the sheep.

Explore and evaluate the advantages and disadvantages of artificial cloning; compare and contrast asexual and sexual reproduction.

Identify natural and human-caused environmental changes that have caused some species to become extinct.

Explain how the use of gene banks to preserve heredity material may prevent some endangered species from becoming extinct.

Analyse and evaluate the available evidence to explain why the dinosaurs suffered mass extinction.

Questions

Questions 1–7

See how well you have understood the ideas in the chapter.

1. Which statement about selective breeding is correct? [1]

   a) It produces offspring that all look very similar.
   b) It cannot produce a new breed of the organism.
   c) Selective breeding can only be used for animals.
   d) It produces offspring that all look very different.

2. How many chromosomes are in a human skin cell? [1]

   a) 23   b) 46   c) 12   d) 92

3. Which of these do animals *not* compete for? [1]

   a) a mate   b) a habitat   c) food   d) light

4. Which of these is the theory proposed by Jean-Baptiste de Lamarck? [1]

   a) Organisms that have the best adaptations survive and pass the feature on to offspring.
   b) Organisms that have the best features develop the feature more and pass it on.
   c) Organisms acquire features that enable them to survive and pass the feature on.
   d) Organisms acquire features that enable them to survive but do not pass the feature on.

5. Name two features that have been selectively bred in cows. [2]

6. What are 'gene banks'? [2]

7. Explain why variation within a species is important. [4]

Questions 8–14

See how well you can apply the ideas in this chapter to new situations.

8. Which of these features of butterflies is an example of discontinuous variation? [1]

   a) area of wings   b) length of body   c) length of legs   d) number of legs

9. A fruit fly has 8 chromosomes in its body cells. How many will it have in its sex cells? [1]

   a) 16   b) 4   c) 2   d) 8

10. A liver cell in a mouse contains 40 chromosomes. How many of these have come from the male parent? [1]

    a) 40   b) 20   c) 10   d) 8

11. Suggest a variation of a feature that would be disadvantageous to a tiger. [1]

12. Why do sex cells have only half the normal number of chromosomes? [2]

13. Megan's father has a genetic disorder. How can doctors find out if Megan has the disorder too? [2]

14. Dan is a rose breeder. He has a rose that produces large, scented blooms – but it has large thorns. How can he breed a thornless variety of this rose? [4]

Questions 15–16

See how well you can understand and explain new ideas and evidence.

15. A scientist is investigating inheritance in mice. He bred two brown mice together. They had 15 brown mice and 5 white mice. How did some of the offspring come to have white fur? [2]

16. Marvin is investigating shoe size among men. He measured the feet of 118 men. Figure 3.1.15 shows his results. [4]

    a) What is the sample size?

    b) What is the range?

    c) What type of variation is shown in the graph?

    d) What is the mode value of shoe size?

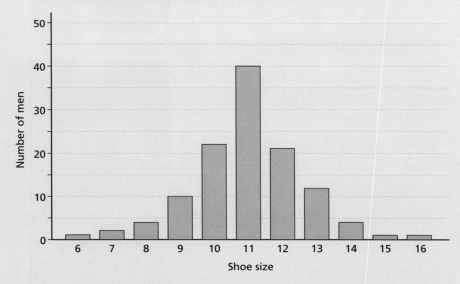

FIGURE 3.1.15: Graph showing the results of an investigation into men's shoe size

Our Health and the Effects of Drugs

Ideas you have met before

Body systems

Our breathing system moves gases in and out of the body. It provides the body with oxygen for respiration and removes waste carbon dioxide.

Our digestive system breaks down large food molecules into smaller molecules, thus providing glucose for respiration.

The lungs are damaged by smoking. Cigarettes contain many poisonous chemicals including nicotine and tar.

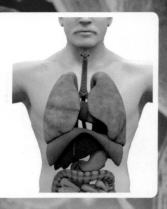

Anabolic steroids

Anabolic steroids increase muscle mass. They can be misused by sportspeople and have serious side effects, such as liver damage and risk of heart attack.

Role of blood

Blood carries substances such as oxygen and glucose to all the cells of our body, where they are needed in respiration.

Blood carries carbon dioxide produced during respiration to our lungs to be breathed out.

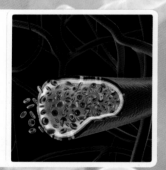

Microbes

Microbes are tiny organisms that cannot be seen with the naked eye. They include bacteria, viruses and fungi.

Yeast is a fungus that is used in brewing and baking. It uses sugar as a food source and produces alcohol and carbon dioxide. Carbon dioxide causes bread to rise and froth to form on beer.

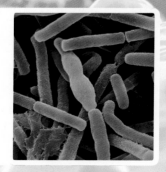

In this chapter you will find out

Cigarettes and alcohol

- Cigarettes and alcohol can affect many organs of the body.
- Passive smoking poses dangers for non-smokers.
- Addiction affects the brain and is very difficult to overcome.
- Alcoholism causes problems in society.

Effects of drugs

- People take drugs for medical reasons, but there is also much use of 'recreational' drugs.
- Drugs have side effects that can harm the body. For example paranoia can be caused by cannabis and heart failure can be caused by ecstasy.
- There are arguments for and against legalising cannabis.

Preventing and treating infection

- Blood contains white blood cells, which are part of our immune system, helping us to fight infections.
- Antibiotics can work against bacterial infections but sometimes they are not used properly.
- The discovery of vaccines allowed huge advances in the fight against infection.

Disease

- We need to use our knowledge of the characteristics of different microbes and how they infect the body to try to limit the spread of diseases.

Exploring types of drugs

We are learning how to:
- State examples of the four main groups of drugs.
- Describe the effects of different types of drugs on the body.
- Explain the effects of each type of drug on the body.

Drugs can be both beneficial and harmful. We may take paracetamol for a headache or decongestants for a blocked nose. Used like this, drugs are helpful. However, drugs can also be misused, causing harm to the body that may be irreversible. For example, taking too many paracetamol tablets can cause liver damage and even death.

Types of drugs

A drug is any substance that affects the way that the body functions. Drugs can be grouped into four main types:

- **Painkillers** relieve pain. Examples are paracetamol, codeine and morphine.

- **Stimulants** speed up body systems. Examples are caffeine, cocaine, ecstasy and amphetamines.

- **Depressants** slow down body systems. Examples are alcohol, cannabis, tranquillisers (sleeping tablets) and heroin.

- **Hallucinogens** cause us to see things that do not exist. Examples are LSD and psilocybin mushrooms.

Some drugs can be bought legally. These include caffeine (e.g. in coffee and chocolate) and paracetamol. **Prescription drugs** are prescribed by a doctor and are used to treat medical conditions. Sometimes these drugs can be misused and taken for the feeling they give, rather than for medical reasons. Other drugs, such as heroin and amphetamines, are bought illegally and are taken for the feeling that they give. Drugs that are not used for medical reasons are **recreational drugs**.

FIGURE 3.2.2a: What type of drug is in psilocybin mushrooms (magic mushrooms)?

Did you know...?

Ritalin is a stimulant used to treat attention-deficit hyperactivity disorder (ADHD). However, in the doses used to treat ADHD, it acts more like a depressant.

1. Describe the four types of drugs, giving examples.

2. Explain the difference between prescription drugs and recreational drugs.

3. Suggest why people may take drugs recreationally.

Each type of drug affects the body in a different way.

TABLE 3.2.2a: How different drugs affect the body

Type of drug	Effect on the body
painkiller	feelings of pain are reduced or removed; pain messages are blocked in the nervous system
stimulant	temporary increase in alertness and energy; brain activity is increased
depressant	relaxed feelings or sleepiness; the nervous system is slowed down
hallucinogen	sense of reality is distorted as chemicals in the brain are interfered with

4. Suggest why people drink coffee if they need to stay awake at night.

5. Ketamine is an anaesthetic that is used to put animals to sleep while they are operated on. Describe and explain which group of drugs ketamine belongs to.

Considering the negative effects of prescription drugs »»»

Drugs can have **side effects**. These are unwanted effects caused by drugs. For example, antibiotics prescribed for an ear infection may cure the ear infection but may cause diarrhoea as a side effect. Often it is worth the risk of the side effect if the medical condition is treated.

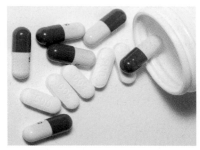

FIGURE 3.2.2b: Painkillers interfere with the nervous system.

TABLE 3.2.2b: The side effects of drugs

Drug	Possible side effects
painkiller	can cause vomiting, nausea and constipation because the drugs affect chemicals in the gut
stimulant	period of fatigue follows the 'high'; risk of heart attack because of increased heart rate; risk of weight loss
depressant	can cause depression in the long term; risk of death if overdosed because the drugs slow body systems down
hallucinogen	can lead to depression and anxiety because the drugs affect the balance of chemicals in the brain; risk of weight loss

Key vocabulary

painkiller

stimulant

depressant

hallucinogen

prescription drug

recreational drug

side effect

6. Explain what 'side effects' are, giving examples.

7. Explain the risks of taking:

    a) ecstasy   **b)** LSD.

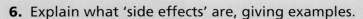

Understanding the impact of smoking

We are learning how to:

- Describe the effects of smoking on the body.
- Explain the risks of smoking on the body.
- Examine the link between smoking and cancer.

Smoking is harmful to the breathing system, contributing to lung infections and lung cancer. However, smoking can also have negative effects on many other parts of the body.

The effects of smoking

Cigarettes contain chemicals including **nicotine** and **tar**. Nicotine is a stimulant drug that increases the heart rate. This can overwork the heart, making smokers more susceptible to heart attacks than non-smokers. Nicotine is also addictive, making it difficult for smokers to quit.

Some tar from cigarettes remains in the lungs and builds up in the alveoli (air sacs). This prevents gases from passing freely in and out of the lungs and the smoker may feel breathless. The tar also supports the growth of bacteria, leading to lung infections.

The tubes of the breathing system have tiny hairs inside them called cilia. Cilia sweep out dust and other particles that can irritate and damage the lungs. Cigarette smoke paralyses these cilia, allowing dust and other particles travel into the lungs. A smoker's cough is the result of the person trying to remove these irritants.

Nicotine and other chemicals in cigarettes affect the blood vessels, which become narrower. Circulation is reduced and less oxygen and nutrients are delivered to parts of the body. This leads to wrinkles forming in the skin and even to the loss of a limb.

FIGURE 3.2.3a: What causes a smoker's cough?

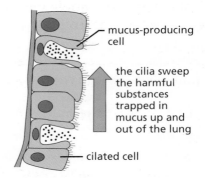

mucus-producing cell

the cilia sweep the harmful substances trapped in mucus up and out of the lung

cilated cell

FIGURE 3.2.3b: Cigarette smoke prevents the cilia from working properly.

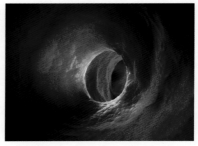

FIGURE 3.2.3c: Smoking can cause the blood vessels to narrow.

1. Describe how three different parts of the body are affected by smoking.

2. Name two chemicals in cigarettes and give an example of their effect.

The dangers of passive smoking 〉〉〉

When a cigarette burns or is smoked, the smoke is released into the air. This smoke may then be breathed in by others around the smoker – this is **passive smoking**.

The smoke from cigarettes can remain in the air for hours after a cigarette has been burned, even when a window is open.

The problems caused by passive smoking are similar to those caused by smoking, including an increased risk of lung **cancer**, heart disease and breathing problems.

3. Describe what 'passive' smoking is.

4. Explain how smokers could avoid damaging people around them with cigarette smoke.

5. Suggest how children in a house could be affected by smoke from cigarettes burned in another room.

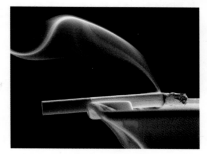

FIGURE 3.2.3d: Cigarette smoke can linger for hours.

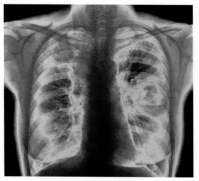

FIGURE 3.2.3e: The risk of lung cancer is increased greatly by smoking.

The link with cancer 〉〉〉〉

Smoking is the single biggest cause of cancer in the world. Studies show that smoking greatly increases the risk of lung cancer. A large study in 2011 suggested that four in every five lung cancers are caused by smoking. Those at the highest risk are people who smoke the most cigarettes and who started smoking at a young age.

Genetics appears to play a part in determining whether we develop cancer or not. Some people appear to be more prone to developing cancer, based on their genes.

6. Explain why people smoke even though the link with cancer is clear.

7. Explain why a person may develop lung cancer from passive smoking alone, while another person may smoke 40 cigarettes a day and never develop lung cancer.

8. In 2002, almost 40 000 people died from lung cancer. Predict how many of these cases were caused by smoking.

Did you know…?

Electronic cigarettes provide the nicotine that the user craves without the smoke and other harmful chemicals. There is debate about whether they help with quitting smoking or 'normalise' cigarette use and lead to more young people becoming addicted to nicotine.

Key vocabulary

nicotine

tar

passive smoking

cancer

Considering the dangers of cannabis

We are learning how to:

- Describe the medicinal uses for cannabis.
- Describe the negative effects of cannabis on the body.
- Give a balanced argument about whether cannabis should be legalised.

Cannabis is made from the dried flowers of the cannabis plant – hashish is formed from the leaves and stems. Cannabis is known for the relaxed feeling that it gives. However, it also has serious side effects.

FIGURE 3.2.4a: The cannabis plant

Uses of cannabis

Cannabis falls into two groups of drugs – it is a depressant but can also be a hallucinogen. It is the most widely used illegal drug in Britain. Many people choose to use cannabis because of the 'chilled-out' feeling that it gives. However, some hospital doctors also prescribe cannabis for medical purposes.

Multiple sclerosis (MS) causes muscle spasms and the sufferer may shake. Cannabis can be prescribed to relieve these spasms. Cannabis can also be prescribed to relieve pain – for example pain caused by cancer, HIV or MS. Cannabis increases the appetite and can be prescribed for patients whose illnesses have caused weight loss.

1. Name the two groups of drugs to which cannabis belongs.
2. Describe one use of cannabis to reduce pain.
3. Give an example of a medical use of cannabis as a depressant.

Harmful effects of cannabis

Cannabis affects the way that the brain functions. It can cause feelings of anxiety, panic and paranoia as well as problems with concentration. In the long term, cannabis has been shown to increase the risk of developing mental illness such as schizophrenia.

Cannabis is usually smoked, although it can also be eaten. Cannabis contains some of the same harmful

FIGURE 3.2.4b: Cannabis can help multiple sclerosis sufferers.

chemicals that tobacco does. In fact, it contains a higher concentration of both tar and other cancer-causing chemicals. Smoking cannabis can cause lung infections and cancer, just as smoking tobacco can. If people smoke cannabis mixed with tobacco, their risks are increased. It is also thought that smoking cannabis can reduce fertility in both men and women.

Cannabis does not contain nicotine and so is less addictive than tobacco.

> 4. Name the chemical in cannabis that causes cancer.
>
> 5. Describe how cannabis can affect mental health.
>
> 6. Compare the harmful effects of smoking cannabis and tobacco.

FIGURE 3.2.4c: Cannabis can reduce the ability to concentrate.

Should cannabis be legalised? >>>>

It is illegal to possess cannabis and anyone caught could be given a five-year prison sentence. Criminals supplying cannabis could spend up to 14 years in prison.

Arguments about whether or not cannabis should be **legalised** have raged for many years.

TABLE 3.2.4: Some of the reasons for and against legalisation of cannabis

Arguments for legalisation	Arguments against legalisation
helpful for patients of MS, cancer, HIV	can cause mental health problems such as paranoia and schizophrenia
does not cause as many health problems as alcohol	may lead to the use of harder drugs
helps people to relax	has a negative effect on concentration and motivation
problems caused by dealing cannabis would be reduced	can cause cancer

> 7. Explain why supplying cannabis is given a longer prison sentence than possession.
>
> 8. Suggest what problems are caused by the dealing of cannabis.
>
> 9. Read the arguments in Table 3.2.4 and then create your own piece of writing, arguing for or against the legalisation of cannabis.

Did you know...?

The risk of having an accident after smoking cannabis *and* drinking alcohol is shown to be 16 times higher than when either substance is used on its own.

Key vocabulary

cannabis

illegal

legalise

Understanding the effects of alcohol

We are learning how to:

- Describe the short-term effects of alcohol on the body.
- Explain the long-term effects of alcohol.
- Suggest how alcoholism affects society.

Most people who drink alcohol will experience a hangover. The headache and sickness that can come with a hangover are not pleasant. However, there are more serious long-term effects linked with drinking alcohol regularly.

The effects of alcohol

Alcohol is a depressant drug. It slows down brain functioning. Soon after drinking alcohol, a person may feel more confident. This is because alcohol suppresses parts of the brain that make us feel shy. As more alcohol is consumed, problems with balance may occur, as well as an inability to speak properly. Some people become aggressive when they are drunk. Alcohol affects the speed at which people can react to external factors, making it dangerous for people to drive after drinking alcohol.

If people continue to drink past the stage of 'being drunk', alcohol poisoning can occur. The heart rate and breathing rate drop dangerously low and the person may slip into a coma. This can lead to death.

1. Describe some of the effects of alcohol on the body.

2. Explain why a person may feel more confident when they drink alcohol.

3. Describe how a person could die from alcohol poisoning.

1 Co-ordination and reaction time are affected

2 Control of emotions (e.g. anger) is lost. Risk of blackout

3 Heart rate and body temperature drop. Risk of possible fatal unconsciousness

FIGURE 3.2.5a: How increasing amounts of alcohol affect the body

Long-term damage

The government makes recommendations on safe levels of alcohol. The recommended maximum per week for women is 14 **units of alcohol** and for men it is 21 units. Generally, women break down alcohol more slowly than men (due to their smaller mass and lower water content in the body) and so they are advised to drink less. Drinking more alcohol than this on a regular basis can cause long-term damage to the body.

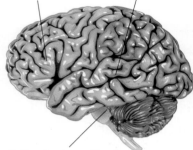

an average glass of wine has 2 units

half a pint of beer or cider has 1.5 units

a measure of spirit (a 'short') has 1.5 units

FIGURE 3.2.5b: One unit is 10 ml of alcohol. The alcohol content of drinks varies, depending on the strength of the drink.

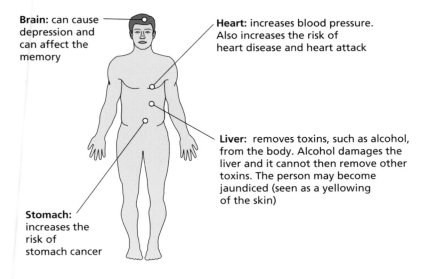

Brain: can cause depression and can affect the memory

Heart: increases blood pressure. Also increases the risk of heart disease and heart attack

Liver: removes toxins, such as alcohol, from the body. Alcohol damages the liver and it cannot then remove other toxins. The person may become jaundiced (seen as a yellowing of the skin)

Stomach: increases the risk of stomach cancer

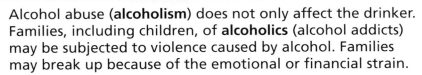

FIGURE 3.2.5c: Some of the long-term effects of alcohol

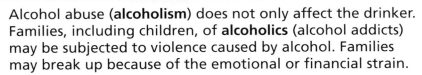

4. A single measure of vodka contains 1.5 units of alcohol. Calculate the maximum number of measures that a woman should drink in a week.

5. A large glass of wine contains 3 units of alcohol. Each bottle contains three large glasses.

   a) How many units does a bottle of wine contain?

   b) How many bottles of wine could a man safely drink in a week?

6. Draw up a table to summarise the long-term effects of alcohol on different organs in the body.

How does alcohol affect society? 〉〉〉

Alcohol abuse (**alcoholism**) does not only affect the drinker. Families, including children, of **alcoholics** (alcohol addicts) may be subjected to violence caused by alcohol. Families may break up because of the emotional or financial strain.

Alcohol abuse costs society an enormous amount of money because of people repeatedly missing work or because they are not productive in the workplace. Alcohol can also contribute to accidents in the workplace.

Alcohol plays a massive part in road traffic accidents. Injuries and deaths caused by drunk drivers change people's lives forever.

7. Explain how alcohol abuse can affect the family of an alcoholic.

8. Explain how alcohol can affect society as a whole.

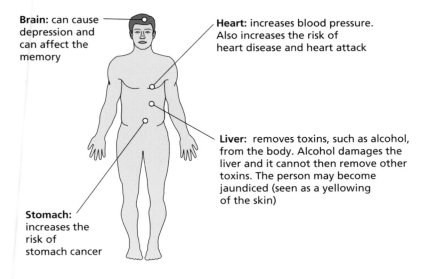

2.5

Did you know...?

Alcohol leads to dehydration by causing more water to be passed in urine than is taken in. This dehydration causes the brain to shrink away from the skull, resulting in a hangover headache.

Key vocabulary

alcohol

unit of alcohol

alcoholism

alcoholic

Exploring the effects of other drugs

We are learning how to:

- Describe the effects of different drugs on the body.
- Compare the dangers of different drugs.

Ecstasy, cocaine and heroin are all **class A drugs**. These are considered to be the most harmful types of drugs. Data shows that, after cannabis, cocaine and ecstasy are the most widely used illegal drugs.

Effects of ecstasy, cocaine and heroin

Ecstasy and **cocaine** are both stimulants. They cause an increase in heart rate and in body temperature. Both drugs cause users to feel energised and confident. After the effects wear off, users of both drugs experience a 'come down'. This can make people feel depressed and flu-like.

Ecstasy is rarely pure. The substances mixed in with it can be fatal. Cocaine is highly addictive. Both drugs are extremely dangerous for people with heart conditions.

Heroin is a depressant. It slows the breathing rate and heart rate. It gives users a feeling of warmth and relaxation. Heroin can cause vomiting, which is dangerous because the highly relaxed user cannot cough and may choke. Heroin is highly addictive, and is either smoked or injected. Injecting drugs can spread infections such as HIV.

1. Describe some of the problems caused by ecstasy and cocaine.

2. Explain why vomiting is dangerous after taking heroin.

3. Explain why ecstasy and cocaine are especially dangerous for those with a heart condition.

The size of the problem

Statistics are gathered on the use of different drugs every year. Information is collected about which drugs are used, the average age of users and the number of deaths caused by different drugs.

FIGURE 3.2.6a: Some ecstasy users have died after taking the drug just once.

Did you know...?

Drug dealers often mix drugs with other, cheaper, substances to maximise their profit. Heroin has even been mixed with brick dust and gravel.

FIGURE 3.2.6b: How could the user know that this drug is mixed with brick dust?

FIGURE 3.2.6c: Number of deaths caused by drugs in 2011 in England.

ecstasy plus other drugs — 20

ecstasy — 6

cocaine plus other drugs — 122

cocaine — 17

heroin plus other drugs — 255

heroin — 103

4. Suggest why it is difficult to monitor the number of deaths caused by drugs.

5. Explain what can be deduced from the data shown in Figure 3.2.6c.

Comparing the negative effects ⟫⟫

TABLE 3.2.6: The negative effects of drug-taking

Ecstasy	Cocaine	Heroin
possibility of up to 7 years in prison for possession	possibility of up to 7 years in prison for possession	possibility of up to 7 years in prison for possession
often impure, containing lethal ingredients	'snorting' may lead to loss of cartilage in the nose; injecting can cause ulcers and damage veins	injecting can cause ulcers and damage veins
may become a habit	highly addictive	highly addictive
can lead to depression and anxiety	can lead to problems with depression and paranoia	over time the addiction becomes stronger and full dependency results
risk of heart problems and dehydration	high doses can cause heart attack and heart failure	can cause coma and death as breathing rate slows

FIGURE 3.2.6d: Injecting drugs carries risks of ulcers, collapsed veins and infections such as HIV, if needles are shared.

6. Describe some similarities of the dangers associated with ecstasy, cocaine and heroin.

7. Explain whether you agree that possession of each of these drugs should carry the same prison sentence.

8. Suggest which of these dangers you consider to be most important when trying to persuade people not to take these drugs.

Key vocabulary

class A drug

ecstasy

cocaine

heroin

Learning about addiction

We are learning how to:

- Define addiction.
- Describe how drugs affect the brain.
- Explain the effects of withdrawal on the body.

Although most people take drugs voluntarily at first, over time some drugs can change the brain in a way that makes the person addicted. Drug addicts are dependent on a drug, which may be illegal or prescribed, and they crave that drug both mentally and physically.

What is addiction?

Casual drug use can lead to **addiction**. Addicts crave more of a drug, even when they know the harm that it is causing to themselves and those around them. The body becomes physically dependent on the drug and without it the person does not feel normal.

Vulnerability to addiction varies from person to person and there is no unique description of 'the addict'. Factors that influence whether or not a person becomes addicted include:

- genetic make-up
- traumatic experiences in childhood
- mental health issues such as depression
- how early in life drugs are experimented with
- the way that drugs are taken (smoking and injecting can lead more quickly to addiction).

Examples of addictive drugs include nicotine, alcohol, cannabis, sedatives, cocaine and heroin.

FIGURE 3.2.7a: Addiction can occur with both legal and illegal drugs.

1. Describe what 'addiction' is.
2. List some examples of drugs that become addictive.
3. Explain why some drug users become addicts whereas others do not.

Changes in the brain

Drugs interfere with the way that the brain sends and receives messages. Some drugs, such as cannabis and heroin,

Did you know...?

Addiction is not restricted to drugs. People may become addicted to gambling, extreme sports, exercise or shopping, for example. This is because the chemicals that are produced during these activities can give a 'buzz'.

are similar to other chemicals in the brain. They fool the brain and abnormal messages are sent. Other drugs, such as cocaine, cause nerve cells to release large amounts of dopamine. Dopamine is a 'feel good' chemical that is usually released when we are happy. Drug users reach a point where they need to take the drug again to try to repeat these feelings.

Brain-imaging studies of drug-addicted individuals show physical changes in areas of the brain that are critical to judgement, decision making, learning and memory, and behaviour control. This explains why drug addicts may take risks that put themselves in danger to get more drugs.

4. Describe the changes in the brain caused by cannabis and heroin.

5. Explain why cocaine addicts continue to take cocaine.

6. Explain why drug addiction may be described as a disease, rather than just a habit.

Overcoming addiction

It is not easy for someone who is addicted to stop taking drugs, but it is possible. **Withdrawal** is the process of coming off drugs and needs to be done in controlled steps. It can be dangerous for some addicts, such as alcoholics or heroin addicts, to stop taking their drug completely.

During withdrawal, physical and emotional symptoms may be experienced.

- Emotional withdrawal symptoms are experienced when coming off all drugs. Examples of emotional withdrawal symptoms include anxiety, insomnia, headaches, depression and poor concentration.

- Physical withdrawal symptoms are also experienced when coming off alcohol, heroin and tranquillisers. Examples of these include sweating, muscle tension, difficulty breathing, tremors, nausea, vomiting and diarrhoea.

Medical help should be sought when overcoming any addiction. **Rehabilitation** clinics allow drug addicts to stay during the withdrawal process. Counselling is also provided at the clinics.

7. Suggest why medical help should be sought when overcoming an addiction.

8. Suggest why rehabilitation clinics are often successful in helping addicts to overcome their addictions.

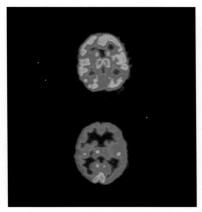

FIGURE 3.2.7b: Drugs affect chemicals in the brain. The yellow areas show the regions of high activity in the brain, in a healthy person (top) and in a cocaine addict (bottom) who has been drug-free for 4 months.

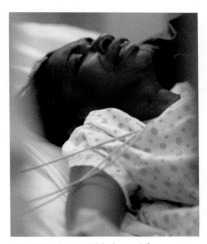

FIGURE 3.2.7c: Withdrawal from drugs can be traumatic.

Key vocabulary

addiction

withdrawal

rehabilitation

Applying key ideas

You have now met a number of important ideas in this chapter. This activity gives an opportunity for you to apply them, just as scientists do. Read the text first, then have a go at the tasks. The first few are fairly easy – then they get a bit more challenging.

Driving under the influence

Most people know that driving while under the influence of alcohol is dangerous. It is also common knowledge that if found to be over the legal level of alcohol, a driver can be charged, leading to a driving ban, a fine and a possible prison sentence.

FIGURE 3.2.8a: Breath testing

Alcohol level in the breath is assessed first using a breathalyser test at the side of the road. If this gives a positive result, the driver is then taken to a police station where the breath may be tested again or blood may be tested. The legal limit is 80 mg (milligrams) of alcohol per 100 ml (millilitres) of blood.

Alcohol is a depressant drug, which means that it will slow down body systems, including the ability to react. After consuming alcohol, drivers are also more likely to take risks.

There is less awareness about the dangers and the consequences of driving under the influence of other drugs. Driving under the influence of drugs carries the same penalties as drink-driving.

If a police officer believes that a driver may be under the influence of drugs other than alcohol, they may carry out a 'field impairment test' at the roadside. This involves the driver carrying out five activities that are simple when not under the influence of any drug, but difficult after taking drugs. The tests include standing on one leg while counting out loud, touching the tip of the nose with a finger while the eyes are closed and walking toe to heel in a straight line.

The description of driving under the influence of drugs does not differentiate between prescription drugs and illegal drugs. It is the responsibility of the driver to ensure that any prescription drugs do not affect their ability to drive safely.

In the last 30 years, the number of deaths caused by drink-driving has fallen dramatically. However, in 2011, there were still 230 fatalities due to drink-driving. It is believed that deaths caused by drug-driving are on the increase. Statistics show that in 2011 drug users were almost twice as likely to drive 'under the influence' than alcohol drinkers. One in five drug users admitted to driving after taking drugs. One in every 100 drug users admitted to driving under the influence almost every day.

FIGURE 3.2.8b: Drugs and alcohol increase the risk of road traffic accidents.

Task 1: Recognising effects

Compare the methods that are used to determine whether a driver is under the influence of alcohol or other drugs.

Task 2: Identifying the drug

Explain why it may be more difficult to determine that a driver is under the influence of drugs other than alcohol.

Task 3: Reaching the limits

Explain why different people can drink different amounts of alcohol before they reach the legal alcohol limit. Suggest why many other countries have stricter laws on drinking than the UK (with the legal level set, for example, at 50 mg of alcohol per 100 ml of blood).

Task 4: Gathering statistics

Compare the percentage of drug users and alcohol drinkers that admitted to driving 'under the influence' in 2011. Suggest why it is difficult to be sure that the data is accurate. Explain which of these statistics it would be most difficult to gather evidence for.

Task 5: Making the most of punishment

Discuss whether or not the current punishments for driving 'under the influence' are working as a deterrent. Suggest other ways to deter people from driving 'under the influence' of alcohol and other drugs.

Task 6: Arguing for drug testing

Provide an argument about whether or not regular, random drug tests should be carried out on drivers. Remember that you should present both sides of the argument and then make a clear conclusion.

Understanding how diseases are spread

We are learning how to:

- Describe how diseases are spread.
- Consider ways of reducing the spread of specific diseases.

Some micro-organisms (microbes) cause 'infectious diseases' that can be spread from one person to another.

What is disease?

A disease is a disorder of a function in our body that is not caused by physical damage. When a disease is caused by an infection it is an **infectious disease** – examples are influenza and chickenpox. Infections can be passed from one person to another. Other diseases, such as diabetes and cancer, cannot be passed on – these are **non-infectious diseases**.

If a disease-causing microbe enters your body, damage is caused to your cells and toxins (poisons) are released. You then start to notice some **symptoms** of the infection – you may get a fever (high temperature), a rash or feel pain.

FIGURE 3.2.9a: What are the symptoms of chickenpox?

1. Describe the difference between infectious and non-infectious diseases. Give examples of each.

2. How can we tell when we have an infectious disease?

How do diseases spread?

Infectious diseases can be spread in a variety of ways.

TABLE 3.2.9a: How infectious diseases are spread

How is it spread?	Details	Examples of disease
air	airborne droplets from the mouth and nose, for example when sneezing	chickenpox, common cold, influenza
faeces/ urine	tiny amounts of urine or faeces are passed from person to person or via an object	threadworms
blood	blood from one person comes into contact with another, such as during a blood transfusion or when sharing needles	HIV, hepatitis B and C
food/water	contaminated water or food is eaten	typhoid, salmonella
sex	body fluids are mixed during sexual contact	HIV, hepatitis B, chlamydia
animals	animal or insect bite	rabies, malaria

3. Suggest why typhoid is much more common in developing countries than in developed countries.

4. Suggest why threadworms are common in young children.

Preventing the spread of disease

It is impossible to keep ourselves completely free of infection throughout our lives. However, steps can be taken to reduce the risk of infection spreading.

TABLE 3.2.9b: How to prevent the spread of some diseases

Disease	How is it spread?	Action taken to avoid spread	Explanation
influenza	air	cover mouth when coughing or sneezeing	traps air-borne droplets
HIV	sex/blood	use a condom during sex	prevents mixing of body fluids that carry the virus
typhoid	water	boil water before drinking	destroys the microbes that cause typhoid
threadworms	faeces	wash hands after using the toilet	removes traces of urine or faeces

FIGURE 3.2.9b: Some types of mosquitos spread malaria.

5. Justify each of these measures used to reduce the spread of infection:

   a) Using alcohol gel as you enter hospital wards.

   b) Screening the blood given by donors before being used in transfusions.

6. Dogs entering the UK from some countries are held in quarantine. Explain how this may reduce the spread of rabies and suggest why some people object to it.

Did you know...?

Some infections cause no symptoms in the patient – an example is chlamydia. This can be easily treated but can cause infertility if left untreated. Screening is important for such diseases.

Key vocabulary

infectious disease

non-infectious disease

symptom

Exploring the body's defences

We are learning how to:

- Describe how the body resists infection.
- Explain the role of white blood cells in fighting infection.

Microbes are all around us and some of these microbes can cause disease. We have barriers to prevent microbes from entering the body but if microbes do enter, cells in our blood act as the next line of defence.

Our body as a barrier

The body has several barriers; these are our 'first lines of defence'.

1. Explain why a cut quickly forms a scab.

2. Describe the ways that the body defends against microbes trying to enter through the nose.

3. Why are these methods are called 'the first line of defence'?

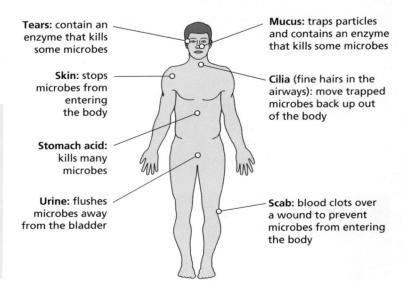

Tears: contain an enzyme that kills some microbes

Skin: stops microbes from entering the body

Stomach acid: kills many microbes

Urine: flushes microbes away from the bladder

Mucus: traps particles and contains an enzyme that kills some microbes

Cilia (fine hairs in the airways): move trapped microbes back up out of the body

Scab: blood clots over a wound to prevent microbes from entering the body

FIGURE 3.2.10a: The 'first lines of defence'

Defence by white blood cells

If disease-causing microbes manage to get past the barriers, **white blood cells** act as the next line of defence. The cells form part of our **immune system** – the system in the body that protects against disease.

There are three types of white blood cell:

- **Phagocytes** ingest microbes and destroy them.
- 'B-cells' produce **antibodies** – these are protein molecules that attach to the microbes and destroy them.
- 'T-cells' produce antitoxins – these are chemicals that neutralise the toxins produced by the microbes. These cells also co-ordinate the attack on the microbes.

FIGURE 3.2.10b: A white blood cell surrounding bacteria

When microbes infect the body, white blood cell numbers increase and blood flows to the site of the infection.

4. Explain why the number of white blood cells would increase in someone with an infection.

5. Suggest why an infected cut may appear red and hot.

6. Draw an annotated diagram to show the roles of the three types of white blood cell.

Memory cells >>>>

Once an infection is overcome, the number of white blood cells returns to normal levels. However, some of both the T-cells and B-cells remain as **memory cells**. If the same type of microbe infects the body again, these memory cells react quickly. Antibodies are produced and microbes are destroyed before they have the opportunity to reproduce. This is why we rarely catch the same disease twice – we become immune to the disease.

Some microbes, such as those that cause influenza, regularly change their structure very slightly. This means that the body has no memory of the microbes and is why people can get flu each year.

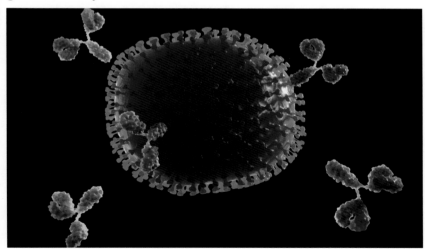

FIGURE 3.2.10d: This shows how antibodies attack a microbe.

Did you know...?

Platelets in the blood are responsible for blood clotting, which leads to a scab developing. Haemophilia is a genetic condition in which the blood does not clot. Without treatment, the person could bleed to death.

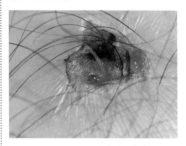

FIGURE 3.2.10c: How does a scab help to protect us?

7. Explain why it is rare to catch measles twice.

8. Antibodies produced by the immune system recognise proteins on the surface of microbes. Suggest how the microbe that causes influenza avoids us becoming immune to it.

9. Explain why it is helpful to have memory cells of both B-cells and T-cells.

Key vocabulary

white blood cell

immune system

phagocyte

antibody

memory cell

Comparing microbes

We are learning how to:

- Describe the characteristics of different types of microbe.
- Recall examples of diseases caused by bacteria, viruses and fungi.
- Evaluate a model of a microbe.

Micro-organisms (microbes) are too small to be seen with the naked eye. There are three main types – bacteria, viruses and fungi. Each infectious disease is caused by a specific type of microbe.

Comparing microbes

Each type of microbe has a different structure. Microbes are usually much smaller than animal cells.

Fungi are usually the biggest type of microbe. **Bacteria** (the singular is 'bacterium') are usually smaller than fungi but larger than viruses. **Viruses** are the smallest type of microbe – and they can only reproduce inside a host cell. For this reason, some people argue that viruses are not living things.

TABLE 3.2.11a: Diseases caused by microbes

Diseases caused by bacteria	Diseases caused by viruses	Diseases caused by fungi
salmonella food poisoning	common cold	athlete's foot
chlamydia	influenza	thrush
tuberculosis (TB)	chickenpox	
cholera	HIV	
typhoid	measles	

1. Construct a table to show if each type of microbe contains a cell wall, cell membrane and nucleus.

2. Give one reason why some people claim that viruses are not living things.

3. Suggest whether or not there is a relationship between:

   a) the size of a microbe and its complexity

   b) the size of a microbe and its ability to cause disease.

Single-celled fungus

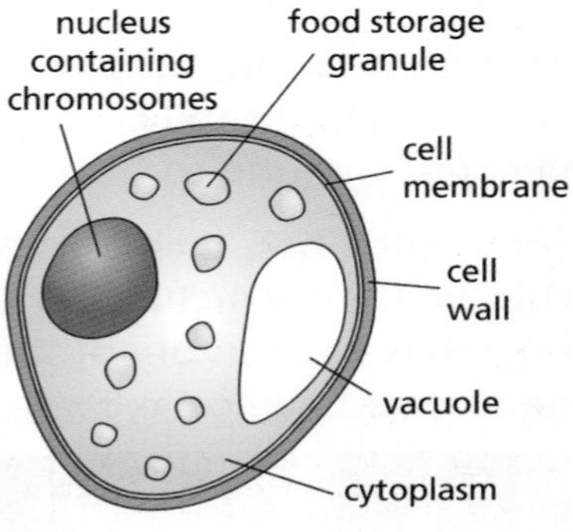

Bacterium

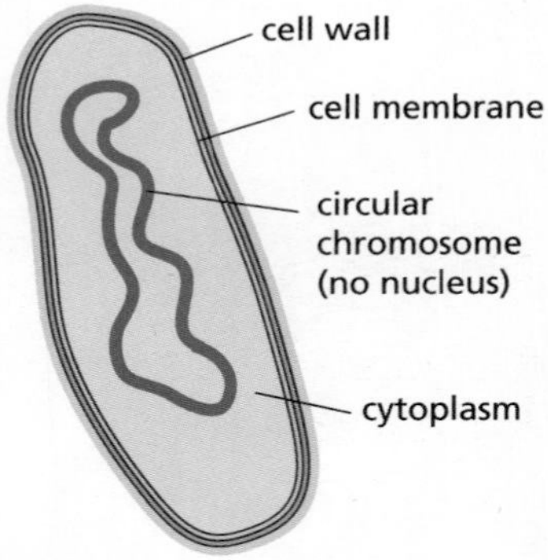

Virus

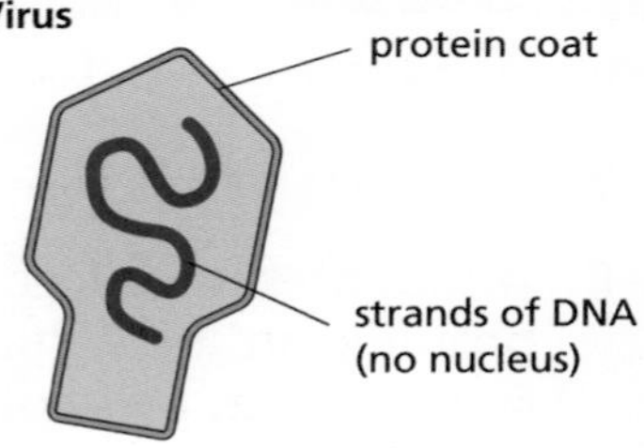

FIGURE 3.2.11a: Microbes vary in structure.

Which microbe is to blame? ⟩⟩⟩

We have not always known that microbes cause disease. An early theory was that 'bad air' produced by dead bodies caused disease. In the 1800s, a doctor called Robert Koch proved that microbes cause disease. He proved that the same type of microbe always caused the same disease.

4. Describe the discovery made by Robert Koch.

5. According to Robert Koch, which type of microbe would always be found in a case of athlete's foot?

6. Suggest why people may have believed that bad air from dead bodies caused disease.

Different shapes and sizes ⟩⟩⟩

Although each type of microbe has general features, within each group, bacteria, fungi and viruses can vary in shape and size.

Microbes are measured in **micrometres** (μm). One micrometre is a millionth of a metre, or a thousandth of a millimetre.

TABLE 3.2.11b: Bacteria and viruses come in different shapes and sizes

Shape and appearance	Size	Example of infection caused
round bacteria	1 μm	pneumonia
rod bacteria	1–2 μm	anthrax
spiral bacteria	2–5 μm	syphilis
bacteriophage	0.1–0.2 μm	infects bacteria, not humans
adenovirus	0.1 μm	conjunctivitis

7. The head of a pin is approximately 2 mm in diameter. Estimate how many:

   a) round bacteria could fit on a pin head

   b) adenoviruses could fit on a pin head.

8. Compare how many times bigger the largest bacterium is than the virus shown in Table 3.2.11b.

FIGURE 3.2.11b: Robert Koch proved that tuberculosis is caused by a bacterium.

Did you know...?

Cold sores are caused by a virus. Most of us carry the virus but only a small proportion ever see any symptoms. It is likely that you were given the virus when you were kissed by someone carrying the virus when you were little.

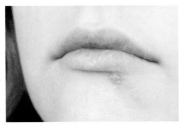

FIGURE 3.2.11c: Cold sores are caused by a virus – herpes simplex.

Key vocabulary

fungus

bacteria

virus

micrometre

Investigating the growth of bacteria

We are learning how to:

- Describe what bacteria need to survive.
- Investigate bacterial growth in different conditions.
- Analyse bacterial growth data.

Bacteria are all around us, on every surface, including our skin. They are found in a wider variety of habitats than any other organism. Bacteria need certain conditions to keep them alive. Sometimes, the conditions in our homes promote the growth of disease-causing bacteria.

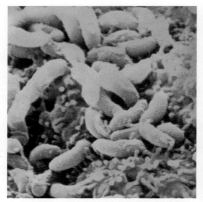

FIGURE 3.2.12a: Bacteria feeding on mucus

What do bacteria need to survive?

Bacteria have adapted to survive in many different conditions. Therefore, their requirements vary from species to species.

- **Nutrients:** Most bacteria need an external source of nutrients. They use enzymes to break down food such as carbohydrates and fats into glucose.

- **Moisture:** Most foods contain enough water for bacteria to survive.

- **Temperature:** Most bacteria like warm temperatures, with the optimum being 37 °C.

- **Oxygen:** Bacteria vary in their oxygen requirements. Some can survive with no oxygen (for example, those that live deep in the sea).

- **pH:** Most bacteria prefer neutral conditions (pH 7). But some can survive in acid or alkaline conditions.

1. Describe how bacteria obtain nutrients.

2. Explain why bacteria would not grow in dried foods such as milk powder.

3. Describe the temperature and pH conditions favoured by bacteria that live in the stomach.

Growing bacteria in the laboratory

In order to study the structure, growth and effects of bacteria, we must grow them in the laboratory. This is a simple and commonly used technique. Bacteria are

> **Did you know...?**
>
> Some bacteria can survive in the hot springs of Yellowstone National Park, USA. The springs contain highly toxic, sometimes boiling water. The bacteria are fuelled by hydrogen and sulfur in the water.
>
>
>
> FIGURE 3.2.12b: Bacteria produce many of the brilliant colours in Yellowstone's hot springs.

transferred onto a plate containing nutrient **agar** jelly and then incubated to allow bacteria to grow.

When investigating bacterial growth, it is important that cultures are not contaminated with other bacteria. The **sterile technique** is used to avoid this.

- Petri dishes and nutrient agar jelly must be sterilised before use.
- Inoculating loops or cotton buds used to transfer bacteria onto plates must be sterile.
- Hands must be clean.
- After plates have been **inoculated** with bacteria, they are sealed before the plates are incubated over night.

Plates are then incubated to allow the growth of bacteria. Incubation is usually carried out at approximately 25 °C.

4. Describe what the 'sterile technique' is and why it is used.

5. Explain why agar plates are sealed after inoculation with bacteria.

6. Suggest the danger of incubating the inoculated plates at 37 °C.

FIGURE 3.2.12c: Why is it important to wear clean gloves or have clean hands when inoculating plates?

TABLE 3.2.12: Numbers of bacteria found in a study

Location	Number of bacteria per cm²
toilet bowl	3.2 million
kitchen worktop	488
TV remote control	70
pet food dish	2110
computer keyboard	64
kitchen cloth	134 630

Bacteria around the home ⟩⟩⟩

When bacteria grow on agar plates, **colonies** are formed. These are circular shapes that are formed from the growth of a single bacterium.

A study was carried out to compare the number of bacteria in different locations around the home. The results are shown in Table 3.2.12.

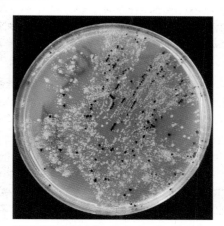

FIGURE 3.2.12d: Bacteria can be seen as colonies on agar plates.

7. Describe and explain what the results in Table 3.2.12 show.

8. Suggest why the results may vary if this investigation was repeated.

9. Suggest what else it would be useful to know about the bacteria, in addition to the number of them.

Key vocabulary

agar

sterile technique

inoculate

colony

Understanding how antibiotics work

We are learning how to:

- Investigate the effect of antibiotics on bacteria.
- Explain how bacteria can become immune to antibiotics.
- Evaluate the impact of superbugs on our health.

Antibiotics are drugs that are used to kill bacteria inside the body – their use has helped human health enormously. However, their overuse and misuse is threatening to do us harm.

Killing microbes

Cleaning products that claim to 'kill bugs' usually contain a **disinfectant**. Disinfectants kill bacteria on contact when they are used at the correct concentration. Disinfectants include bleaches and alcohols. They are used to clean surfaces such as floors, toilets and worktops. Disinfectants are toxic.

Antiseptics also kill bacteria but these are used on the skin, rather than on surfaces. Some antiseptics are weak forms of disinfectants. Antiseptics are important in hospitals – for example to clean the skin before surgery and to clean hands before entering a ward.

FIGURE 3.2.13a: Disinfectant and antiseptic both kill bacteria.

1. Describe the difference between disinfectants and antiseptics.

2. Explain why both disinfectants and antiseptics are important in hospitals.

3. Suggest why surgery was more dangerous before antiseptics were widely used.

The effects of antibiotics

Antibiotics are drugs that kill bacteria without damaging human cells. They are used as a medicine to treat bacterial infections. Different antibiotics affect bacteria in different ways. For example some antibiotics disrupt the cell wall of the bacteria and they burst, whereas others prevent the bacteria from respiring and so they die.

To test the effectiveness of different antibiotics on bacteria, discs of paper soaked in antibiotic can be used. Figure 3.2.13b shows a Petri dish in which bacteria have been spread before laying antibiotic discs onto the plate.

A clear zone can be seen around each of the antibiotic discs where the bacteria have not grown.

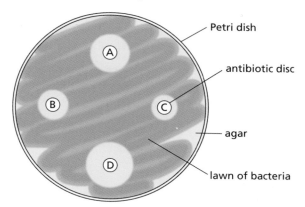

FIGURE 3.2.13b: Testing the effectiveness of different antibiotics

4. Describe some of the effects that antibiotics have on bacteria.

5. Look at Figure 3.2.13b. Explain:

   a) which antibiotic a doctor should prescribe for an infection with this bacterium

   b) whether the doctor should prescribe the same antibiotic for other bacterial infections.

6. Explain why a doctor will not prescribe antibiotics for a common cold.

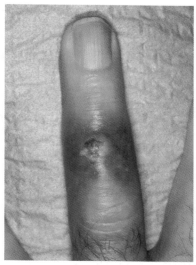

FIGURE 3.2.13c: Infection caused by MRSA can be very serious.

Superbugs ▶▶▶

As the use of antibiotics has increased, so too has the number of bacteria that are resistant to the drugs. When antibiotics are used, any bacteria that have a genetic **resistance** survive the medicine and reproduce to form whole populations of resistant bacteria. The antibiotics are then ineffective at fighting infection.

Antibiotic resistance is a huge problem in hospitals. There are some strains of bacteria that are resistant to many different antibiotics – these are called **superbugs**. One superbug is MRSA (methicillin-resistant *Staphylococcus aureus*). An infection by MRSA can be very difficult to treat.

7. Explain why some people believe that more money should be spent on developing new antibiotics.

8. Suggest why MRSA is more common in hospitals and nursing homes than in the rest of the population.

9. Discuss whether or not you think that antibiotics should be sold without a prescription.

Did you know...?

Following the discovery of the superbug MRSA, hospital doctors were required to stop wearing ties and long-sleeved shirts. It was thought that their clothing was carrying bacteria from one patient to another.

Key vocabulary

disinfectant

antiseptic

antibiotic

resistance

superbug

Learning about vaccination

We are learning how to:

- Describe how vaccines were discovered.
- Explain how vaccines prevent a viral infection.
- Evaluate the risks involved with vaccination.

Children are given vaccines for several diseases, including measles, mumps, rubella and tuberculosis. Before vaccines were developed, children died of these diseases. The discovery of vaccines has had a huge impact on society.

Discovery of vaccines

Smallpox was once a deadly disease, killing an estimated 30 million people in the 20th century. One in every three people who became infected by the smallpox virus died.

Edward Jenner was a country doctor. He noticed that milkmaids who caught the much less serious cowpox did not catch smallpox. He took fluid from a cowpox blister and inoculated a small boy with it. The boy became ill but made a full recovery. Jenner then scratched the boy's arm with smallpox but the boy did not show any symptoms of smallpox. The boy was immune to smallpox. This was the first use of a **vaccine**. Use of the smallpox vaccine worldwide led to the eradication of the smallpox virus.

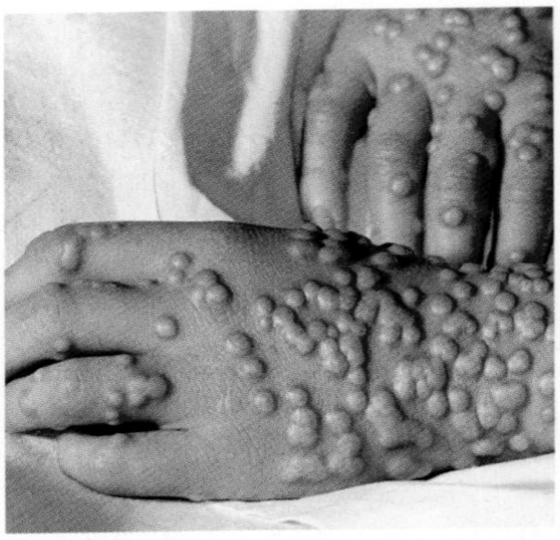

FIGURE 3.2.14a: Smallpox once killed people all over the world.

1. State what causes smallpox.

2. Explain how Edward Jenner vaccinated against smallpox.

How do vaccines work?

A vaccine is a weakened or dead form of the disease. This means that the microbe from which the vaccine is made cannot reproduce inside the body. Vaccines are usually given by injection, although a recently developed influenza vaccine is sprayed up the nose.

Vaccines bring about an immune response in the body:

- The vaccine enters the body and causes white blood cells to produce antibodies.

- The microbe is quickly destroyed.

- Memory cells are formed inside the body.

Did you know...?

The first attempts to prevent people from catching smallpox involved scratching prisoners with fluid from smallpox blisters. Prisoners were used because they were not considered as important as other people. Many of them died.

- If the live form of the microbe enters the body, memory cells produce antibodies and antitoxins. The microbes are destroyed quickly before the person shows any symptoms.

3. Explain why a microbe is changed before it is used in a vaccine.

4. Draw a cartoon strip to show how a vaccine leads to immunity.

5. Suggest why some people may prefer to have a vaccine as a nose spray rather than as an injection.

Vaccines and side effects ⟫⟫

As with any medicine, vaccines carry risks and side effects can occur. These side effects vary with vaccines but are usually minor, such as:

- pain and itching at the injection site

- headache

- fever

- mild rash.

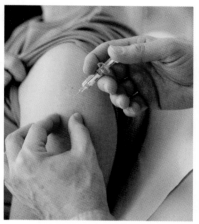

FIGURE 3.2.14b: Most vaccines are injected.

The risks of these side effects outweigh the damage that could be caused by the disease.

In 1998, claims were made that the vaccine for measles, mumps and rubella (**MMR**) was linked to autism and bowel disease. The claims led to a huge decrease in the uptake of the MMR vaccine by parents for their children. Large-scale studies made since these claims have shown that there is no link between the MMR vaccine and either of these conditions. It is thought that the original studies may have been flawed.

6. Explain how you would respond to a parent considering not having their child vaccinated because of the side effects.

7. Explain how the claims that the MMR vaccine causes autism and bowel disease affected the number of cases of measles, mumps and rubella.

8. Suggest how the number of parents having their children vaccinated with the MMR vaccine could be increased further.

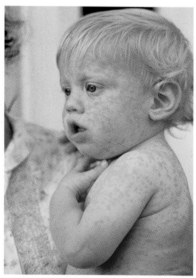

FIGURE 3.2.14c: Measles can have serious complications in children.

Key vocabulary

smallpox

vaccine

MMR

Checking your progress

To make good progress in understanding science you need to focus on these ideas and skills.

Give examples of some different types of drugs.

Describe the effects of different types of drugs on the body.

Explain the effects of different drugs on the body, including harmful effects.

Identify parts of the body damaged by smoking.

Explain how the body is damaged by smoking and by passive smoking.

Examine data about smoking and cancer, and draw a conclusion about the correlation.

Describe the effects of cannabis on the body.

Suggest some reasons why people use cannabis.

Present, using evidence, arguments for and against the legalisation of cannabis.

Describe some effects of alcohol on the body.

Describe and explain several effects of alcohol on the body.

Suggest how alcoholism affects society.

Describe what addiction is and give examples.

Describe the changes in the brain caused by drugs and how this can lead to addiction.

Explain the effects of withdrawal from drug dependency on the body, including the brain.

Describe and give examples of a way in which diseases are spread.

Describe several examples of how specific diseases are spread and suggest how their spread may be reduced.

Consider suggestions to reduce the spread of specific diseases and justify decisions.

☐ Describe the body's mechanisms to prevent infection.

☐ Describe the roles of white blood cells in fighting infection.

☐ Explain why we rarely catch the same infectious disease twice, but may catch influenza over and over again.

☐ State examples of diseases caused by microbes.

☐ Describe the characteristics of different microbes.

☐ Evaluate a model of a type of microbe.

☐ Describe the conditions that bacteria need to survive.

☐ Compare bacterial growth in different parts of the home.

☐ Analyse data about bacterial growth.

☐ Describe the effect of antibiotics on bacteria.

☐ Explain how bacteria become resistant to antibiotics.

☐ Explain what superbugs are and evaluate their impact on society.

☐ Describe what a vaccine is and how vaccines were discovered.

☐ Explain how vaccines prevent a viral infection.

☐ Evaluate the risks associated with vaccination.

Questions

Questions 1–7

See how well you have understood the ideas in the chapter.

1. What type of drug is paracetamol? [1]

    a) stimulant   b) depressant   c) painkiller   d) hallucinogen

2. Which drug in cigarettes causes the heart rate to increase? [1]

    a) tar   b) nicotine   c) carbon monoxide   d) carcinogen

3. Salmonella infection is mainly spread by: [1]

    a) contaminated food   b) blood   c) sex   d) air

4. What are the protein molecules called that attach to microbes and destroy them? [1]

    a) platelets   b) mucus   c) antibiotics   d) antibodies

5. Explain the difference between antiseptics and disinfectants. [2]

6. Give two examples of features that bacteria contain that viruses do not. [2]

7. Explain what drug addiction is, using examples. [4]

Questions 8–14

See how well you can apply the ideas in this chapter to new situations.

8. What group of drugs would a substance that causes a person to see imaginary spiders and monsters belong to? [1]

    a) hallucinogens   b) painkillers   c) stimulants   d) depressants

9. An unknown drug causing a person to become hyperactive is most likely to be: [1]

    a) heroin   b) ecstasy   c) tranquilliser   d) anaesthetic

10. If infection of a person with one microbe gives resistance to another microbe infection, which of the following is likely? [1]

    a) The microbes have similar structure.

    b) The person will not be infected by any microbe in the future.

    c) The immune system of the person is not working properly.

    d) Antibiotics may be needed.

11. Explain two measures that a school could take to reduce the spread of a disease-causing microbe that seems to be spread by air. [2]

12. You can reduce the spread of disease in a number of ways. Which is the only row in Table 3.2.16 that correctly states how you could best reduce the spread of the stated disease? [1]

TABLE 3.2.16

	Disease	Method of reducing spread
a)	threadworms	cover mouth when sneezing
b)	influenza	use a condom during sex
c)	rabies	wash hands after going to the toilet
d)	typhoid	boil water before drinking

13. Passive smoking may be banned in cars. Explain how this may affect the number of cases of lung cancer. [2]

FIGURE 3.2.16a

14. A student tested how well four different handwash products killed bacteria. Figure 3.2.16b shows the agar plate after incubation with discs soaked in the four samples of handwash. Explain what these results show, including which handwash you would recommend for use in a bathroom. [4]

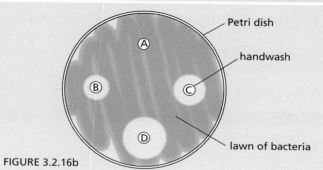

FIGURE 3.2.16b

Petri dish

handwash

lawn of bacteria

Questions 15–16

See how well you can understand and explain new ideas and evidence.

15. A unknown microbe has been seen in a sample of faeces from a patient. Identify what type of microbe this is, with reasons, and explain whether or not antibiotics may be suitable to treat the patient. [2]

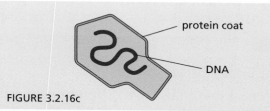

protein coat

DNA

FIGURE 3.2.16c

16. Scientists have manufactured a new antibiotic drug. Explain why the effectiveness of this drug may decrease over time and suggest how this could be tested. [4]

Obtaining Useful Materials

Metals

Metals are materials with many useful applications. All metals are good conductors of heat and electricity. Some, such as copper, are better conductors than others.

Many metals, like iron and steel, are strong and hard. Metals such as aluminium and sodium are light. The properties of metals determine their applications.

Reactions of metals

Sodium and magnesium are much more reactive than iron and copper. If sodium is put in some water, it catches fire. An extremely vigorous reaction occurs between sodium and an acid. When iron or copper are put in water or an acid, a very slow reaction occurs.

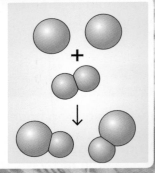

Changes in chemical reactions

Chemical reactions occur when the atoms of reactants are rearranged to form new products. Word equations and balanced symbol equations summarise the changes involved. Mass is conserved in all chemical changes.

Many chemical reactions, such as combustion, transfer energy as heat and light.

Properties of materials

Different materials have different properties. We may be able to change the properties of materials to suit our purposes. Small amounts of metals can be added to each other to make alloys, like adding magnesium to aluminium to make duraluminium. Alloys are stronger than the original metals.

In this chapter you will find out ⟩⟩

Metal ores

- Most metals are found in rocks known as ores.

- In an ore the metal is combined with other elements, both chemically and physically. Changes are needed to remove the metal from its ore so it can be useful.

- Metal ores are obtained from mines, but these can have wide-scale negative environmental impacts.

Reactivity

- The reactivity series is a list of metals arranged in order of their reactivity.

- More reactive elements will remove less reactive metals from their compounds. Carbon is more reactive than iron, copper, lead and zinc, and is used to obtain these metals from their ores.

- Metal carbonates can be decomposed by heat. The carbonates of more reactive metals are harder to decompose than those of less reactive metals.

Reaction energy and catalysts

- Some reactions transfer energy to their surroundings – these are known as exothermic reactions. Other reactions take in energy from their surroundings – these are known as endothermic reactions. Photosynthesis is the most common endothermic reaction.

- Catalysts are substances that can speed up or slow down a reaction, without taking part in it. Enzymes are examples of biological catalysts.

Special materials

- Ceramics, polymers and composite materials have been in use for many thousands of years. Today, many new types of materials are being made, based on the chemistry of these earlier materials. These have exciting applications – as in racing cars, rockets and modern buildings.

Obtaining metals from ores

We are learning how to:

- Recognise how abundant common ores are in the Earth.
- Explain how ores are extracted from the Earth.

We rely on the use of metals to carry out different jobs. Metals are mined as ores from the Earth's crust. How are metals extracted from their ores?

What is an ore?

Only a few metals are found in their pure form on the Earth's surface. Gold, silver and platinum are examples of these 'native' metals.

The majority of other metals are found chemically combined with other elements in the form of an **ore**. An ore is a rock that contains a sufficient quantity of the metal to make it worth extracting the metal from it.

Ores are often mixtures of different **minerals**. Usually a combination of physical and chemical processes is needed to remove the metal from the other elements in the ore. Many ores contain a metal oxide or metal carbonate.

> **Did you know...?**
>
> The world's deepest iron ore mine in Sweden operates at 1.3 km below the surface.

Lead ore – galena PbS

Iron ore – haematite Fe_2O_3

Copper ore – malachite $CuCO_3(OH)_2$

Lead metal – Pb

Iron metal – Fe

Copper metal – Cu

FIGURE 3.3.2a: The names and chemical formulas of some common metal ores and their metals

1. Why do many ores look very different from the metal they contain?

2. Why do you think gold is found uncombined?

First extraction of metals from ores

Copper exists in its native form, as well as in ores. We know that it was used in its native form as early as 6000 BCE. Around 4000 to 3000 BCE, it was discovered that copper could be extracted from ore. It may be that potters accidentally included copper ore in their furnaces. The temperature of around 1000 °C would have decomposed (split up) the ore.

Lead and tin were also extracted from their ores thousands of years ago. These ores require only about 200 °C to decompose them. It may be that the ores fell into camp fires.

Carbon, in the form of charcoal, played a major part in producing the metals from the ores, but people in those times would not have understood carbon's role.

3. Suggest why some metals were found much earlier than others.

4. Aluminum is the most abundant metal in the Earth's crust. It was not discovered until 1825. Suggest why it took so long to discover.

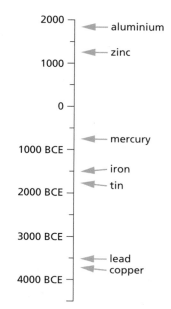

FIGURE 3.3.2b: A timeline showing the discovery of the extraction of metals from their ores

Extracting ores

Many metal ores make their way to the surface of the Earth's crust as a result of volcanic activity. The molten ores are pushed into seams of rock where they cool over many thousands of years. Some seams are very close to the surface. Others are deep within the crust and have to be mined. Many, beneath the ocean floor, are still to be uncovered.

Very reactive metals, like sodium, are extracted from their ores using electricity – this process is known as electrolysis. Less reactive metals, like iron, can be obtained by **smelting** (the ore is roasted with carbon). The ores of very unreactive metals, like copper, are heated to decompose the ore first, before smelting is carried out.

5. Why were most reactive metals not discovered until the late 1800s?

6. Why is it harder to remove metals from the compounds of reactive metals than from the compounds of unreactive metals?

7. Why are many metal ore seams beneath the ocean floor still to be uncovered?

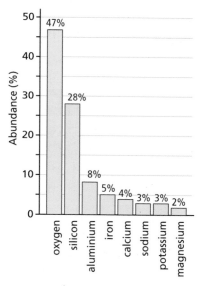

FIGURE 3.3.2c: The elements most commonly found in the Earth's crust

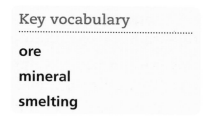

Key vocabulary

ore

mineral

smelting

Understanding reactivity

We are learning how to:

- Use evidence to identify the reactivity series of metals.
- Represent reactions using formulas and equations.

Many metal ores take the form of carbonates. By using heat to decompose (split up) metal carbonates, we can find out how reactive the metals are in comparison with each other. Do more reactive metal carbonates decompose more easily than less reactive metal carbonates?

Sodium and water
(immediate reaction)

Signs of how reactive metals are ⟩⟩

Some metals are clearly more reactive than others. If a piece of sodium is dropped into water, it fizzes and pops, releasing a gas that burns. If an iron nail is added to water, signs of a chemical change will be seen after a few days; but if copper is added to water, there is no change. The **reactivity** of the different metals can be compared by observing their reactions – the more vigorous the reaction, the more reactive the metal.

TABLE 3.3.3a: How different metals react with an acid. The general word equation for the reaction is: metal + hydrochloric acid → metal chloride + hydrogen

Name of metal	Observations with acid
sodium	explosive reaction occurs; any hydrogen produced catches fire spontaneously
copper	no visible change occurs
magnesium	vigorous production of hydrogen bubbles; the test tube becomes hot quickly

Iron nail and water after a week

1. Use the observations in Table 3.3.3a to place the metals in order of reactivity with the most reactive metal first.

2. Zinc is less reactive than sodium but more reactive than iron. Predict how it will react with an acid.

3. Write word equations for the reactions of zinc, potassium and gold with hydrochloric acid.

Copper and water after a week

FIGURE 3.3.3a: The reaction between sodium and water, an iron nail and water, and copper in water. Which metal is the most reactive?

Why is reactivity important?

By understanding the reactivity of metals, we can make predictions about how to extract metals from compounds.

Some **metal carbonates**, like limestone (calcium carbonate), decompose on heating – a process known as **thermal decomposition**. Thermal decomposition of a metal carbonate can be the first stage in the extraction of a metal.

TABLE 3.3.3b: Energy is needed in varying amounts to decompose different metal carbonates.

Metal carbonate	Energy for thermal decomposition (kJ/mol)
magnesium carbonate	101
strontium carbonate	235
barium carbonate	269
calcium carbonate	178

4. Use Table 3.3.3b to put the metals magnesium, strontium, barium and calcium in order of reactivity.

5. Which metal(s) could you extract easily using thermal decomposition? Explain your answer.

Decomposing metal carbonates

The more reactive the metal in the carbonate, the harder it is for the carbonate to decompose. The reason is that metals with a high reactivity make stronger bonds with carbonate.

Strong bonds are harder to break because they require more energy to break. Higher temperatures will be needed to decompose their carbonates. The bonds formed by less reactive metals are easier to break because they require less energy.

The general word equation for decomposing a carbonate is:

metal carbonate → metal oxide + carbon dioxide

6. Suggest which metal carbonate will require the highest temperature for decomposition – iron carbonate, copper carbonate or potassium carbonate. Give a reason for your choice.

7. Write a balanced symbol equation for the thermal decomposition of sodium carbonate, which is Na_2CO_3. Sodium oxide is Na_2O.

Did you know...?

As you go down a group in the Periodic Table, the metal carbonates tend to be more stable. They are harder to decompose. What does this tell you about the reactivity of metals as you go down a group?

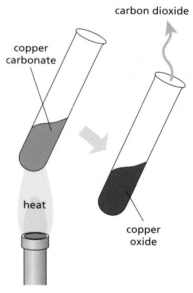

FIGURE 3.3.3b: Copper carbonate can be decomposed by heating.

Key vocabulary

reactivity

metal carbonate

thermal decomposition

Making use of displacement reactions

We are learning how to:

- Represent and explain displacement reactions using formulas and equations.
- Make inferences about reactivity from displacement reactions.

We can use the order of reactivity of elements to make predictions about reactions. Reactive metals can be thought of as 'chemical bullies'. Why might this be so?

Chemical bullies

When a reactive metal reacts with a compound of a less reactive metal, the more reactive metal 'pushes out' or 'displaces' the less reactive metal. The more reactive metal forms a chemical bond with whatever the less reactive metal was bonded to.

The situation is a bit like a basketball match. Imagine a weak player with the ball. A stronger player takes the ball from him, displacing the weaker player and leaving him on his own.

An example of such a **displacement reaction** is when iron is added to a blue copper sulfate solution. Iron is more reactive than copper. A chemical change occurs – iron displaces the copper, bonding with the sulfate to make iron sulfate, which is a pale green solution.

FIGURE 3.3.4a: Iron and copper sulfate solution – before and after the displacement reaction. Over time, the blue copper sulfate solution becomes paler, and the iron nail becomes covered with a brown coating of copper.

The word equation for the reaction is:

iron + copper sulfate → iron sulfate + copper

1. When magnesium is added to a solution of copper sulfate, the solution changes from blue to colourless much faster than with iron. Which is more reactive, magnesium or iron?

2. Write a word equation for the reaction between iron sulfate and magnesium.

Did you know...?

Old copper mines often become flooded, and a blue solution of copper sulfate results. By adding cheap scrap iron to this solution, copper metal is produced. This makes extra money for the mine owners.

Using displacement reactions

When reactive metals react with acids, a displacement reaction occurs and hydrogen is displaced. As long as a metal is above hydrogen in the **reactivity series**, they will react to displace hydrogen and form bubbles of the gas:

zinc + hydrochloric acid → zinc chloride + hydrogen

Non-metals also undergo displacement reactions. Chlorine is more reactive than iodine. When chlorine gas is passed through sodium iodide solution, the chlorine displaces the iodine as follows:

chlorine + sodium iodide → sodium chloride + iodine

This method is used to make iodine on an industrial scale.

> **3.** Copper is more reactive than silver. Predict what would happen when copper foil is put in silver nitrate solution.
>
> **4.** Write a balanced symbol equation for the reaction in question 3. Silver nitrate is $AgNO_3$; copper nitrate is $Cu(NO_3)_2$.
>
> **5.** Bromine displaces iodine from sodium iodide, but there is no reaction when it is added to sodium chloride. What is the order of reactivity between chlorine, bromine and iodine?

Making predictions

The reactivity series is shown in Figure 3.3.4c. The further elements are from each other in the series, the more vigorous the displacement reaction between the more reactive element and a compound of the less reactive element.

> **6.** Write a balanced symbol equation for the reaction between the most reactive metal and the least reactive metal nitrate.
>
> **7.** Why is no hydrogen produced when copper is added to hydrochloric acid?
>
> **8.** Copper is a valuable metal. Suggest why it is not made commercially by reacting copper oxide with a more reactive metal, like sodium.

FIGURE 3.3.4b: Displacement of iodine by chlorine. The iodide particles in a potassium iodide solution are oxidised to form iodine – this gives the brown colour.

Most reactive

K	potassium
Na	sodium
Ca	calcium
Mg	magnesium
Al	aluminium
C	carbon
Zn	zinc
Fe	iron
Sn	tin
Pb	lead
H	hydrogen
Cu	copper
Ag	silver
Au	gold
Pt	platinum

Least reactive

FIGURE 3.3.4c: The reactivity series

Key vocabulary

displacement reaction

reactivity series

Using carbon to extract iron

We are learning how to:

- Represent displacement reactions with carbon, metal oxides and iron using formulas and equations.
- Explain how mass is conserved in the extraction of metals.

Carbon has been used to obtain metals for thousands of years. What is so special about it and how does it work?

Using carbon to extract metals

Humans have burned wood, which is mostly carbon, for thousands of years. It is thought that the accidental addition of lead ore (galena) and tin ore (cassiterite) to wood fires resulted in the formation of lead and tin.

Coal is a richer source of carbon than wood. When it is burned slowly to temperatures over 1000 °C, in the absence of oxygen, **coke** is made. This was discovered in the 18th century. Coke is used in industry today to extract some metals from their ores.

Carbon is more reactive than metals such as iron, tin, lead and copper. When ores of these metals are roasted with carbon, a displacement reaction occurs. Carbon removes the oxygen or sulfur they are combined with, and displaces the metal.

When oxygen is removed from a metal, we call this **reduction**. It is the opposite of adding oxygen, which is known as **oxidation**. The carbon acts as a reducing agent.

1. What would happen if carbon was roasted with an ore of zinc sulfide?
2. Write a word equation for the displacement of lead from lead oxide with carbon.

Extraction of iron

Iron ore occurs in the form of iron oxide (Fe_2O_3) – it is called haematite.

To extract the iron, powdered coke is added to the crushed iron ore along with limestone, which removes impurities. All the ingredients are roasted in a large furnace about 30 metres in height, known as a **blast furnace**. Air is injected into the bottom of the furnace to improve the reducing properties of the carbon. A blast furnace operates at temperatures up to 1650 °C.

FIGURE 3.3.5a: Coke can provide much more heat than wood, and is a concentrated form of carbon.

Did you know...?

Iron, initially found native in meteorites, has been used since 4000 BCE. It is the sixth most abundant element in the Universe.

FIGURE 3.3.5b: An ancient iron spearhead

3. Why do you think the coke is powdered and the iron ore crushed?

4. What is the advantage of operating the blast furnace at this high temperature?

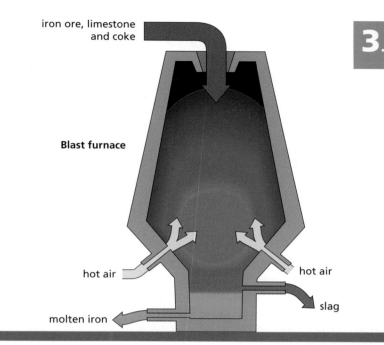

iron ore, limestone and coke

Blast furnace

hot air

hot air

slag

molten iron

FIGURE 3.3.5c: In a blast furnace, the carbon reduces the iron oxide ore to make iron metal.

Predicting the mass of iron >>>>

The symbol equation for the overall reaction in a blast furnace is:

$$2Fe_2O_3 + 3C \rightarrow 3CO_2 + 4Fe$$

By knowing the quantity and purity of the iron ore and carbon added to the furnace, and knowing that mass is always conserved, you can predict the theoretical amount of iron made.

An example is given here.

If 100 tonnes of iron ore was added to the furnace and it had a purity where 20 per cent of the mass of the ore was iron, how much iron metal could theoretically be made?

The amount of iron entering the furnace = amount of ore × percentage purity = 100 × 0.2 = 20 tonnes.

Because mass is conserved, the amount going in should equal the amount coming out.

So the theoretical amount of iron metal made would be 20 tonnes.

FIGURE 3.3.5d: Molten iron in a blast furnace

5. Magnetite (Fe_3O_4) is another ore of iron used in the blast furnace. Write a balanced equation to show the products made.

6. How much iron metal could be made from 250 tonnes of magnetite with a purity where 30 per cent of its mass is iron?

Key vocabulary

coke

reduction

oxidation

blast furnace

Extracting copper, lead and zinc

We are learning how to:

- Explain how copper, lead and zinc are extracted from their ores.
- Calculate the yield of the extraction process.

Copper, lead and zinc are all below carbon in the reactivity series. This enables carbon to play an active role in the extraction of these metals.

Extracting copper

Malachite is copper carbonate, a form of copper ore. You can see its striking green colour in Figure 3.3.6a. In order to extract the copper, the carbonate first has to be heated to over 200 °C. This causes thermal decomposition and carbon dioxide is released. Copper oxide is made. The reaction is:

$$CuCO_3 \rightarrow CuO + CO_2$$

The copper oxide is then heated with carbon in the form of coke. Because carbon is more reactive than copper, the copper from copper oxide is displaced:

$$2CuO + C \rightarrow 2Cu + CO_2$$

The copper will still have other impurities. A process known as electrolysis further purifies the copper.

Malachite ($CuCO_3$) is heated to over 200°C to form copper oxide.

Copper oxide is roasted with carbon to make copper metal.

This is copper metal.

FIGURE 3.3.6a: Extracting copper from copper carbonate

1. Which product occurs in both the thermal decomposition of copper carbonate and the reduction of copper oxide?

2. Which reactant is reduced?

Extracting lead and zinc

One of the ores of lead is galena, which is lead sulfide. To extract the metal, the ore is first crushed into small particles. These are added to a mixture of oil and water. Air is blown upwards to push the lead ore particles to the top, separating them from other impurities – this is called 'froth flotation'.

Oil is needed because lead sulfide is very dense and this helps it to rise to the top. The lead sulfide is then heated in air at high temperatures, converting it to lead oxide. The word equation for the reaction is:

lead sulfide + oxygen → lead oxide + sulfur dioxide

Roasting lead oxide with carbon reduces it to lead. The word equation for the reaction is:

lead oxide + carbon → lead + carbon dioxide

Zinc ore (sphalerite) is zinc sulfide. Before it can be displaced with carbon, the zinc sulfide needs to be changed into zinc oxide. This is achieved by blowing hot air through a concentrated mixture of zinc sulfide and water, by froth flotation. The concentrated zinc sulfide is then roasted in air to make zinc oxide. This is reduced by roasting it with carbon.

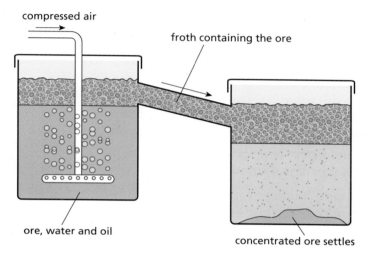

FIGURE 3.3.6b: Froth flotation to concentrate lead sulfide ore

3. Draw a flow chart to show the process for making lead from lead sulfide.

4. Write two word equations for the main reactions in making zinc from zinc sulfide.

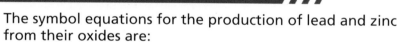

Making predictions from equations 〉〉〉

The symbol equations for the production of lead and zinc from their oxides are:

$$2PbO + C \rightarrow 2Pb + CO_2 \qquad 2ZnO + C \rightarrow 2Zn + CO_2$$

In reality, processes for extracting metals from their ores are inefficient because not all the metal is removed from ores. The **yield** of the process is less than 100 per cent, where the yield is defined by:

$$yield = \frac{\text{actual amount produced}}{\text{theoretical amount}} \times 100\%$$

5. 500 tonnes of zinc is produced from an ore containing 800 tonnes. Work out the yield of the process.

6. 446 tonnes of lead oxide is roasted with coke, and 200 tonnes of lead are made. What is the yield of the process? Assume that the lead oxide is 50 per cent by mass lead, and use ideas from Topic 3.5 to help you.

Did you know...?

75 per cent of the lead produced is used to make batteries; copper is mainly used in electrical wiring and zinc is also a component of batteries.

Key vocabulary

yield

Looking at the impact of metal extraction

We are learning how to:

- Describe the environmental impacts of metal extraction.
- Describe how recycling of metals reduces damage to the environment.

There are about 2500 large-scale mines over the world extracting different metal ores. Our reliance on metals may be costing our planet more than we think.

Surface impacts of metal mining

The largest copper-producing mine in the world is 4 km wide and 1.2 km deep.

Mining involves removing many hundreds of tonnes of rock, often crushing them and putting them somewhere suitable. Much of the waste rock, if it is free of heavy metals, can be crushed and used for road filler or building materials.

FIGURE 3.3.7a: One of the main impacts of mining is that it scars the landscape. This is an open-pit copper mine in Utah, USA.

Once a mine ceases to operate, companies have to plant the area with trees and other plants to restore the landscape – this is known as **reclamation**. The hole caused by mining can often be made into a lake, adding recreational value.

Deep mining can lead to **subsidence**. The ground becomes unstable, causing it to cave in.

1. What can mine owners do to reduce scarring of the landscape?
2. Why might people object to a mine being sited near their home?

Environmental impact of mining

Sometimes, waste rock and materials from processing an ore contain small amounts of heavy metals or other toxic materials. These can dissolve out of the rock over time. This is called 'leaching'. Toxic materials enter the soil, rivers and lakes, and harm aquatic and terrestrial life.

FIGURE 3.3.7b: Nearby houses and buildings can be badly affected by subsidence.

Waste liquids from the mining process are called **leachates**. They have to be stored in specially lined pools to avoid contaminating the ground or water systems.

Some mining processes use carbon to displace the metal from its ore. This produces carbon dioxide, which is a greenhouse gas. In addition, the metal ore is often roasted with carbon, again producing carbon dioxide because fossil fuels are burned to provide the heat.

Metals, such as lead, that come from sulfide ores must be heated in oxygen so that the metal oxide can be made. Sulfur dioxide is produced as a result, which causes acid rain.

Finally, mines are very noisy places. Blasting, heavy machinery and trucks transporting to and from the mine all contribute to a noisy environment.

3. Suggest two other processes involved in mining in which carbon dioxide is produced.

4. Which of the problems caused by mining is the most difficult to solve? Explain your answer.

FIGURE 3.3.7c: Leachates from mining can contaminate water systems.

The importance of recycling metals

Recycling avoids the need to mine and process new material, saving metal reserves and energy. One tonne of new aluminium cans requires five tonnes of aluminium ore and produces five tonnes of waste that is hazardous to the environment.

FIGURE 3.3.7d: Aluminium cans are recycled to produce aluminium.

Recycling metals is by far the most effective way of reducing environmental impact. Aluminium cans are a classic example – it takes as much energy to make one can from newly mined metal as it does to make 20 cans by recycling.

5. Discuss the advantages and disadvantages of recycling.

6. How can we improve the processes involved in recycling metals?

Did you know...?

In 1902, rich deposits of lead were found in Kabwe, Zambia and were mined without preventative measures. Today the levels of lead in the water and soil are high enough to kill people.

Key vocabulary

reclamation

subsidence

leachate

recycling

Applying key ideas

You have now met a number of important ideas in this chapter. This activity gives an opportunity for you to apply them, just as scientists do. Read the text first, then have a go at the tasks. The first few are fairly easy – then they get a bit more challenging.

Metal protection

Understanding the reactivity series has enabled scientists and engineers to develop ways of protecting metals.

Aluminium is near the top of the reactivity series. When exposed to air, it reacts with oxygen quickly. This forms a layer of aluminium oxide over the aluminium's surface and protects the metal beneath from further corrosion. Aluminium oxide is hard, and quite resistant to chemical attack. Figure 3.3.8a shows aluminium and iron after exposure to air for many years. The aluminium has hardly corroded because of its protective oxide layer.

Metals less reactive than aluminium, such as zinc and titanium, may be protected with an aluminium coating. This process is called anodising. Anodised titanium is used in dental implants.

Zinc, which is more reactive than iron or steel, can be used to protect these metals – this process is called galvanising. The iron is cleaned and then dipped in a bath of molten zinc. The zinc coating reacts with oxygen in the air, before oxygen has the chance to react with the iron – this is because zinc is more reactive than iron. The iron is now protected by the zinc, until all the zinc has reacted. This procedure protects iron and steel in underground pipes, large ships and oil tankers. It is an example of sacrificial protection – because zinc is more reactive, it will react with oxygen in the air before the iron does. In this way the iron stays intact.

Sometimes less reactive metals are used to protect more reactive metals. Tin is coated over steel (a much stronger metal) in the manufacture of tin cans. Tin is less reactive than iron so is less likely to react with air than iron. By covering the steel can with tin, the can will last longer. The tin forms a protective coating for the more reactive metal, preventing it from oxidising. Tin is useful because it is non-toxic. It can be safely used for coating food cans.

Copper coins can be plated with silver by dipping them in silver nitrate solution. The more reactive copper displaces the silver, forming copper nitrate, and a thin layer of silver is deposited on the coin.

FIGURE 3.3.8a: Aluminium (top) and iron (bottom) after lengthy exposure to air

FIGURE 3.3.8b: Zinc-coated steel (top) and steel that has not been coated (bottom): both have been exposed to air for some time.

Task 1

Use information from the text to explain what is meant by the following terms:

a) anodising

b) galvanising

c) sacrificial protection.

Task 2

Write word equations to show the following:

a) Formation of oxide layer when aluminium is exposed to air.

b) Plating of silver onto copper using silver nitrate solution.

Task 3

Magnesium is more reactive than aluminium. However, aluminium is used to anodise magnesium. Explain how this works.

Task 4

Write balanced symbol equations to explain the chemistry behind each of the following:

a) Zinc can be used to protect iron.

b) Copper can be plated onto aluminium using copper nitrate solution.

c) Tin is used to protect steel (iron) in tin cans.

> Use the following information:
> aluminium nitrate = $Al(NO_3)_3$
> tin oxide = SnO_2
> zinc oxide = ZnO

Task 5

Explain how the reactivity series is used to extract each these metals from their ores: iron, zinc and copper.

Why is aluminium not extracted from its ore in this way?

Understanding exothermic reactions

We are learning how to:

- Describe examples of exothermic reactions.
- Explain the energy changes taking place during an exothermic reaction.

Many chemical changes result in a very obvious energy change. Fireworks, using glow sticks and burning fuels are common examples of exothermic reactions.

Examples of exothermic reactions

Energy changes occur in all chemical reactions. In some reactions there is a very clear energy change, with the transfer of energy by heat, light and sometimes sound to the surroundings. These are **exothermic** reactions – exothermic means 'to give out heat'. Exothermic reactions can be recognised because the temperature of the products is higher than the temperature of the reactants. The bigger the temperature rise, the more exothermic the reaction.

> **Did you know...?**
>
> Respiration is an exothermic process, releasing energy from glucose and oxygen in a form that our cells can use.

FIGURE 3.3.9a: Fireworks and glow sticks make use of exothermic reactions.

Some examples are:

- Adding strong bases or reactive metals to strong acids, causing the temperature to increase dramatically.
- The reaction between iron wool and oxygen – a type of hand-warmer makes use of the heat produced by this.
- Adding calcium oxide (quicklime) to a bath of cold water, producing such an exothermic reaction that the cold water boils after about ten minutes!
- The thermit reaction, in which aluminium powder reacts with iron oxide using a magnesium fuse – aluminium is

FIGURE 3.3.9b: The thermit reaction is useful in repairing railway tracks. The extreme heat melts the iron, which runs into any crack.

more reactive than iron, displacing it to produce iron metal. The reaction is highly exothermic, and the heat produced melts the iron.

1. Which reaction is the more exothermic – adding calcium oxide to water or the thermit reaction? Give a reason for your answer.

2. Describe an exothermic reaction where in which the main energy transfer is by sound.

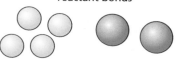

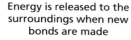

Energy is taken in from the surroundings to break the reactant bonds

Why are some reactions exothermic?

During all chemical changes, the reactant particles undergo collisions. During a collision, energy is absorbed from the surroundings to break bonds between the reactant particles. Once all the bonds have broken down, the reactant atoms are now free to form bonds with other reactant atoms and make new products. During the formation of new bonds energy is transferred to the surroundings, usually in the form of heat.

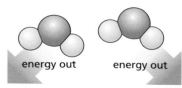

Energy is released to the surroundings when new bonds are made

If the energy transferred to the surroundings during the **bond-making** process is higher than the energy absorbed during the **bond-breaking** process, the reaction is exothermic.

3. Explain, using ideas about particles and atoms, why burning magnesium is an exothermic change.

4. What is happening if there is no overall energy change during a chemical reaction?

energy out   energy out

FIGURE 3.3.9c: Bond-making and bond-breaking processes occur when hydrogen is burned.

Energy diagrams for reactions

Figure 3.3.9d shows how the energy of the reactants and products change during an exothermic reaction. As you can see, the products are always at a lower energy compared to the reactants. The difference in energy has been transferred to the surroundings. Remember the Law of Conservation of Energy – the total energy must always be the same.

$$\frac{\text{energy of}}{\text{reactants}} - \frac{\text{energy of}}{\text{products}} = \text{energy transferred}$$

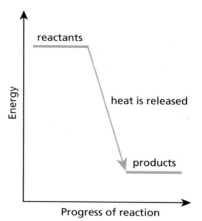

FIGURE 3.3.9d: Energy levels of reactants and products during an exothermic reaction

5. Sketch two separate energy-level diagrams to compare the following two reactions:

   a) a neutralisation reaction, in which the temperature difference between the reactants and products is 10°C

   b) the thermit reaction.

Key vocabulary

exothermic

bond-making

bond-breaking

Comparing endothermic and exothermic changes

We are learning how to:

- Describe examples of endothermic reactions.
- Compare the energy changes during exothermic and endothermic reactions.

Energy is given out in an exothermic change. What do you think will happen in an endothermic change?

Describing endothermic changes

In an **endothermic** reaction more energy is absorbed than is given out. Endothermic means 'to take in heat'. This results in a reaction in which the temperature is seen to fall as the reaction proceeds. These reactions are not very common, but have some useful applications.

When some salts like potassium chloride, ammonium chloride and ammonium nitrate are dissolved in water, the temperature decreases. Cold packs make use of this. Water and ammonium nitrate are sealed in separate chambers in a sealed bag – squeezing the bag causes the water and ammonium nitrate to mix, cooling the mixture rapidly.

1. Why is there a drop in temperature during an endothermic change?

2. Would an endothermic change occur faster or slower in a very cold environment?

FIGURE 3.3.10a: The most important endothermic reaction for life is photosynthesis. More energy is absorbed by plants from the Sun than is given out when glucose and oxygen are made.

FIGURE 3.3.10b: When an ammonium salt is dissolved in water, the temperature drop is enough for ice to form on the outside of the flask.

Energy changes

Figure 3.3.10c shows energy diagrams for an exothermic change and an endothermic change. The energy of the products in the endothermic change is at a higher level than the energy of the reactants. The 'extra' energy comes from the surroundings, causing a cooling effect.

3. Draw a table summarising the differences between exothermic changes and endothermic changes. Include one example of each in your table.

> ### Did you know...?
>
> It is estimated that about 4×10^{16} kJ of energy are absorbed by plants every year during photosynthesis. This is six times more than the amount used by the human race in a year.

4. The endothermic reaction between barium hydroxide crystals and ammonium chloride can produce a temperature drop to –20 °C in about 5 minutes. This is a much greater temperature drop than in the reaction between ammonium salts in water, used in cold packs and shown in Figure 3.3.10b. Sketch a graph to compare the energy changes in these two processes.

Explaining endothermic changes ⟫⟫⟫

The reason why some reactions are endothermic relates to bond-making and bond-breaking. If the energy absorbed from the surroundings to break the reactant bonds is higher than the energy released on forming new product bonds, the process is endothermic. This results in a decrease in temperature. By calculating the difference between the energy needed to break bonds and that released on making bonds, you can determine if a reaction is exothermic or endothermic.

Some endothermic processes are physical changes. When salts dissolve in water, energy is needed from the surroundings to break the bonds between the solute particles. A smaller amount of energy is released when new attractions are formed between the solute and the solvent particles. Other endothermic physical processes include melting ice and evaporating water.

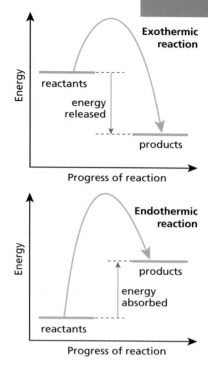

FIGURE 3.3.10c: Energy-level diagrams for exothermic and endothermic reactions

TABLE 3.3.10: Bond energies involved in different reactions

Reaction	Energy to break reactant bonds (kJ/mol)	Energy released in making product bonds (kJ/mol)
a) between carbon and oxygen to make carbon dioxide	496	1486
b) between hydrogen and chlorine to make hydrogen chloride	678	862
c) between nitrogen and hydrogen to make ammonia (NH_3)	2252	2328
d) decomposition of hydrogen bromide to make hydrogen and bromine	732	629

5. Use the data in Table 3.3.10 to determine whether the reactions are exothermic or endothermic.

6. Why do you think some bonds are harder to break than others?

Key vocabulary
....

endothermic

Explaining the use of catalysts

We are learning how to:

- Describe what a catalyst is.
- Explain how catalysts work.

Without catalysts, we would not be able to make many of the products we rely on today. In fact, without biological catalysts (enzymes), life would not exist!

What are catalysts?

A **catalyst** is a substance that is added to a chemical reaction, causing it to happen faster or slower. Catalysts are not changed by the reaction – they alter the **rate of reaction**.

Catalysts are usually specific to particular reactions – a catalyst used in one reaction will not necessarily work in another. Different catalysts can be used for the same reaction. An important thing about a catalyst is that it does not actually take part in the reaction, and can be fully recovered afterwards.

Hydrogen peroxide (H_2O_2) is a colourless liquid that decomposes very slowly over time making water and oxygen. Different catalysts can speed up this process, including manganese dioxide and catalase (an enzyme found in liver, potatoes and apples).

1. How could you prove that something was a catalyst and not a reactant?

2. Why is it sometimes important to speed up a reaction?

Using data to interpret the effect of catalysts

Enzymes are examples of biological catalysts. Many billions of reactions take place in our cells every second. Without enzymes, these reactions would not happen fast enough for life to exist.

Many industrial processes rely on catalysts to make the reactions fast enough to be profitable. In the manufacture of ammonia, the catalyst is made from iron or platinum. Many industrial catalysts are metals or metal oxides.

To investigate the effect of catalysts, you can observe how fast a reaction occurs. This can be done by either recording how quickly a product is made, or how quickly a reactant is used up.

FIGURE 3.3.11a: Decomposition of hydrogen peroxide can be catalysed by manganese dioxide (black powder).

> Did you know...?
>
> Catalysts can increase the rate of a reaction by up to 10^{17} times.

3. Which graph plotted in Figure 3.3.11b represents the reaction with a catalyst? Explain your answer.

4. How would you find out if catalase was a better catalyst than manganese dioxide?

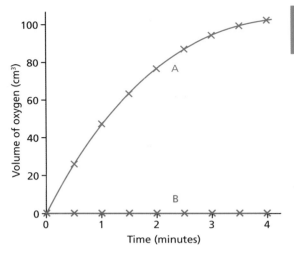

FIGURE 3.3.11b: How the decomposition of hydrogen peroxide proceeds with and without a catalyst

How do catalysts work?

Most catalysts provide an alternative 'pathway' for the reaction. This lowers the amount of energy needed for the reaction to proceed, and helps reactions to occur faster.

Catalytic converters in car exhausts remove harmful gases. Platinum and rhodium in the converter remove oxides of nitrogen and convert them into nitrogen gas and oxygen gas:

nitrogen oxide → nitrogen gas + oxygen gas

The catalyst is not part of the reaction. It strips nitrogen atoms from the nitrogen oxide and holds onto them. These react with one another to make nitrogen gas and are then freed from the catalyst.

Carbon monoxide and hydrocarbons in the exhaust gases react with oxygen gas:

carbon monoxide + oxygen → carbon dioxide

hydrocarbon + oxygen → water + carbon dioxide

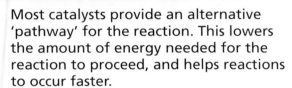

harmful exhaust gases – nitrogen oxides, carbon monoxide, hydrocarbons – enter

platinum and rhodium lining acts as a catalyst

nitrogen oxides are converted to nitrogen

carbon monoxide is converted to carbon dioxide

hydrocarbons react to form carbon dioxide and water

less harmful gases released into air

FIGURE 3.3.11c: A catalytic converter

Enzymes involved in digestion catalyse reactions in which large molecules are broken down. They have a specific shape that locks onto food molecules and keeps hold of them. Water molecules then break down the food molecules. The enzyme is then free to work on other food molecules.

5. Draw an annotated diagram to show how an enzyme works.

6. In which form would you use a catalyst – as a lumpy solid, as small granules or in powdered form? Explain your answer.

Key vocabulary

catalyst

rate of reaction

enzyme

catalytic converter

Exploring ceramics and their properties

We are learning how to:
- Describe what is meant by the term ceramic.
- Describe the properties of ceramics.

We think of a 'ceramic' as clay or pottery. This group of materials has greatly changed over the centuries, with the development of a wide set of very useful properties.

What is a ceramic?

Archaeologists have uncovered human-made **ceramics** dating back to 24 000 BCE. Animal and human figurines were made from animal fat, bones, bone ash and fine clay and fired in a kiln. Ceramic pottery vessels have been used since 9000 BCE to store grain and other foods. In 4000 BCE, glass was first discovered and in 1600 BCE the first porcelain ('china') was made in China.

A ceramic is an inorganic (not carbon-based), non-metallic solid. It is prepared by the action of heat followed by cooling. Ceramics are used for making tiles, glass, bricks, plates and vases and ornamental objects.

1. List three items made from ceramics in your home.

2. Ceramic materials have been uncovered since earliest human history. What does this tell you about the nature of ceramics?

General properties of ceramics

Ceramics are very useful because of their properties. Most are:

- hard and resistant to wear
- relatively light
- brittle – they can break easily if a force is applied
- thermal insulators – they keep heat in
- electrical insulators – they do not allow electric current to pass through
- non-magnetic
- chemically stable – they do not break down in air
- non-toxic – they can be used for food and drink
- non-ductile – they cannot be drawn out into wire.

FIGURE 3.3.12a: A Bronze Age ceramic pot

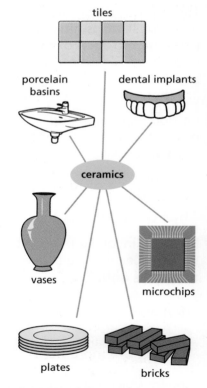

FIGURE 3.3.12b: Some of the uses of ceramics

tiles

porcelain basins

dental implants

ceramics

vases

microchips

plates

bricks

3. Draw a table to compare the properties of ceramics with metals.

4. Suggest why ceramics may be used for some purposes instead of metals.

The chemistry of ceramics

Clay, sand and other natural materials were important ingredients in early ceramics. Nowadays, advanced ceramics are based on oxides like aluminium oxide – nitrides, silicides and carbides, for example boron carbide (B_4C), are also used. Hardly any natural materials are used now. The ingredients are carefully manufactured to produce exact properties.

There are two main types of ceramic, although with modern materials the classification is less simple:

- **crystalline** – usually made from one or more varieties of a metal oxide
- **amorphous** (which means without shape) – glass based ceramics come into this category.

The atoms are bonded in a regular 3D pattern. Powdered raw materials are used, and additives and water added to form specific shapes. The mixture is then heated to a high temperature, which expels water and causes the particles to take up a permanent regular structure.

When molten glass mixtures are thrust in very cold conditions quickly, they cannot form a regular structure and as a result they can be 'blown' or moulded into very specific shapes. Once they are cooled they form permanent irregular structures.

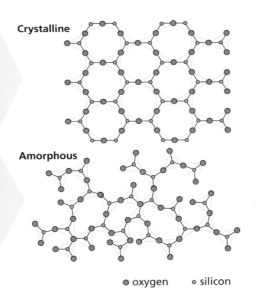

● oxygen   ○ silicon

FIGURE 3.3.12c: Some ceramic materials, like silicon dioxide (SiO_2), can exist in either amorphous or crystalline form.

5. Summarise the key differences between crystalline ceramics and amorphous ceramics.

6. Why are ingredients that are taken directly from nature no longer used in making ceramics?

FIGURE 3.3.12d: The world's most expensive Chinese vase

Key vocabulary

ceramic

crystalline

amorphous

Matching properties of ceramics to their uses

We are learning how to:

- Explain how the properties of ceramics determine their uses.

Ceramics are probably the most widespread materials in use today. The ability to manufacture them to have particular properties has provided an edge over more traditional materials like metals.

Different uses of ceramics

Ceramics can be classed according to their main uses:

- Refractory uses These are industrial uses such as linings for furnaces, gas-fire linings, steel-making and glass-making crucibles.

- Structural uses These include roofing tiles, floor tiles, pipes and bricks. Ordinary clay is used for these purposes with ingredients like sand, lime and iron oxide added to change the characteristics.

- Whiteware These include tableware, cookware, wall tiles, toilets, basins and baths. They are largely made from **earthenware**, **stoneware**, **porcelain** or fine china-clay ceramics. Earthenware and stoneware tend to be used for tableware and cookware. Porcelain is harder and more durable and is used for making baths and toilets. China clay-based ceramics are the hardest and most durable of all these types.

1. What properties of ceramics are shown in the photos?

2. Which of the above uses are specific only to ceramics?

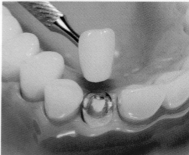

FIGURE 3.3.13a: Ceramics are used in bathrooms. Porcelain is used in dentistry, as well as for tableware.

Matching properties to uses

Refractory ceramics retain their strength at high temperatures, and resist corrosion and chemical attack. Oxides of aluminium, silicon, calcium and magnesium are some of the ingredients used to make refractory ceramics. They are used in furnaces, like the blast furnace, where metals are extracted from their ores.

Advanced applications of ceramics include specialist uses such as tiles for space shuttles, high temperature parts for aeroplane engines, turbo-jet engine blades, gas burner

FIGURE 3.3.13b: Refractory ceramics like these bricks are used to line kilns.

nozzles and missile nose cones. They are also of great importance in the electronics industry.

TABLE 3.3.13: Properties of some common ceramics – with metals for comparison

Type of material	Name of material	Melting point (°C)	Measure of hardness*	Density (g/cm³)	Measure of expansion on heating*
ceramic	aluminium oxide	2050	9	3.8	8.2
ceramic	silicon carbide	2800	9	3.2	4.3
ceramic	zirconium oxide	2660	8	5.6	6.6
ceramic	porcelain	1840	7	2.3	8
metal	mild steel	1370	5	7.9	15
metal	aluminium	660	3	2.7	24

*The higher the number, the bigger the hardness, or the greater the amount of expansion.

3. Describe, in general, how the properties of ceramics differ from metals.

4. **a)** Which properties would be most important when lining a furnace?

   b) Which ceramic would be most suitable for this purpose? Explain your answer.

Problems with the use of ceramics

Manufacturing ceramics relies on both chemical and physical processes. The formation of bonds between ceramic particles depends on the perfect composition of the raw materials, and the conditions under which they are heated. These are not always attainable, and defects may be found after manufacture.

Another problem is that ceramics are very brittle compared to metals, shattering on impact.

Producing ceramics is a high-energy and expensive process. Clay has to be dug from the ground and many raw materials need to be manufactured to high specifications.

5. Are ceramics compounds or mixtures? Explain your answer.

6. Consider whether the statement 'ceramic could completely replace metals' is true or false. Justify your answer.

Did you know...?

Tantalum hafnium carbide is a refractory ceramic that can withstand extremely high temperatures. It has a melting point of over 4200°C.

Key vocabulary

earthenware

stoneware

porcelain

refractory ceramics

Exploring natural polymers

We are learning how to:

- Explain what a polymer is.
- Describe examples of natural polymers.

Polymers are chemicals that have been around since the start of life. Natural polymers make up the constituents of living organisms. But what makes them so special?

What is a polymer?

Polymers can be found in nature. They are chemicals made of long chains of repeating chemical units – the repeating molecule is called a **monomer**.

One of the most familiar natural polymers is starch. Plants store glucose in the form of starch – glucose is its monomer.

Figure 3.3.14b shows a glucose molecule and the structure of starch. There are about 10 000 glucose monomers in a starch molecule. Plants store glucose as starch, which is insoluble in cold water – this means that starch can be stored within plants. Glucose, however, is soluble in cold water. When a plant needs glucose, enzymes break bonds in the starch. This releases glucose molecules for the plant to use.

1. Polymers can be broken down to the molecules they are made from. Is this a physical or a chemical change?

2. Why is it useful to store small molecules (such as glucose) in the form of polymers (such as starch)?

Examples of natural polymers

Proteins are some of the most important natural polymers. The monomers of proteins are called amino acids – there are over 20 different types. This means that different combinations of amino acids can give rise to an enormous variety of different proteins, each with different properties. Enzymes, muscle fibres, collagen (found in skin, ligaments and bones), haemoglobin (in red blood cells) and antibodies are all proteins.

FIGURE 3.3.14a: This beetle has a hard covering of a polymer called chitin.

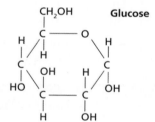

Glucose

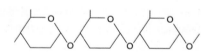

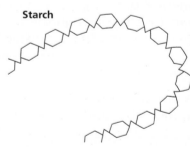

Starch

FIGURE 3.3.14b: Starch is made up of many glucose monomers.

DNA, shown in Figure 3.1.9b in Topic 3.1, is another polymer. It was one of the first polymers to appear on Earth, enabling life to reproduce.

Cellulose is the polymer that makes up the cell wall of plants, providing them with strength. Cotton is the purest form of cellulose.

Insects and crustaceans have a hard covering to their bodies made from the polymer **chitin**. It is waterproof, but flexible so that the animal can move inside it and grow.

Silk and rubber are natural polymers made by living organisms. Silk is made by silk worms – rubber is a polymer found in the sap of rubber trees.

Collagen

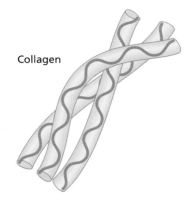

Haemoglobin

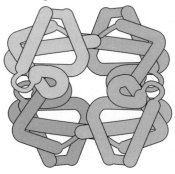

3. Which of the following are likely to be polymers?

   a) water

   b) keratin, the component of nails and hair

   c) sugar

4. Plants store sugar in the form of starch; animals store it in the form of glycogen. What prediction(s) can you make about glycogen?

FIGURE 3.3.14c: Different proteins have different shapes.

Some properties of natural polymers

Polymers have very large molecules. Their structure often has a particular shape that provides them with particular properties. The arrangement of molecules within a polymer defines this shape.

Cellulose and starch are both made from glucose, but in different arrangements. Cellulose is very hard to break down, extremely tough and strong enough to make fibres for clothes. Starch is easy to break down.

Many polymers are strong because of the number of chemical bonds within their structure. Some are elastic, like muscle fibre and rubber. In elastic polymers the long chains are tangled up in their natural state and they straighten to long lengths when a force is applied.

> **Did you know...?**
>
> Cellulose is the most abundant compound made from plants.

Key vocabulary

polymer

monomer

protein

cellulose

chitin

5. Do you think that polymers are chemically the same as the monomers that make them? Explain your answer.

6. Draw a model to represent a polymer with elastic properties.

Using human-made polymers

We are learning how to:

- Describe how human-made polymers are made in simple terms.
- Describe uses for human-made polymers.

The usefulness of polymers in nature has inspired people to imitate their chemistry. We have designed a range of synthetic polymers, which we now depend on.

Making synthetic polymers

Humans have been using natural polymers for thousands of years, largely in the form of cellulose from cotton and hemp, and also rubber from rubber plants. But there was no chemical understanding of how polymers worked until the 1900s, when **synthetic** polymers began to be developed. Herman Staudinger won a Nobel Prize in 1953 for his research in explaining how polymers work.

In the development of synthetic polymers, carefully selected monomers were heated under great pressure. Catalysts were added until, almost by chance, polymers were made. **Polythene** is a synthetic polymer, which has many uses. It is a type of plastic.

FIGURE 3.3.15a: Polythene has many uses including the construction of polytunnels for growing plants.

1. What are the similarities between synthetic polymers and natural polymers?
2. Why did it take so long for chemists to find out what polymers are made from?

Uses of synthetic polymers

The name of a polymer is derived from its monomer. In polystyrene, the monomer is styrene; in polyvinyl chloride (**PVC**) the monomer is vinyl chloride. Most synthetic polymers are derived from monomers that come from crude oil. They are mostly made of hydrogen and carbon.

Table 3.3.15 shows different types of polymers and their uses.

3. What do all monomer units have in common?
4. Describe some examples of uses of polymers in place of metals.

Ethene

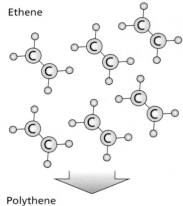

Polythene

FIGURE 3.3.15b: Polythene can be made from its monomer, ethene.

TABLE 3.3.15: Uses of some polymers

Name of polymer	Uses of polymer
polythene	plastic bags, plastic containers, cling film, plastic milk bottles
polystyrene	packaging, model kits, containers
acrylics	aircraft canopies, covers for car lights
nylon	ropes, fabrics, gear wheels
polypropylene	ropes, containers
polychloroethene	water pipes

Properties of synthetic polymers ⟩⟩⟩

The types of monomer, the way they are bonded and the length of a polymer chain all determine the properties of synthetic polymers. By understanding the chemistry, scientists have found ways to improve on their properties.

FIGURE 3.3.15c: Contact lenses are made from polyacrylamide, which is cross-linked and holds water molecules inside its structure.

The length of a polymer chain alters the melting and boiling points of the polymer. The longer the chain, the higher the melting and boiling points, and generally the more viscous the polymer is in the liquid state.

The overall structure of a polymer affects its properties. **Cross-links** within the polymer can be made by inserting small amounts of other elements. The natural polymer rubber is strengthened by adding small amounts of sulfur. These sulfur cross-links enable tyres to be made from rubber. Cross-links also allow polymers to hold other molecules within them, forming gels.

The amount of branching in a polymer chain affects its properties. Low-density polythene is used for plastic shopping bags – it is light, flexible and has chains with many branches. High-density polythene is made of single straight chains – it is rigid, strong and dense, and so is used to make plastic buckets. Both are made from the same monomer, ethene.

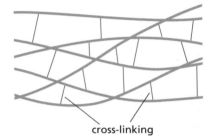
cross-linking

branching

FIGURE 3.3.15d: Cross-linking and branching determine the properties of a polymer.

5. Draw a model of a polymer molecule with a high melting point which is very light.

6. Explain how cross-linked polymers might be used in the delivery of medicines into our bodies.

Key vocabulary

synthetic

polythene

PVC

cross-link

Explaining composites

We are learning how to:

- Explain what is meant by the term 'composite'.
- Describe some uses of natural composites.

There is a saying that 'two is better than one'. In the case of making composite materials this is certainly the case.

What are composites? ⟩⟩

Composites are formed when two or more materials, often with different properties, are combined. The composite is usually stronger, more durable or has other desirable properties compared to the materials it is made from. The materials involved are not often chemically combined together, and are ususally recognisable within the composite.

Around 1500 BCE, Ancient Egyptians were making bricks from mud – this is an early example of a composite. Straw was added to the mud mixture, resulting in stronger and more durable bricks. The straw was not chemically combined with the mud and acted to enhance its properties.

In the 12th century the Mongols improved the design of their archery bows by adding cattle tendons, horn, bamboo or birch, silk and pine resin. These were far stronger, superior bows compared with their bows constructed of single materials.

FIGURE 3.3.16a: These bricks are made from mud and straw, in an ancient traditional method.

1. Define the term 'composite'. Give one everyday example of a composite.

2. Draw a diagram to show how straw might add strength to bricks made from mud.

Explaining concrete ⟩⟩⟩

Concrete is a composite made from natural materials, some of which have been processed. First, limestone and clay are heated to over 700 °C in a kiln to make cement. This is then added to sand, water and gravel to make concrete. The proportions of the ingredients determine the overall properties of the concrete.

FIGURE 3.3.16b: The Three Gorges Dam in China is made from concrete.

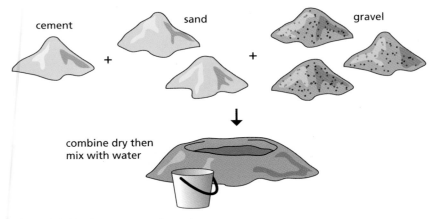

FIGURE 3.3.16c: How concrete is made

3. a) Civil engineers routinely test the strength, density and ability of concrete to soak up water. Why might the results of such tests not be reliable for all the concrete samples they test?

b) What could be done to improve the reliability of the tests?

Composites in nature 》》》

Composites are normally made from two parts. One acts as a **matrix** or 'binder'. The other is the **reinforcement**, which is usually fibres, crystals or fragments.

Wood is a natural composite – it is composed of cellulose and lignin. Without the lignin, the cellulose is much weaker (as in cotton which contains cellulose but no lignin). Together, they bond to make a much stronger material. The lignin acts like a glue, binding the fibres of cellulose together.

Bone is another composite found in nature. It is composed of a soft, flexible protein called collagen and a hard, brittle mineral made from calcium phosphate. The mineral reinforces the collagen making it stronger, so the bone is strong but also slightly flexible and not brittle.

4. Explain which is the binder and which is the reinforcement found in wood and bone.

5. Wood from the Brazilian Cherry is four times harder than wood from the Douglas Fir. Draw a model of the wood from each tree, showing how the structure of the composite materials might account for these differences.

6. Osteoporosis is a condition in which bones break easily and become less dense. Which part of the composite material is lacking in a person with osteoporosis?

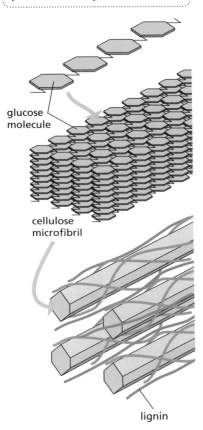

glucose molecule

cellulose microfibril

lignin

FIGURE 3.3.16d: Cellulose forms long fibres, composed of long chains of glucose molecules. Lignin, found in wood, binds the fibres together.

Key vocabulary

composite

concrete

matrix

reinforcement

Using human-made composites

We are learning how to:

- Explain how human-made composites were developed.
- Describe the properties and uses of human-made composites.

Human-made composites are relatively new, with plastics paving the way. Nowadays, we use a host of new materials with improved features. Will the world of composites finally replace metals?

FIGURE 3.3.17a: Denver International Airport is made from fibreglass.

Development of human-made composites 》

In 1935, scientists developed **fibreglass** by adding short glass fibres to a plastic matrix (polyester). An incredibly strong material was created, which was also lightweight. Fibreglass dominates the world of composites today, accounting for 90 per cent of the market.

The space race in the 1950s led to new metal-matrix composites in which fibres of ceramic, plastic or metal were fixed in a metal matrix. These were able to withstand very high temperatures, without causing too much thermal expansion.

In the 1960s, fibres of carbon (from the graphite) were investigated, leading to carbon fibres being added to a plastic matrix. The product, called **carbon fibre**, is the strongest material on the planet.

Today there are many types of composites. These have combinations of plastic, ceramic and metal matrices and different types of materials to reinforce these, depending on the properties required. Glass and carbon fibres are still mostly used to reinforce the matrix.

1. What makes glass and carbon fibres a popular choice as reinforcers?

2. Suggest why plastic matrices were preferred to metal or composite ones for the development of carbon fibre composites.

Some uses of human-made composites 》》

Fibreglass is lightweight, strong, impact-resistant, corrosion-resistant, waterproof and can be moulded into many shapes. It is also relatively cheap to make and the raw materials are abundant. This set of unique properties has made it ideal for

manufacturing boats, ships, swimming-pool linings, house insulation and roofing materials.

Carbon fibre is one of the most lightweight and strongest materials. It has many applications including making car, aircraft and spacecraft bodies, the construction of buildings, manufacture of bikes and audio equipment, and sports equipment such as tennis racquets.

Cermets are composites in which a ceramic matrix, often titanium carbide, has metal particles added. They are particularly useful where high temperatures are needed, such as in some electrical applications. They are also used for making machine tools, dental fillings and hip replacements. Some cermets are being considered for use in spacecraft shielding to resist high-speed space debris and small meteors.

FIGURE 3.3.17b: Cermets are used in power tools.

3. Fibreglass is waterproof. Suggest why carbon fibre might be preferred in the construction of buildings.

4. Can you think of other uses of fibreglass and carbon fibre?

Comparing human-made composites >>>

Table 3.3.17 shows some data about different types of composite – some metals are included for comparison.

TABLE 3.3.17

Type of material	Material	Density (g/cm³)	Strength (MPa)*	Strength/ weight ratio
composite	fibreglass	1.9	3400	1307
composite	carbon fibre	1.6	4300	2457
metal	aluminium	2.8	600	214
metal	stainless steel	7.86	2000	254
composite	concrete	2.3	12	4.35

*The pressure needed to squash the material until it breaks.

5. What conclusions can you draw from the data in Table 3.3.17?

6. Explain what might cause the differences in data between carbon fibre and fibreglass. Use diagrams and models to help your explanation.

Did you know...?

Formula One racing cars are made almost entirely of carbon fibre. Each costs over one million dollars to build.

FIGURE 3.3.17c: A racing car made from carbon fibre

Key vocabulary

fibreglass

carbon fibre

cermet

Checking your progress

To make good progress in understanding science you need to focus on these ideas and skills.

Write word equations to represent the decomposition of metal carbonates.

Use observations from thermal decomposition reactions to make inferences about metal reactivity.

Write balanced symbol equations for the decomposition of metal carbonates.

Give uses of displacement reactions and write word equations to represent them.

Use models to explain displacement and relate it to the reactivity series.

Write balanced symbol equations for displacement reactions.

Describe different ways to extract metal ores from the Earth and describe the associated environmental issues.

Explain how metals are recycled and how this affects the environment.

Evaluate the positive and negative aspects of metal mining and extraction.

Describe the use of carbon in extracting iron from its ore.

Describe the process of extracting iron from its ore in a blast furnace.

Use balanced symbol equations to make predictions about the mass of iron produced when extracted from ore, showing that mass is conserved, and explain the advantages of using carbon.

Write word equations for the reactions between carbon and metal ores.

Describe the extraction processes for lead, copper and zinc.

Work out the yield of an extraction process.

Describe what is meant by the terms exothermic and endothermic reactions, with examples.

Explain the energy changes taking place during an exothermic and endothermic reaction.

Use energy-level diagrams to compare the energy in the reactants and products of exothermic and endothermic reactions, explaining the energy changes in the particles.

Describe what a catalyst is and give examples.

Interpret data to explain how a catalyst affects a reaction.

Explain how a catalyst works.

Describe what is meant by the term 'ceramic', describing their properties and uses, with some examples.

Explain how different types of ceramic vary in their properties.

Explain how the chemistry and bonding within a ceramic affects its properties.

Describe what is meant by the term 'polymer', using examples of natural and human-made polymers.

Describe the properties of polymers, explaining how these relate to their uses.

Explain how the properties of polymers are affected by their bonding, using simple models.

Describe what is meant by the term 'composite' using examples of natural and human-made composites.

Describe the properties of composites, explaining how the properties relate to their uses.

Use models to explain how composites are constructed and use these to explain their properties.

Questions

See how well you have understood the ideas in the chapter.

1. Which of the following is a natural polymer? [1]

   a) cement   **b)** protein   **c)** plastic   **d)** brick

2. Which is the most reactive element in this list? [1]

   a) sodium   **b)** silver   **c)** carbon   **d)** copper

3. Which of the following is an example of an endothermic change? [1]

   a) burning magnesium   **b)** dissolving calcium chloride
   c) photosynthesis   **d)** firework

4. Which of the following are *not* extracted by using carbon? [1]

   a) zinc   **b)** iron   **c)** copper   **d)** aluminium

5. Explain what is meant by the term 'catalyst'. [2]

6. Describe the difference between a polymer and a composite. [2]

7. Burning hydrogen is an exothermic change. Explain how an exothermic change occurs. Use ideas about bond-making and bond-breaking in your answer. [4]

See how well you can apply the ideas in this chapter to new situations.

8. Rubidium is more reactive than sodium. Which of the following correctly shows the word equation between rubidium and sodium chloride? [1]

   a) rubidium chloride + sodium → sodium chloride + rubidium
   b) rubidium + sodium chloride → rubidium chloride + sodium
   c) sodium + rubidium → sodium chloride + rubidium
   d) sodium chloride + rubidium → sodium chloride + rubidium

9. The carbonates of metals X, Y and Z are decomposed. It is found that Z is easier to decompose than X, but harder to decompose than Y. What is the correct order of reactivity of the metals, with the most reactive first? [1]

   a) Y, Z, X   **b)** X, Y, Z   **c)** X, Z, Y   **d)** Z, X, Y

10. Which of the following is likely to be a very viscous polymer with the highest melting and boiling point? [1]

   a)   **b)**

   c)   **d)**

11. Which of the following statements about the energy diagrams in Figure 3.3.19a is true? [1]

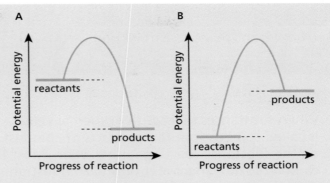

FIGURE 3.3.19a: Exothermic and endothermic energy diagrams

   a) A shows the diagram for dissolving ammonium nitrate in water.

   b) A greater difference in energy would be observed in A when a weak acid reacts with a weak alkali compared to burning magnesium.

   c) B shows that more energy is absorbed in bond-breaking than is released in bond-making.

   d) If the energy of the reactants is the same as the products, an endothermic change has occurred.

12. Zinc ore is 40 per cent pure. Carbon is used to extract the zinc from its oxide. The process has a yield of 50 per cent. If 100 tonnes of zinc ore were processed, how much zinc would be obtained? [2]

13. Which will have the biggest impact on the metal underneath – scratching a 'tin' can or scratching a galvanised steel plate? Explain your answer. [2]

14. A mine owner wants to start a copper mine in an area of outstanding natural beauty. Explain the issues involved that will impact on the environment. [4]

Questions 15–16

See how well you can understand and explain new ideas and evidence.

15. Hydrogen peroxide decomposes to make oxygen and water. The graph in Figure 3.3.19b shows the effect of a catalyst on the reaction. Sketch a graph to show the effect of a better catalyst. What is similar about the two graphs? [2]

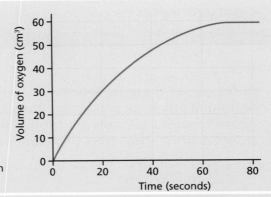

FIGURE 3.3.19b: Graph showing the rate of decomposition of hydrogen peroxide with a catalyst

16. Titanium metal produces fewer bubbles when placed in acid, compared to aluminium. It oxidises more quickly than copper in air. Explain, using ideas about reactivity, how:

   a) aluminium b) copper can be used to protect titanium in a new application. [4]

Using our Earth Sustainably

Ideas you have met before

Combustion

When substances react with oxygen to release energy it is called combustion. The products of combustion depend on the substance reacting with oxygen. Most fuels release carbon dioxide and water during combustion.

Useful materials

The Earth has many useful resources, such as metal ores. The extraction process can damage the environment by, for example, digging mines, pollution caused by waste and subsidence of land. Some metals are extracted from their ores using carbon, which leads to increased levels of carbon dioxide in the atmosphere.

Recycling

There are cycles in nature. The water cycle, for example, is the continuous movement of water on, above and below the surface of the Earth.

Waste metals can be recycled instead of extracting new raw materials. This reduces greenhouse gas emissions, uses less energy than making metal from its ore and conserves natural resources.

Rocks

Rocks can be grouped together based on their appearance and simple physical properties, such as whether they have grains or crystals. Fossils are formed when organisms are trapped within the layers of sedimentary rock.

In this chapter you will find out

The atmosphere

- The Earth's atmosphere has changed over time and is still changing now.

- Some human activities are thought to affect the rate at which the atmosphere is changing.

- Technological advances impact on the quality of our atmosphere.

Damage to the Earth's resources

- The Earth's resources are limited and they may be damaged by human activities.

- The need to use land for homes, industry and farming must be balanced against the impact on the Earth's resources.

Recycling

- Nature constantly recycles materials – for example carbon in the carbon cycle.

- There are benefits and limitations to the recycling of materials.

- Some recycled materials are 'down-cycled' into less desirable products.

The rock cycle

- There is a relationship between the shape of a volcano and the type of magma it produces.

- Magma solidifies to form igneous rock.

- There are different ways that fossils can form in sedimentary rock.

- Rocks are continually being broken down and new rocks are formed. This is described by the rock cycle.

- The constant movement of the Earth's crust causes rocks deep underground to be brought to the surface and mountain ranges to form.

Understanding our atmosphere

We are learning how to:

- Describe the composition of our atmosphere.
- Describe how the atmosphere has changed over time.
- Explain why the atmosphere has changed.

Our atmosphere consists of the gases around the Earth and is unlike that of any other body in the Solar System. What gases are in our atmosphere? How did they get there?

What is the composition of our atmosphere? »

The Earth's **atmosphere** consists mainly of nitrogen and oxygen. There is also a small amount of argon and even smaller amounts of other gases (see Table 3.4.2). Our atmosphere has remained about the same for the past 200 million years.

Nitrogen is the most abundant gas in the atmosphere, followed by oxygen. These two gases make up about 99 per cent of the gases in the atmosphere. The remaining gases, including carbon dioxide, are found in much smaller amounts.

1. What is the atmosphere?
2. Describe the composition of the Earth's atmosphere.

TABLE 3.4.2: Percentages of the main gases in the Earth's atmosphere

Gas	Percentage
nitrogen	78
oxygen	21
argon	0.9
carbon dioxide	0.04
water vapour	variable
other gases	trace

How has the Earth's atmosphere evolved? »

The Earth is about 4.6 billion (4 600 000 000) years old. Originally it was a molten mass and its early atmosphere was probably formed from the gases released by volcanic activity. Gradually the Earth cooled and about 4 billion years ago the first solid rocks started to form a crust over the molten mass. The atmosphere at that time is believed to have been similar to that of Mars and Venus today – about 95 per cent carbon dioxide, with water vapour and small amounts of ammonia and methane.

FIGURE 3.4.2a: Volcanic activity added water vapour to the atmosphere.

About 3.8 billion years ago, the temperature of the Earth is thought to have cooled to below 100 °C. Water vapour in the atmosphere started to condense and form the oceans. Most of the carbon dioxide and ammonia dissolved in these oceans.

The first life forms appeared about 3 billion years ago. They used up carbon dioxide to make food and transfer energy, and released oxygen into the atmosphere. Eventually the levels of oxygen and carbon dioxide settled to what we have today.

3. Describe how the atmosphere has changed since the Earth was formed.

4. Suggest why it took over a billion years for living organisms to appear after the Earth formed.

What caused the changes in composition? 》》》

The amount of oxygen in the atmosphere increased because plants photosynthesised, producing oxygen as a 'waste' product. The amount of carbon dioxide in the atmosphere then decreased because:

- it became bound up in sedimentary rocks – for example limestone ($CaCO_3$) – and in fossil fuels
- it was absorbed by green plants for photosynthesis
- it dissolved into the oceans.

FIGURE 3.4.2b: Trees absorbed carbon dioxide for photosynthesis. They also used a small amount of the oxygen they released, for respiration.

5. Explain how and why the amounts of carbon dioxide and oxygen have changed over time.

6. Explain why the composition of the atmosphere has remained almost stable for the past 200 million years.

Did you know...?

There is no clear defining line between the Earth's atmosphere and outer space, but most figures estimate that space starts between 80 and 120 km above the surface of the Earth.

Key vocabulary

atmosphere

Exploring the effects of human activity

We are learning how to:

- Describe examples of human activity that cause air pollution.
- Explain the effects of smog, acid rain and damage to the ozone layer.

In some places around the world, human activities have added gases to the atmosphere that would not be there in such amounts naturally – these are pollutants. Which activities cause air pollution, and how can we keep the air clean?

What causes air pollution?

Air pollution results from both human and natural activities. Natural air pollution is caused by forest fires, volcanic eruptions, wind erosion, pollen dispersal and natural radioactivity.

Human activities that result in air pollution include:

- emissions from industry and manufacturing
- emissions from fossil fuel-burning vehicles
- household and farming chemicals – for example pesticides, cleaning products and paints
- cigarettes – smoking is one of the main causes of indoor air pollution.

FIGURE 3.4.3a: Exhaust fumes contain carbon monoxide, oxides of nitrogen, hydrocarbons and particulates.

1. What are pollutants?
2. Describe the natural causes of air pollution.

What are the effects of air pollution?

Air pollution damages the atmosphere. Most scientists believe that releasing too much carbon dioxide into the atmosphere is one of the main causes of global warming.

The **ozone layer** helps to protect us from harmful rays from the Sun that can cause cancer. It is damaged by methane gas released by cattle and by chemicals used in spray cans, called 'CFCs'.

Acid rain is created when gases released from burning dissolve in water vapour in the atmosphere. This can damage forests and kill fish. Carbon dioxide dissolves in rain water to form a weak acid called carbonic acid:

carbon dioxide + water → carbonic acid

Sulfur dioxide is also released when fossil fuels are burned. It can also form acid rain:

sulfur dioxide + water → sulfuric acid

In the 1950s 'smog' was the mixture of smoke and fog experienced in London. Smog occurs when emissions from industry, vehicles and burning build up under certain weather conditions.

FIGURE 3.4.3b: Smog is still a major problem in parts of China.

3. How is acid rain formed?

4. Explain why the damage caused to the ozone layer by pollutants is a concern.

Did you know...?

Pollution in China can change weather patterns in the USA. It takes five days for the air currents to carry heavy air pollution from China across the Pacific Ocean.

Technology and air quality ⟫⟫⟫

Scientists are trying to improve air quality by:

- researching safer alternatives to CFCs

- removing sulfur from fossil fuels so that they do not produce sulfur dioxide when they burn

- removing sulfur dioxide produced by power stations and industry using filter systems in chimneys, and removing particulates from smoke using electrostatic precipitators

- developing engines that burn hydrogen – the only waste product is water

- developing renewable energy technology – for example, wind, solar and wave power

- fitting catalytic converters (see Topic 3.11) to car exhausts to reduce carbon monoxide and nitrogen oxide emissions.

FIGURE 3.4.3c: In 2012, 4.1% of UK energy consumption came from renewable sources, compared with 3.8% in 2011.

5. Explain how technological advances could have reduced the 'Great Smog' in London in 1952.

6. Evaluate the development of renewable energy technology in the UK.

Key vocabulary

ozone layer

acid rain

smog

Understanding the global warming debate

We are learning how to:

- Describe the effects of global warming.
- Explain the consequences of global warming for living things.
- Evaluate the arguments for human activity impacting on global warming.

The greenhouse effect is a natural phenomenon that allows the Earth to be warm enough to support life. Without it the average temperature of the Earth would be −18 °C. What causes the greenhouse effect and how does human activity affect it?

What is global warming?

The Sun's radiation passes through the atmosphere, is absorbed by the Earth's surface and is re-radiated as heat. This heat is absorbed or reflected by greenhouse gases in the air instead of escaping into space, causing the atmosphere to warm up.

Human activities have caused higher concentrations of greenhouse gases in the atmosphere. Scientists think that this increase has thrown the natural **greenhouse effect** out of balance. The atmosphere is trapping too much heat and causing the temperature of the Earth to rise. This is known as the 'enhanced greenhouse effect' or **global warming**.

> 1. What is the natural greenhouse effect and why is it important for life on Earth?
>
> 2. Name four greenhouse gases and identify where they come from.

The impact of global warming

A rise in the global mean temperature will cause climate change, which may result in:

- polar ice sheets melting, causing sea levels to rise, low-lying areas of the world becoming submerged and habitat loss for many species
- some areas having less available water, causing food shortages, drought and desertification of land
- longer growing seasons in temperate regions and faster growth for some crop species due to increased carbon dioxide concentrations

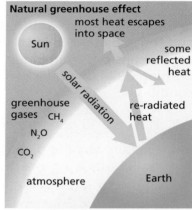

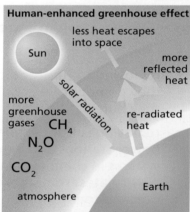

FIGURE 3.4.4a: Human activities increase levels of greenhouse gases (carbon dioxide, methane, nitrogen oxide and CFCs).

Did you know...?

The Kyoto Protocol is an international agreement on climate change that was set up by the United Nations. The Protocol involves agreed targets to collectively help fight against global warming.

- agricultural pests thriving in warmer environments
- tropical diseases, for example malaria, affecting a larger area
- an increase in severe weather events

Scientists agree that the Earth's temperature has risen over the last century and that carbon dioxide is one of the greenhouse gases that cause global warming. Some disagree over whether global climate change is part of a normal cycle or not, and about how big a problem it could become.

FIGURE 3.4.4b: If the polar ice caps melt, will the wildlife survive?

3. Explain how global warming might affect polar bears, penguins and mosquitoes.

4. Suggest how global warming might affect global food security.

Are we to blame? >>>

The Earth's average temperature increased by about 0.5 °C over the last century. It is projected to rise between 1.4 and 5.8 °C in the next 100 years. The Earth's climate has changed naturally throughout its history, but the current rate of change has not been seen in the last 10 000 years.

The debate is about whether or not human activities are to blame. Most of the research shows that human activities are accelerating global warming. However, some scientists think that data is being interpreted incorrectly by climate scientists, who are not looking at the evidence objectively. And some think that any increase in global temperatures could be a natural climate shift, or due to factors other than human activity.

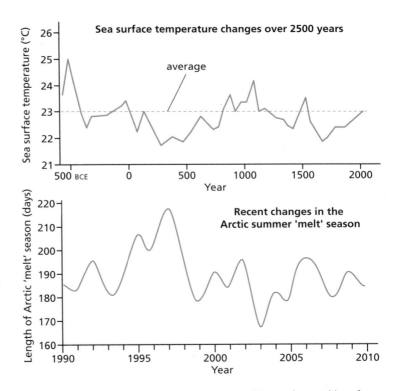

FIGURE 3.4.4c: Two graphs of data relating to climate change (data from University of Illionois Arctic Climate Research Group)

5. Explain why scientists believe that global warming is happening.

6. Look at the data in the graphs in Figure 3.4.4c. Describe what each graph shows. What conclusions can you draw about global warming from each set of data?

Key vocabulary

greenhouse effect

global warming

Understanding how carbon is recycled

We are learning how to:

- Describe the carbon cycle.
- Explain how human activity increases the amount of carbon in the atmosphere.
- Explain what is meant by a 'carbon footprint'.

Carbon is found in all living organisms. Most of the chemicals that make up our tissues and organs contain carbon. Where does the carbon come from? What happens to it when we die?

Natural recycling

Living organisms have been recycling materials for millions of years. Decomposers such as bacteria and fungi break down waste along with dead and decaying organisms. They make the chemical elements they contain, including carbon, available again for living organisms to use for growth. Carbohydrates, proteins and fats all contain carbon.

The main way that carbon enters food chains is as carbon dioxide from the air. All producers in the oceans and on land use carbon dioxide to make carbohydrates such as glucose. The carbon is then passed on to the next organism in the food chain.

1. Write the word equation for photosynthesis. Explain what is happening to the carbon.

2. What is the role of decomposers in the carbon cycle?

FIGURE 3.4.5a: These are phytoplankton – microscopic plants. Why are plants so important in the carbon cycle?

Explaining the carbon cycle

Carbon, in carbon dioxide, is released by respiration and combustion into the atmosphere. Green plants remove carbon dioxide from the air when they photosynthesise. They trap the carbon in compounds such as glucose. The carbon then passes from organism to organism along food chains. Each organism returns carbon dioxide to the air during respiration.

Decomposers return carbon dioxide to the air when they feed on dead and decaying matter. In certain conditions, decomposition cannot happen and the carbon in dead organisms is trapped in the Earth. Over millions of years this trapped carbon is changed into fossil fuels.

Combustion (burning) then returns carbon dioxide to the atmosphere. These processes form the **carbon cycle**, summarised in Figure 3.4.5b.

The weathering of limestone rock (made from compressed animal shells containing calcium carbonate) also returns carbon dioxide to the atmosphere, as does volcanic activity.

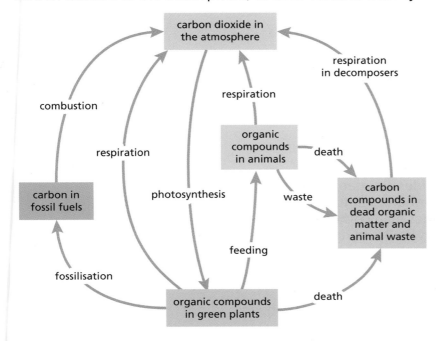

FIGURE 3.4.5b: A simple summary of the carbon cycle

3. Name four sources of the carbon dioxide in the atmosphere.

4. How is carbon removed from the atmosphere?

Carbon footprint ▶▶▶

A '**carbon footprint**' is a measure of the impact that all your activities have on the environment. It calculates the total amount of greenhouse gases that you are expected to produce, measured in units of carbon dioxide. The footprint reflects the amount of carbon-based natural resources consumed by a person, company, community or country over a given period of time. More-developed countries tend to have higher carbon footprints. The world average is about 4 tonnes of carbon dioxide per person per year.

5. Explain what a 'carbon footprint' is.

6. Look at Table 3.4.5. Suggest why developed countries have far bigger carbon footprints than other countries.

TABLE 3.4.5: Average estimated carbon footprints (2012), calculated by measuring the total emissions and dividing by the total population. (Data from European Commission and Netherlands Environmental Assessment Agency)

Country	CO_2 emissions (tonnes/person/year)
Australia	18.8
USA	16.4
Canada	16
UK	7.7
China	7.1
Brazil	2.3
India	1.6

Did you know...?

The oceans and some rocks can store carbon for many years and are known as carbon 'sinks'.

Key vocabulary

carbon cycle

carbon footprint

Exploring damage to the Earth's resources

We are learning how to:

- Describe resources that the Earth provides.
- Explain how human activity limits these resources.
- Justify decisions about making changes to the environment.

The Earth has limited resources that we rely on for survival. How have our activities affected these resources? How can we protect them for the future?

The Earth's vital resources

The Sun's energy, the wind, the tides and geothermal heat are some of the Earth's natural resources that you have already studied. The Earth provides many other resources, from the air we breathe and the wood and rocks used for building, to the minerals that we refine into metals. Life as we know it would not be possible without these precious resources, but as we process them, pollution is produced.

Other natural resources that are vital to our survival include:

- biological resources (plants and animals)
- land
- fossil fuels
- metal ores
- water

FIGURE 3.4.6a: Which natural resources can be seen here?

Natural resources are often classified as **renewable** or **non-renewable resources**.

1. Choose six natural resources. Describe why we need each one and how we use it.

2. Classify each of the resources identified in question 1 as renewable or non-renewable.

> **Did you know...?**
>
> Water is abundant on the Earth, but 97 per cent of the water is salt water in the oceans. Only 3 per cent is in fresh water lakes and rivers.

As the human population increases, so does pollution and environmental damage. Developed countries use the majority of the world's resources. About 25 per cent of the world's population are causing 75 per cent of the damage to the environment. Areas that are most vulnerable to damage are those that are easily accessible and supply natural resources that are in high demand.

Mining provides precious gems, coal for making electricity, and ores from which metals are extracted. It also causes pollution and leaves scars on the landscape. This environmental impact means that the mining is not **sustainable**. Other examples of unsustainable activities are oil extraction, deforestation, over-fishing the seas and intensive farming (producing more food from the same area of land). To get the most out of their land, farmers who use intensive farming sometimes cut down hedgerows, which results in habitat loss and affects food chains. They also use chemicals – for example pesticides and fertilisers, which pollute the land and waterways, killing organisms and disrupting food chains.

FIGURE 3.4.6b: Drainage from surface coal mines can pollute nearby streams.

3. Why are some natural resources more vulnerable to human activities than others?

4. Look at Figure 3.4.6b. How has this damage occurred?

Making sustainable decisions ▶▶▶

Deforestation in the Amazon rainforest is becoming a major issue. Huge areas of the rainforest are cleared annually to:

- increase the land available for farming soya and cattle
- allow mining
- flood the land for use in hydro electric power stations
- sell the timber.

However, once the trees have been cut down, the soil quickly becomes less fertile, making farming difficult. Wildlife is lost and local tribespeople are forced off the land and lose their traditional cultures. Global impacts include loss of biodiversity (including valuable medicinal or crop plants) and increased carbon dioxide levels in the atmosphere.

FIGURE 3.4.6c: The lush biodiversity of the Amazon rainforests is being destroyed.

5. Explain why there has been a loss of biodiversity in the Amazon.

6. Suggest how we could manage the Amazon's resources in a more sustainable way.

Key vocabulary

renewable resource

non-renewable resource

sustainable

Considering the importance of recycling

We are learning how to:

- Describe examples of recycling.
- Explain the benefits and limitations of recycling schemes.
- Compare the efficiency of recycling methods.

Recycling is the collection and processing of waste materials to make new products. What materials can be recycled and why do we recycle?

Why recycle?

UK households produce about 82 000 tonnes of rubbish every day. Each week, a typical family in England or Wales uses an average of:

- 7 glass bottles or jars
- 14 food or drinks cans
- 8 plastic bottles
- 4 kilograms of paper.

Continuing to burn or dump this amount of rubbish is unsustainable – recycling is a sustainable alternative. It reduces the demand for natural resources, including fossil fuels. It also causes less pollution and release of greenhouse gases, and less waste is sent to **landfill**.

Many materials can be recycled, including batteries, mobile phones, clothes and wood. Currently we recycle about 43 per cent of our household waste, though this varies across the country.

1. Name ten materials that can be recycled.

2. Use Table 3.4.7a to draw a bar chart showing the time taken for different materials to decompose.

3. Suggest why paper milk cartons take so long to decompose.

The limitations of recycling

Disadvantages of recycling are that recycling sites can produce pollution and they may be unsafe and unhygienic. The initial costs of recycling plants can be very high and some processes use a lot of energy. The separation of useful

FIGURE 3.4.7a: How do landfill sites damage the environment?

TABLE 3.4.7a: Some materials take hundreds of years to decompose.

Material	Time taken to decompose
paper	2–4 weeks
paper milk cartons	5 years
plastic bags	1020 years
cans	100 years
plastic bottles	450 years
glass bottles	500 years
rubber	80–2000 years

material from waste can be difficult and recycled products are often not high quality (for example paper) or durable (for example textiles). Finally, many of the resources saved are not that rare.

4. Why is reducing the demand for natural resources an advantage of recycling?

5. Suggest why recycling sites may be unsafe and unhygienic.

Making sustainable decisions >>>

There is much debate over the efficiency of recycling. Experts have conducted detailed life cycle analysis of recycled goods, estimating the energy used from collecting to processing. The efficiency compared to using new raw materials varies dramatically depending on the material. However, in most cases the energy needed to extract and process natural resources is much higher than that used to recycle the same material. Recycling therefore reduces the carbon footprint.

Recycling materials like metals and glass is fairly efficient. However, some materials have to be 'down-cycled' into products that cannot themselves be recycled. For example, soft-drink bottles made from PET (a plastic) end up as polyester fibres in clothes or carpets.

There is no economic incentive for people to recycle – the cost is zero for the consumer whether they throw their rubbish away or recycle it. The industry has therefore struggled for consistent amounts of materials to recycle. China now imports vast amounts of waste in order to recycle things like paper.

FIGURE 3.4.7b: Why is this worker at a recycling plant wearing a mask?

TABLE 3.4.7b: How much more efficient is aluminium recycling compared to glass recycling?

Material	Reduction in energy needed to recycle rather than use raw material (%)
aluminium	96
glass	21
plastic	76
newsprint	45

6. Explain why it is efficient to recycle aluminium.

7. Suggest why China imports waste paper to recycle.

Did you know...?

In Brazil old car tyres are cut up to make the soles for beach sandals. The rubber is hard wearing, waterproof and gives a good grip.

Key vocabulary

landfill

down-cycle

Applying key ideas

You have now met a number of important ideas in this chapter. This activity gives an opportunity for you to apply them, just as scientists do. Read the text first, then have a go at the tasks. The first few are fairly easy – then they get a bit more challenging.

Washable-nappy service

More than 8 million used disposable nappies are taken to landfill sites every day. Some parts of these nappies take up to 200 years to degrade, and cause soil and water contamination. Many people believe that reusable nappies have less environmental impact than disposable nappies. However, over 95 per cent of parents choose disposables because they are very convenient. The UK has a major problem with the amount of household waste sent to landfill and 2 per cent of this is nappies.

The washable-nappy service is a scheme that may encourage more parents to use reusable cloth nappies. These do not contain chemicals and are made from natural materials that are better for a baby's sensitive skin. The soiled biodegradable nappy liners are flushed down the toilet, and the used cloth nappies are stored in a special bin until the weekly collection. The nappies are reused repeatedly over a long period.

The main disadvantages of the service are:

- collection only once a week
- the energy (electricity) used in washing and drying
- the volume of water used in washing
- the fuel used for the collection service.

Initial studies found no significant difference in the environmental impact of disposable and reusable nappies. But recent research has shown that washable nappies have a much reduced impact. They produce far fewer greenhouse gas emissions (than the same number of disposables) if they are washed at (40–60 °C) with a full machine load and hung on a line to dry. Using 'A'-rated appliances also reduces the energy and water used.

On the other hand, chemicals in laundry detergents pollute the environment. Some are toxic to marine life and may also irritate human skin, lungs and eyes. In addition, cloth nappies are made from cotton, which is the crop treated with the most fertilisers and pesticides in the world. The majority of cotton is also bleached, which again uses chemicals that are potentially harmful to the environment.

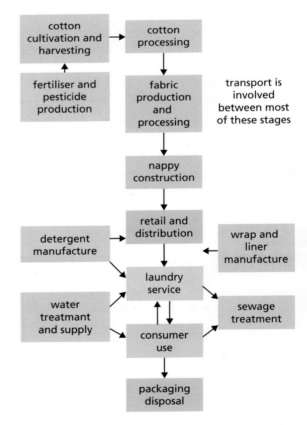

FIGURE 3.4.8a: The processes involved in a washable-nappy service that may impact on the environment.

Task 1: Exploring damage to the Earth's resources

Describe the environmental problems caused by disposable nappies.

Task 2: Considering the importance of recycling

Explain why people may decide to use a washable-nappy service.

Task 3: Understanding how carbon is recycled

Referring to the carbon cycle (Figure 3.4.5b), explain what happens to the waste matter on nappies after it has been flushed away. How is this beneficial to other organisms?

Task 4: Considering the importance of recycling; exploring damage to the Earth's resources

Research and explain why people are being encouraged to recycle materials, with reference to the materials used in washable and disposable nappies.

Task 5: Exploring damage to the Earth's resources

Analyse the effect of using disposable nappies compared with reusable nappies on local environments. Come to a final decision about which option you think is better for the environment.

Task 6: Understanding the global warming debate

Explain what global warming is and then analyse and evaluate how the nappy-washing service could impact on global warming and the environment.

Understanding the structure of the Earth

We are learning how to:

- Describe the layers of the Earth.
- Describe the characteristics of the different layers.
- Explain how volcanoes change the Earth.

The Earth has various layers, some of which are constantly moving. What are the different layers of the Earth called? What are their features?

The Earth's layers

The Earth is made up of different layers:

- inner core (solid)
- outer core (liquid)
- **mantle** (semi-liquid and solid)
- **crust** (solid).

The crust and the outer (solid) part of the mantle are called the **lithosphere**. This consists of pieces called **tectonic plates** that float on the semi-liquid mantle and move about slowly.

It is difficult to study the structure of the Earth directly because the crust is too thick to drill right through. However, scientists can study how waves made by earthquakes and explosions travel through the Earth. This gives them evidence of the different types of material in the different layers.

1. What is the lithosphere?

2. Why do the tectonic plates float on the mantle?

Features of the layers

The Earth's core is very hot. The outer core is made of liquid nickel and iron; the inner core is made of solid nickel and iron.

The mantle is the very thick middle layer. It contains silicon, magnesium and iron, in the form of oxides. The outer part is solid but the lower part can flow very slowly and has convection currents in it.

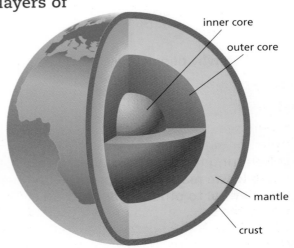

FIGURE 3.4.9a: The crust is the outer layer of the Earth – it is the land on which we live.

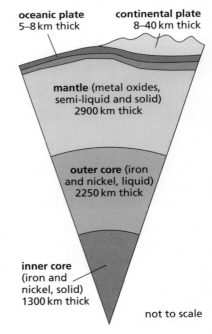

oceanic plate 5–8 km thick

continental plate 8–40 km thick

mantle (metal oxides, semi-liquid and solid) 2900 km thick

outer core (iron and nickel, liquid) 2250 km thick

inner core (iron and nickel, solid) 1300 km thick

not to scale

FIGURE 3.4.9b: What is the distance from the crust to the centre of the core?

The crust is relatively thin (5 to 100 km thick) and rocky. There are two types – the dense, thinner oceanic crust (made of basalt) and the less dense continental crust (which is granite).

The Earth's lithospere is a relatively cold part of the Earth. It is made up of about 20 tectonic plates. These move at a rate of about 2.5 cm per year on average. Over millions of years this has allowed whole continents to shift thousands of kilometres apart. This process is called 'continental drift'.

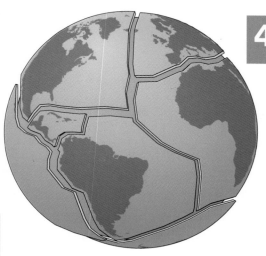

FIGURE 3.4.9c: The map of the Earth is changing very slowly because the plates are constantly moving.

3. Explain the difference between the two types of crust.

4. How do continents move?

Changing the Earth's surface ⟩⟩⟩

Where tectonic plates meet, they can push against each other, or move under or over each other. Earthquakes and volcanic eruptions occur at these points, and the crust may crumple to form mountain ranges. **Magma**, which is molten rock from the mantle, is less dense than the crust. It can rise to the surface through volcanoes (weak areas of the crust). **Lava** is the molten rock that escapes onto the Earth's surface. As this cools down it solidifies.

Geologists study volcanoes to try to predict future eruptions and to study the Earth's structure. Volcanoes can be very destructive. Even so, farming communities may choose to live near them because volcanic soil is very fertile.

Did you know...?

The cinder cone volcano Paricutin appeared in a Mexican cornfield on February 20, 1943. By the end of a year it was 336 m tall, and it reached its tallest height of 424 m in 1952. In geology, that is very quick.

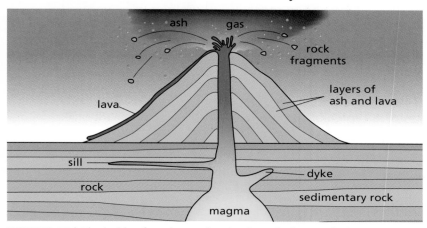

FIGURE 3.4.9d: The inside of a volcano, showing how the layers of ash and lava build up.

Key vocabulary

mantle

crust

lithosphere

tectonic plate

magma

lava

5. How do volcanoes form?

6. What is the difference between lava and magma?

Exploring igneous rocks

We are learning how to:

- Describe how igneous rocks are formed.
- Explain how the pH of the magma affects the formation of rocks.
- Investigate the effect of cooling rate on the formation of crystals.

Some of the oldest rocks on Earth are igneous rocks. Other igneous rocks are being formed right now. The word 'igneous' comes from a Greek word for 'fire'. How do igneous rocks form? What are their features?

What are igneous rocks?

Igneous rocks form when hot molten rock from the Earth's mantle cools down and hardens. They have no layers, may be light- or dark-coloured, usually have crystals and rarely react with acids. They do not contain fossils because these would have melted when the magma formed.

There are two main types of igneous rock:

- **extrusive** – these form when magma flows onto the Earth's surface
- **intrusive** – these form from magma below the Earth's surface in the crust.

Igneous rocks make up most of the rock on Earth, but they are often buried below the surface. One of the most common igneous rocks is granite, which is used for building and making statues. Other examples are pumice, basalt and obsidian.

FIGURE 3.4.10a: The Sierra Nevada mountains in the United States are made of granite.

1. Name four igneous rocks.

2. Describe some of the features of a typical igneous rock.

Looking at magma

Volcanoes formed from acidic magma and volcanic ash – they are typically steep and conical, for example Mount Fuji in Japan. These volcanoes often exceed heights of 2500 m. They have periodic explosive eruptions. The acidic lava that flows from them is very **viscous** (thick and sticky). It cools and hardens before spreading very far. Rocks formed from acidic magma include granite, pegmatite and pumice.

> **Did you know...?**
>
> Obsidian forms from magma that cools so rapidly that no crystals develop – it forms a glass.

FIGURE 3.4.10b: Mount Fuji was formed from acidic magma. Olympus Mons on Mars was formed from alkaline magma.

Volcanoes formed from alkaline magma typically have shallow, sloping sides – for example, Olympus Mons on Mars and the Hawaiian volcanoes. They often eject large amounts of lava onto the ground. The alkaline lava that flows from them is thin and runny. It can travel long distances before it cools and hardens to form rocks. Rocks formed from alkaline magma include basalt and gabbro.

3. How does pH affect magma?

4. What is the relationship between magma viscosity and volcano shape?

Crystal size >>>

The rate at which lava or magma cools determines the size of the crystals in an igneous rock. If the rate of cooling is fast, the rock will have small crystals. If the rate of cooling is slow, the rock will have large crystals. Granite cools slowly and has large crystals; gabbro cools even more slowly and has even larger crystals. Intrusive rocks often cool more slowly than extrusive rocks. However, when **fissures** (cracks) open underground, the magma in them cools quickly to form rocks with small crystals (such as basalt).

FIGURE 3.4.10c: Look at these rocks carefully. What conclusions can you come to about how they cooled?

5. What is the relationship between rate of cooling and crystal size?

6. Compare the rate of cooling in intrusive and extrusive rocks.

Key vocabulary

igneous

extrusive

intrusive

viscous

fissure

Studying sedimentary rocks

Sedimentary rocks are formed over thousands or even millions of years. What are their features? How are they formed?

Rocks in layers ▶▶

Rocks are **weathered** – pieces break off and are transported by wind or water. When river or sea currents slow down, rocks, pebbles and sediments drop to the riverbed or seabed – this is **deposition**. Over millions of years they are buried under more sediments. The weight of the upper layers squeezes the water out and compacts (presses together) and cements (sticks together) the lower sediments to form **sedimentary** rocks.

Sedimentary rocks are usually crumbly, found in layers and can contain **fossils**. Examples are:

- sandstone – made of sand particles
- limestone – made of tiny shells and skeletons of marine organisms
- shale and mudstone – made of silt- and clay-sized particles that are too small to see
- conglomerate – made of rounded pebbles.

1. How do rocks become sediments?

2. Name and describe three sedimentary rocks.

Looking at fossils ▶▶▶

A fossil is the preserved remains of a dead organism. Fossils give clues about the environments the rock formed in. For example, they can tell us if it formed in fresh water or seawater. Fossils form when dead organisms get covered in a layer of sediment before they can rot away. If the covering sediments change into sedimentary rocks, the remains of the animal or plant can also turn into rock but keep their original shape.

FIGURE 3.4.11a: Sedimentary rocks build up in layers and may contain fossils.

FIGURE 3.4.11b: Sedimentary rocks are made of rock particles and are usually porous, meaning water can pass through the gaps between the grains. This shows sandstone under a microscope.

There are three main ways that fossils can form:

- hard body parts (shells or bones) can be covered by sediments and then replaced by minerals
- softer parts of plants and animals can form casts or impressions
- dead plants and animals can be preserved in amber (a sticky tree resin), tar pits or glaciers.

3. Is limestone made in the sea or on land? Explain your answer.

4. How do fossils form?

Breaking rocks >>>

Rocks gradually wear away. Acid rain can dissolve rocks such as marble and limestone. Waves pound on rocks and eventually cause cliffs to crumble. Fast water in rivers or strong waves on beaches pick up rocks, knocking off sharp edges and turning them into smooth pebbles. When the pebbles are deposited on the river or seabed, water seeps through the sediments. Minerals in the water can crystallise between the rock particles and cement them together.

Freeze–thaw weathering of rocks happens when water seeps into cracks in the rock and then freezes. As it freezes it expands, eventually breaking the rock apart.

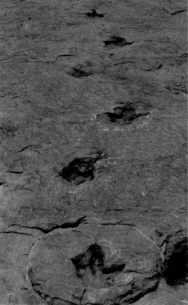

FIGURE 3.4.11c: Fossils give us information. Dinosaur footprints can tell us about the dinosaur's size, weight and how it moved.

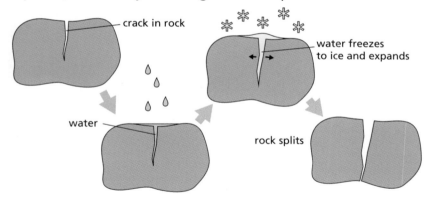

FIGURE 3.4.11d: How does water cause rocks to break apart?

Tree roots can also gradually break rocks apart as they grow. Some living organisms, such as bacteria and algae, produce chemicals that react with the rock and break it up.

5. What causes pebbles to become smooth?

6. Explain the processes of deposition, compaction and cementation.

Did you know...?

Sedimentary rocks cover most of the Earth's surface, but only make up a small percentage of the crust compared to metamorphic and igneous rocks.

Key vocabulary

weathered

deposition

sedimentary

fossil

freeze–thaw

Using metamorphic rocks

We are learning how to:

- Name some examples of metamorphic rocks.
- Describe how metamorphic rocks are formed.
- Explain why metamorphic rocks are suited to their uses.

The word 'metamorphic' comes from the Greek for 'change of form'. What are metamorphic rocks changed from? What are their features?

Making metamorphic rocks ⟩⟩

Existing rocks that are subjected to large amounts of heat and/or pressure can change into another type of rock called **metamorphic** rock. The original rocks are usually found deep in the Earth's crust. The new metamorphic rock is generally very hard-wearing and resistant to weathering and erosion.

Examples of metamorphic rocks are:

- marble formed from limestone
- slate formed from clay
- schists formed from sandstone or shale.

1. Describe how metamorphic rocks are formed.

2. What type of rocks are limestone, clay, sandstone and shale?

Metamorphic changes ⟩⟩⟩

When existing rocks **metamorphose**, they **recrystallise** without melting and new crystals form. The structure of the original rock changes permanently. This can happen in and around volcanoes, for example. The new minerals are more stable in the new conditions of pressure and temperature.

Different minerals form at different temperatures. The new minerals can be used to estimate the temperature, depth and pressure that the original rock metamorphosed at.

Limestone, chalk and marble are chemically identical but only marble is a metamorphic rock. Metamorphic rocks are usually very hard and shiny. Marble is a typical example – it is extremely hard and can be polished. Marble is used by sculptors because it can be carved into complex shapes.

FIGURE 3.4.12a: What are the names of the metamorphic rocks used in these pictures?

Did you know...?

Metamorphic rocks can be formed from igneous, sedimentary or other metamorphic rocks, but the changes from sedimentary to metamorphic are the most dramatic.

TABLE 3.4.12: Examples of metamorphic rocks and their uses

Original rock	Rock after metamorphism	Uses of the metamorphic rock
sandstone (sand grains in layers)	quartzite – much harder; original layers destroyed	building stone
limestone (layers, often with fossils)	marble – much harder; shiny; no fossils left	building stone; statues; work surfaces
mudstone (layers; soft and crumbles easily)	slate – very hard, shiny; splits in a single direction to give flat sheets	roofing; facings for buildings

3. Explain how metamorphic rocks differ from sedimentary rocks.

4. Why are there no fossils (or only very distorted fossils) in metamorphic rocks formed from sedimentary rocks?

Metamorphic rocks in detail 〉〉〉

Formation of metamorphic rocks varies a great deal depending on the temperature and pressure applied. Each set of conditions produces different rocks. The most intense metamorphism is called high-grade metamorphism. It produces gneiss (pronounced 'nice'), which has alternating bands of light and dark minerals. This type of metamorphism is often associated with the collision of tectonic plates and the formation of new mountains.

Heat and high pressure can destroy information contained in rocks. Limestone that is full of marine fossils may metamorphose into marble that is fossil-free. The heat (and pressure) destroys the fossils and hence, clues to the origin of the rock.

5. Why can many different metamorphic rocks be formed from the same sedimentary rock?

6. Metamorphic rocks do not usually provide geologists with much evidence about the past. Explain why not.

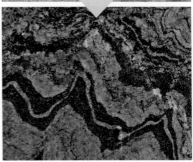

FIGURE 3.4.12b: The effect on shale (sedimentary rock) of exposure to more and more heat and pressure.

Key vocabulary

metamorphic

metamorphose

recrystallise

Understanding the rock cycle

We are learning how to:

- Describe the rock cycle.
- Explain how rocks can change from one type to another.

The three main types of rock on Earth are all related and the amount of each type changes constantly. Which processes link the different rocks?

The rock cycle

The Earth's rocks are continually changing because of processes such as weathering, erosion and large earth movements. The rocks are slowly recycled into other types over millions of years – this is known as the **rock cycle**.

The movement of tectonic plates and the Earth's inner heat drive the rock cycle. Look at Figure 3.4.13a, which describes the processes in the rock cycle. Mountains and hills form when buried rocks are moved to the surface. This is called **uplift**. Rocks at the surface are weathered and pieces break off. Erosion occurs when rock particles are worn away and moved elsewhere.

1. How are rocks changed from one type to another?

2. What is the difference between weathering and erosion?

> **Did you know...?**
>
> A Scottish scientist called James Hutton found evidence that the Earth had experienced extremely high pressures – enough to uplift and tilt rocks – and temperatures high enough to melt rocks and drive the rock cycle we understand today. He is recognised as the founder of modern geology.

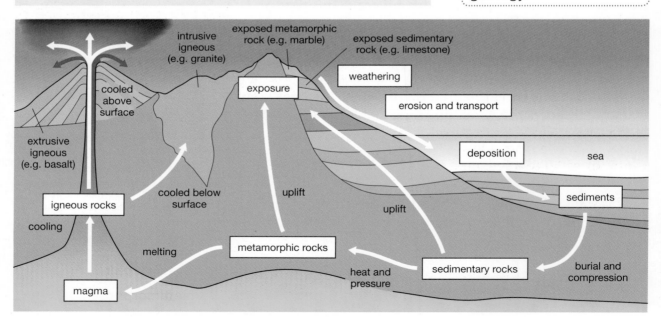

FIGURE 3.4.13a: Uplift causes the continual movement and cycling of rocks.

Earth movements can squeeze layers of rock into massive folds, forming mountains – for example the Alps, Rockies and Zagros mountains. The Alps are so old that the top halves of the folds have been worn away by the weather.

Folding can be seen on a small scale in coastal cliffs. When strata (layers of rock) are pushed up into a dome shape it is called an **upfold** or **anticline**. When strata are forced down into a bowl shape it is called a **syncline**.

Sediments and lava flows are usually deposited in horizontal layers due to the effect of gravity. Earth movements cause these layers to bend, tilt or fracture into pieces.

FIGURE 3.4.13b: Folding formed this structure at Lulworth Cove in Dorset.

3. Explain the part these processes play in the rock cycle:

   a) erosion

   b) sedimentation

   c) heat and pressure.

4. Explain how anticlines and synclines form.

Rocks on the move ▶▶▶▶

The movement of the Earth's crust causes rocks deep underground to be brought up to the Earth's surface, in the process of uplift. Uplift is occurring continually in some areas of the world today, such as Taiwan.

Faulting occurs when rocks break because of the forces acting on them. Stress builds up over years until the rocks move. Rocks can move from a few centimetres up to a few metres. When this happens, huge amounts of energy are released in earthquakes.

FIGURE 3.4.13c: Taiwan is rising by over 1 cm every year. During a big earthquake in 1999, uplift of up to 9.5 metres in some places caused significant damage to many large buildings and structures.

5. Explain how rocks from deep underground can quickly reach the surface of the Earth.

6. Which of the processes in the rock cycle happen quickly and which happen slowly?

Key vocabulary

rock cycle

uplift

upfold

anticline

syncline

Checking your progress

To make good progress in understanding science you need to focus on these ideas and skills.

Name the main gases in the atmosphere and describe the composition of the atmosphere.

Describe how the gases in the atmosphere, and their relative proportions, have changed over time.

Explain how plants and then animals have changed the atmosphere over time using different processes.

Name and describe some examples of human activities that cause damage to the atmosphere.

Name and describe the environmental effects caused by some human activities and suggest how they can be reduced.

Name some technological advances that reduce the effects of human activities on the atmosphere and analyse their impact.

Identify natural resources that the Earth provides.

Explain how human activities limit or damage these resources – for example through agricultural practices.

Analyse the advantages of a development against the disadvantages to the environment and make evidenced judgements about whether the development should be allowed.

Describe what global warming is and identify the effects of global warming on the Earth.

Explain how global warming affects living organisms and identify that scientists across the world have different opinions about global warming and its effects.

Evaluate the arguments for and against human activities enhancing the global warming effect.

Describe the carbon cycle as natural recycling and name the different ways that carbon enters and leaves the atmosphere.

Explain how each stage of the carbon cycle affects the amount of carbon in the atmosphere.

Explain what is meant by 'carbon footprint' and analyse the carbon footprint of different activities.

Describe the benefits of recycling and name some materials that can be recycled.

Explain the advantages and disadvantages of some recycling schemes.

Compare the efficiency of different recycling schemes to extracting the natural resource from the Earth.

Name the layers that make up the Earth and identify that the Earth's surface is made of plates that move constantly.

Describe the characteristics of each layer of the Earth and recall that tectonic plates move very slowly.

Explain that earthquakes, volcanic eruptions and the formation of mountains can happen where tectonic plates meet; explain how volcanic activity changes the surface of the Earth.

Describe how igneous, sedimentary and metamorphic rocks are formed; give examples and describe how they can change from one type to another.

Describe the features and properties of these rocks, including crystals in igneous rocks, recrystallisation in metamorphic rocks and layers (burying fossils) in sedimentary rocks.

Explain the processes involved in the rock cycle and link these to how the rocks are formed.

Questions

See how well you have understood the ideas in the chapter.

1. What caused the amount of oxygen in the Earth's early atmosphere to increase? [1]
   a) respiration   b) volcanic activity   c) photosynthesis   d) earthquakes and uplift

2. Which is the correct order of the layers of the Earth, starting from the centre? [1]
   a) mantle, inner core, outer core, crust   b) outer core, inner core, crust, mantle
   c) inner core, outer core, crust, mantle   d) inner core, outer core, mantle, crust

3. Which statement describes the mantle correctly? [1]
   a) relatively thin and rocky   b) very thick with the properties of a
                                               solid but can flow
   c) made of liquid nickel and iron   d) made of solid nickel and iron

4. What was the major cause of the decrease in carbon dioxide levels in the Earth's early atmosphere? [1]
   a) it was locked up in fossil fuels and sedimentary rocks   b) volcanic activity
   c) it formed the oceans with condensed water vapour   d) photosynthesis

5. What might the effects be if the ozone layer becomes thinner and develops a hole? [2]

6. What are tectonic plates? [2]

7. Give two examples of human activities that can damage the Earth's resources and explain how the damage might occur. [4]

See how well you can apply the ideas in this chapter to new situations.

8. Why does magma come out of volcanoes? [1]
   a) it is less dense than the crust   b) uplift forces it out
   c) an explosion forces it out   d) it is more dense than the crust

9. Look at Figure 3.4.15a. What has caused this to happen? [1]
   a) one tectonic plate has ridden up over another
   b) one tectonic plate has slid under another
   c) two tectonic plates have pushed up against each other
   d) uplift from under the Earth

FIGURE 3.4.15a: The San Andreas fault – this stretches over 1000 km through California.

10. Why does the water content of new sedimentary rock change as it forms? [2]

11. Scientists find a new type of rock that has small crystals. What does this tell them? [4]

12. Why do developed countries tend to have higher carbon footprints than developing countries? [1]

    a) there are more people   **b)** there is more agriculture to produce food

    c) there are more trees and plants   **d)** there are more cars and industries using fossil fuels

13. Why is it important that human activity does not damage or limit natural resources? [1]

    a) natural resources will run out if we do not look after them

    b) some areas are more vulnerable to damage by human activity than others

    c) we need natural resources to survive

    d) air, water and rock are natural resources

14. Describe how an ammonite fossil, like that shown in Figure 3.4.15b, was formed. [2]

FIGURE 3.4.15b: Ammonites were marine invertebrates that lived around the time of the dinosaurs.

Questions 15–16

See how well you can understand and explain new ideas and evidence.

15. What do you think has happened to the sedimentary rock in Figure 3.4.15c? [2]

FIGURE 3.4.15c: The Kharaza Arch in Jordan

16. Over the last 30 years the pH of lakes in southern Norway and the number of fish have been recorded. What pattern is shown by the data in the table? Suggest why. [4]

TABLE 3.4.15: Data from southern Norway

pH of lake	Percentage of lakes with		
	Good fish population	Poor fish population	No fish
4.4	3	41	56
4.7	6	38	56
5.1	16	48	36
over 5.5	71	8	21

PHYSICS
Motion on Earth and in Space

Ideas you have met before »>

Forces

Forces are measured in newtons (N) and can act in any direction. They can have a variety of effects including stretching, compressing and causing changes in the motion of objects. Some types of forces require contact, such as friction – others act without contact, such as gravity.

Speed

The speed of an object can be calculated by dividing the distance travelled by the time taken. Speed is measured in units such as metres per second (m/s) and kilometres per hour (km/h).

Fields

Non-contact forces such as magnetism, static charge and gravity act in a space known as a 'field'. The strength of a field gets weaker the further you move from the centre of the field. The Earth's gravitational field acts over a large distance and affects objects both close to Earth and those in space.

The Solar System and space

The Earth's motion in relation to the Sun explains day and night. The Sun is our nearest star but there is an unimaginable number of other stars.

The speed of light through a vacuum is very high but it is measurable.

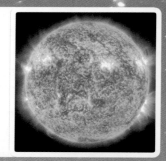

Forces in equilibrium

- If two or more forces acting on a stationary object are balanced, the object will remain still.
- A moving object will continue at the same speed and in the same direction unless an unbalanced force acts on it.

Motion

- An object's motion can be represented on a distance–time graph, which can be analysed to find out more about the motion.
- The motions of two objects can be compared and their relative speeds calculated.

Gravitational fields and the motion of the Earth

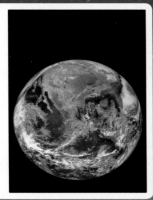

- The gravitational field strength around an object depends on the mass of the object and its distance from the centre of the field.
- Gravitational fields account for most of the patterns of motion in the Universe.
- The motion of the Earth around the Sun and the tilt of the Earth's axis account for variations in day length and for seasonal changes.

Stars and galaxies

- The Sun is our nearest star. Billions of other stars are present in the Universe.
- Distances in space are so vast that special units are used to measure them.

Describing journeys with distance–time graphs

We are learning how to:

- Gather relevant data to describe a journey.
- Use the conventions of a distance–time graph.
- Display the data on a distance–time graph.

Science provides explanations for how the world works and gathers data to test the explanations. Graphs are a useful way of displaying data and can help you to understand the story behind the data.

FIGURE 3.5.2a: Steady speed along a straight, level path

Looking at distance–time graphs

The cyclists in Figure 3.5.2a are travelling at a steady speed along the path. This means that they cover the same distance every second.

The cyclists' journey can be represented on a **distance–time graph**, as shown in Figure 3.5.2b. For every second that passes, the cyclists travel 5 m. After 10 s they are 50 m from the starting point.

You can use information from the graph to find how much distance has been covered at different times, how long it takes to travel different distances, and the cyclists' speed.

1. What unit is used to measure the cyclists' speed in Figure 3.5.2b?

2. How far did the cyclists travel in 10 s?

3. What was the cyclists' speed?

4. Describe or sketch a line graph to show another cyclist who is travelling at half the speed. How does it differ from Figure 3.5.2b?

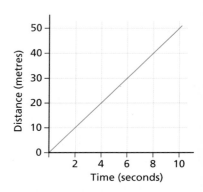

FIGURE 3.5.2b: The cyclists are travelling at a constant speed.

Changing speed

In the distance–time graph in Figure 3.5.2c, the cyclist does not travel the same distance every second. For the first 10 s they travel at a slow speed and cover little distance. However, they gradually **accelerate**. The speed between

30 s and 45 s is faster than before because the cyclist covers more distance every second. The steeper line of the graph indicates that the speed is faster. Subsequently the cyclist stops and then remains **stationary**. The flat part of the graph shows that no more distance is covered.

5. On a distance–time graph, what does it mean when:

   a) the graph is a horizontal line

   b) the graph is a straight upward-sloping line

   c) the graph is an upwards-sloping curve?

6. Looking at Figure 3.5.2c, when is the cyclist stationary?

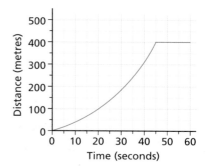

FIGURE 3.5.2c: A distance–time graph for a cyclist who changes speed.

Complex journeys ▶▶▶

Figure 3.5.2.d shows a distance–time graph for a student's journey to school which includes walking (1), waiting for a friend (2), walking with their friend (3), waiting for a bus (4) and riding on the bus (5). Their speed varies during different sections of the journey – at certain times no distance is covered.

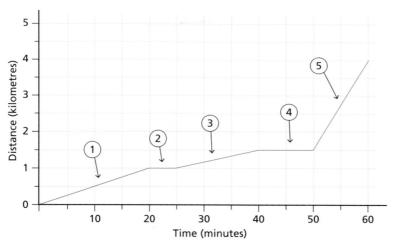

FIGURE 3.5.2d: A distance–time graph for a student's journey to school

7. Looking at Figure 3.5.2d, what is the evidence that the students travelled faster on the bus than at other times during the journey?

8. Compare sections 1 and 3 on the graph. How are they different? Suggest a possible reason for the difference.

9. Imagine a journey where you travel from your home to an overseas holiday destination. Sketch a line graph to represent the journey. Label each part of the graph to explain what is happening.

Did you know...?

From a distance–time graph you can work out the average speed for a whole journey where the speed varies at different times. You can also work out the speed at different parts of the journey.

Key vocabulary

distance–time graph

accelerate

stationary

Exploring journeys on distance–time graphs

We are learning how to:

- Interpret distance–time graphs to learn about the journeys represented.
- Relate distance–time graphs to different situations and describe what they show.

A speeding motorist sees a speed camera and slows down. The car then accelerates and is again breaking the speed limit. Further along the road a second camera comes into view and, again, the driver slows. A few days later a letter from the police arrives in the post...

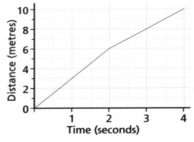

FIGURE 3.5.3a: A speed camera

Speed cameras and distance–time graphs ⟩⟩

Speed measurement on roads is often done by cameras that record the position of a car at the start and at the end of a period of time. The further the distance the car moved during that time, the faster it was going. It is then simple to use the speed formula to calculate the car's speed.

A motorist who realises they are speeding may suddenly slow down when they see a camera. Figure 3.5.3b shows what a **distance–time graph** might look like in such a situation.

1. What is the formula for calculating speed?

2. Looking at Figure 3.5.3b, how can you tell that the car's speed has changed?

3. Calculate the speed of the car in both sections of the graph. Show your working.

FIGURE 3.5.3b: A distance–time graph for a car approaching a speed camera

Using a time-lapse sequence ⟩⟩

Figure 3.5.3c shows a **time-lapse sequence** taken as a candle burned. The photographs were taken at five-minute intervals. The candle burned at a steady rate so it got shorter by a similar amount every five minutes.

The same process of time-lapse photography can be used to record the motion of objects, such as cars. The longer the distance between a car's position in successive photographs, the faster it must have been travelling. For example, if photographs are taken at one-second intervals and a car moves 12 m between each photograph, then the speed of the car is 12 m/s.

FIGURE 3.5.3c: Time-lapse photography of a burning candle – images were taken every 5 minutes

4. Look at Figure 3.5.3c. How long did the candle take to burn?

5. Read the final paragraph on the opposite page. What is the speed of the car in km/h?

6. Assuming the car in question 5 is travelling at a steady speed, draw a distance–time graph to show its motion.

Acceleration >>>

On a distance–time graph, a steep slope shows that an object is travelling faster than an object with a shallow slope. If an object suddenly **accelerates** (increases speed), the slope of the line will suddenly change. However, if the change in speed is more gradual, the gradient will change more gradually.

Figure 3.5.3d shows three different journeys. The change in each slope shows how quickly the speed of each object changes. Change in speed is called acceleration.

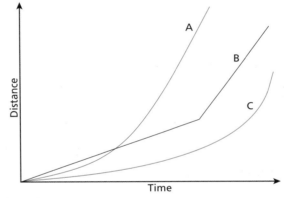

FIGURE 3.5.3d: Looking at acceleration on a distance–time graph

7. Looking at Figure 3.5.3d, which object has:

   a) the fastest speed at the start

   b) the fastest final speed?

8. If speed is measured in m/s, what unit is used for acceleration?

9. Sketch the graph in Figure 3.5.3d and extend the lines to show:

   a) object A continuing at the same speed for a while and then stopping abruptly

   b) object B coming to a gradual halt having travelled a shorter total distance than object A

   c) object C slowing down and then travelling at a steady speed.

Did you know...?

Drag race cars can accelerate from a standstill to cover a 300 m straight-line race track in less than 4 s, reaching speeds of over 500 km/h.

Key vocabulary

distance–time graph

time-lapse sequence

accelerate

Understanding relative motion

We are learning how to:

- Describe the motion of objects in relation to each other.
- Explain the concept of relative motion.
- Apply the concept of relative motion to various situations.

Imagine driving along a motorway. Alongside your car is another car travelling at exactly the same speed. Both cars' speedometers could be reading over 100 km/h, but compared to each other the cars are not moving at all.

Relative motion

When scientists compare the movement of two objects, they talk about **relative motion**. For example, if a car is travelling at 50 km/h and is being caught by a car doing 55 km/h, the speed of the second car relative to the first – its **relative speed** – is 5 km/h.

If you compare a 60 km journey for a cyclist doing 20 km/h and a car doing 60 km/h, the car is 40 km/h faster relative to the cyclist. After 1 hour the car has reached the destination but the cyclist needs a further 2 hours to complete the journey.

FIGURE 3.5.4a: The car travels faster in relation to the bicycle.

1. A person sets off jogging along a canal path at 12 km/h at the same time as a boat sets off at 10 km/h.

   a) How far will each one travel in half an hour?

   b) What is their relative speed?

   c) To the jogger, how would the boat appear to be moving as they travel along the canal?

Journeys and collisions

Figure 3.5.4b shows the distance–time graphs for two cars on a motorway. Car B set off later than car A. You can see when each will have completed their journey and the distance between them.

If the cars were in the same lane, car B would crash into the back of car A. It is the relative speed of two cars in a collision that is important rather than the actual speed of one car alone.

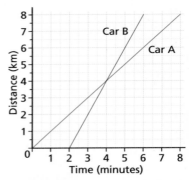

FIGURE 3.5.4b: Two cars travelling at different speeds

Imagine two cars driving towards each other on a road. They could collide head-on. If both cars are travelling at 40 km/h, their relative speed is 80 km/h. The crash would be equivalent to colliding with a stationary car at 80 km/h.

2. Look at Figure 3.5.4b. What are the speeds of the two cars in km/h? What is their relative speed?

3. What is the relative position of the two cars:

   a) 2 minutes after car A sets off

   b) 1 minute later?

4. Explain why head-on collisions are so dangerous.

Looking at events differently

If you look at the sky from a moving car it can be very difficult to tell which way the clouds are moving. They can appear to be stationary if the car is travelling at the same speed as the clouds. If the car speeds up, the clouds may appear to the passengers to be travelling in the opposite direction to the car.

FIGURE 3.5.4c: Two cars travelling at different speeds

FIGURE 3.5.4d: The relative motion depends on the speed and direction of the car and clouds.

5. Explain why in some situations it is hard to tell whether or not you are moving. How could your other senses help your judgement?

6. Explain the similarities and differences between these situations:

   a) a car travelling at 10 km/h and colliding with a parked car.

   b) a car travelling at 70 km/h and colliding with a car doing 60 km/h in the same direction.

   c) a car travelling at 70 km/h and colliding with a car doing 60 km/h in the opposite direction.

Did you know...?

If you travel away from a loud noise faster than 344 m/s, you will never hear the sound. Sound travels through air at just over 343 m/s, so it would never catch you up.

Key vocabulary

relative motion

relative speed

Analysing equilibrium

We are learning how to:

- Analyse situations to identify the various forces that are acting.
- Explore static situations in which objects are held in equilibrium and the nature of the forces involved.

A person asleep on a settee, a car parked in a garage and a coat hanging on a hook. In each case there is no movement at all, but forces are still being exerted.

Forces in balance

When something is not moving, the forces that are acting may not be obvious. In Figure 3.5.5a, each mass is pulling downwards and each spring is pulling upwards with exactly the same force, but in the opposite direction. We say that the forces are **balanced** or in **equilibrium**.

If you hang more mass from the spring, initially the forces are no longer in equilibrium because the downward force of the weight has increased and the mass moves downwards. However, the forces reach equilibrium again as the larger mass becomes balanced by a larger upwards force from the spring.

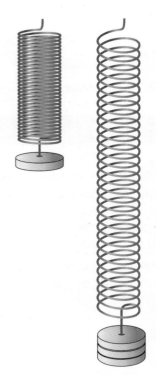

FIGURE 3.5.5a: Forces in equilibrium

1. Look at the right-hand part of Figure 3.5.5a. Describe the forces that are acting on the mass and spring.

2. Draw force diagrams to show the forces acting on:

   a) a small mass hanging from a spring

   b) a larger mass hanging from a spring.

3. Explain why neither mass in Figure 3.5.5a is moving.

Multiple forces in equilibrium

It is possible to have equilibrium between several forces at once. In Figure 3.5.5b, the straw bale is stationary even though the person on the left is pushing harder than the person on the right. The two pushing forces do not balance each other, so there must be another force acting for there to be equilibrium. In this case, the force of friction between the bale and the ground is working in the same direction as the person pushing from the right. Together they balance the larger pushing force exerted from the left.

FIGURE 3.5.5b: Why is the straw bale not moving?

4. Based on Figure 3.5.5b, draw a force diagram to show all the horizontal forces acting on the straw bale.

5. Explain why the straw bale might still not move if the person on the left pushed with a little less force.

Analysing forces in equilibrium ⟫⟫⟫

Figure 3.5.5c shows a car pulling a caravan at a constant speed. For the forces to be in equilibrium, the air resistance plus the friction opposing the movement of the car and the caravan need to be balanced by the pulling force provided by the car's engine.

FIGURE 3.5.5c: This car and caravan are travelling at a steady speed.

6. Referring to Figure 3.5.5c and the text above, the air resistance on the car is 300 N and on the caravan it is 400 N. The car has frictional forces of 250 N and the caravan's frictional forces are 200 N.

   a) In which direction is each force acting?

   b) What is the total of all the forces acting to the left?

   c) What is the total of all the forces acting to the right?

   d) Explain why the car and caravan are not speeding up or slowing down.

7. Suggest and explain ways of reducing the force that the car needs to produce in order to tow the caravan at a steady speed.

> **Did you know...?**
>
> When a car is towing a caravan, the car's engine has to produce more force and this increases the amount of fuel used. The cost of the extra fuel to tow a caravan from Edinburgh to London is over £100 more than if the car went alone.

Key vocabulary

balanced forces

equilibrium

Exploring motion and equilibrium

We are learning how to:

- Explore dynamic situations which may involve equilibrium.
- Apply ideas about equilibrium to a situation in which an object is moving.

When an ice hockey player hits the puck, it glides across the ice with little friction. Once the puck has left the stick, there is no pushing force and if there was no friction at all the puck would glide forever.

Forces in equilibrium

Two forces act on a sycamore seed when it falls from a tree – the force of weight acts downwards and the force of air resistance acts in the opposite direction. Once a sycamore seed starts to fall and spin, the force of air resistance is the same size as the force of weight. The two forces cancel each other out and the seed descends at a constant speed. The forces are in **equilibrium**.

air resistance   weight

FIGURE 3.5.6a: The forces are in equilibrium as the seed falls steadily.

1. What does the word 'constant' mean?

2. Describe the forces acting on a sycamore seed as it falls and spins downwards.

3. Why does a sycamore seed not keep accelerating downwards?

Newton's ideas about equilibrium

Sir Isaac Newton realised that a stationary object will stay still unless an unbalanced force acts on it. He also noted that if an object is already moving, it will continue in the same direction at the same speed unless an **unbalanced force** acts on it.

An important word in the explanation above is 'unbalanced'. There may be forces present but as long as they are balanced by other forces, they will not alter the object's movement.

air resistance

pushing force

friction

FIGURE 3.5.6b: This train is accelerating – the pushing force from the engine and the resistive force are not in equilibrium.

In Figure 3.5.6b the resistive force is half the size of the pushing force from the train's engine. Only half the pushing force is balanced, so the train accelerates.

4. Explain what is meant by the term 'balanced forces'.

5. Look at Figure 3.5.6b and describe the forces acting on the train.

Applying ideas about equilibrium 〉〉〉

When a car is travelling at a constant speed along a straight road, all the forces are in equilibrium. The passengers feel no pushing force from the car but continue in a forwards direction at the same speed.

Imagine the car crashes into a wall – it suddenly stops. If the passengers are wearing seat belts, they will stop too because they are attached to the car. The force from the wall, which stopped the car, is transferred to the people.

However, if the passengers are not wearing seat belts, there is no force from the wall acting on them. They will continue at the same speed in the same direction until another force acts, such as the one provided by the windscreen if they hit it.

FO4305OZ02

FIGURE 3.5.6c: Some forces are in equilibrium here; some are not.

6. Imagine a car driving into a gusty wind at a constant speed and direction. Explain how well the driver would be able to maintain equilibrium on the car during the gusts.

7. How could you help a non-scientist to understand how and why seatbelts are a good idea? Include scientific ideas and use different examples.

> **Did you know...?**
>
> Although seat belts reduce injuries to car drivers and passengers, they work best in conjunction with a range of other systems. Air bags, head restraints and crumple zones in the body of a car all make useful contributions to reducing injuries.

Key vocabulary

equilibrium

unbalanced forces

Applying key ideas

You have now met a number of important ideas in this chapter. This activity gives an opportunity for you to apply them, just as scientists do. Read the text first, then have a go at the tasks. The first few are fairly easy – then they become a bit more challenging.

Crossing the English Channel

There are various ways that people can travel across the English Channel from Kent to northern France. Two popular options are the ferry between the ports of Dover and Calais, and the train that goes through the Channel Tunnel from Folkestone to Calais. Both allow people to take their cars. Table 3.5.7 gives information about the journey using each of these routes.

TABLE 3.5.7: Journey information for crossing the English Channel

Time (minutes)	Distance covered by ferry (km)	Distance covered by train (km)
0	0	0
10	0	0
20	0	0
30	0	0
40	2	10
50	4	26
60	9	42
70	15	52
80	21	52
90	27	52
100	33	
110	39	
120	42	
130	42	
140	42	

FIGURE 3.5.7a: A cross-Channel ferry

FIGURE 3.5.7b: Trains are able to use the Channel Tunnel.

You will notice that at the start and end of both journeys no distance is covered – this is the time taken for cars to be loaded onto and off the ferry or train. Also the distance covered by the tunnel (52 km) is slightly longer because the tunnel entrance and exit are not on the coast next to the where the ferry docks.

Task 1: What makes a good graph?

You are going to plot graphs to show the journeys by ferry and by tunnel on the same axes. Write a list of bullet points to describe how you will correctly plot the graphs. Indicate how you will show which line represents which mode of travel.

Task 2: Distance–time graphs for crossing the English Channel

Plot distance–time graphs to display the journeys by ferry and by tunnel on the same axes. Indicate clearly which line represents which mode of travel.

Task 3: Interpeting the distance–time graph

Compare the positions of the ferry and the train 25 minutes after they set off. Calculate the mean (average) speed in km/h for each journey, not counting the time that the ferry and train are stationary.

What does the gradient of each line indicate?

What does the horizontal section of each line indicate?

Task 4: Swimming the English Channel

A top-level swimmer can cross the Channel in about 8 hours. The straight line distance is 36 km. Calculate the mean (average) speed for the journey. Add an additional line to your distance–time graph from Task 2 to show the progress of the swimmer, setting off from 0 minutes and swimming for 150 minutes. Explain why the actual speed of the swimmer may vary from the mean speed during the journey.

Task 5: Forces in action

With the help of diagrams, describe the forces in action during the journey of the ferry. Include setting off, cruising steadily mid-journey and coming into port at the end of the journey. Explain how the motion of the ferry can be accounted for by analysing the forces.

Task 6: A crash in the tunnel

Many people crossing the Channel by tunnel sit inside their cars on the train. Explain what would happen to the cars and the people if the train crashed.

Explain how the outcome might be affected if the people were **a)** wearing seat belts **b)** walking around the train instead of sitting in their cars.

Understanding gravitational fields

We are learning how to:

- Describe gravity as a non-contact force.
- Explore the concept of gravitational field and weight.
- Relate this concept to life on Earth.

Non-scientists may be puzzled by certain scientific concepts, such as mass and weight being different, and that an object's weight can be different in different places. By understanding gravitational fields, it is possible to explain these ideas.

Gravitational fields

The region around a planet where its gravity acts is called its **gravitational field**. Within this field objects are pulled towards the planet. This pull is a non-contact force because it acts at a distance – objects do not have to be on a planet's surface to be affected.

On Earth, as with other planets, the **gravitational field strength** gets weaker the further you move from the Earth's surface. It also varies slightly in strength across the surface.

Gravitational fields can extend over long distances. Even though the Moon is over 350 000 km from Earth, they are affected by each other's gravitational fields.

FIGURE 3.5.8a: The rise and fall of the tide is largely due to the Moon's gravitational field.

1. Describe what is meant by a gravitational field.

2. What evidence exists that the Moon's gravitational field affects the Earth?

3. List the main differences between the pulling force due to gravity and the pulling force from a rope in a tug-of-war.

Weight and gravitational field strength

The **weight** of an object depends on the **mass** of the object and the strength of the gravitational field acting on it. The formula used to calculate weight is:

weight of object (W) = mass (m) of object × gravitational field strength (g)

Weight is measured in newtons (N) and mass is measured in kilograms (kg), so the gravitational field strength is measured in newtons per kilogram (N/kg).

On the surface of the Earth the gravitational field strength is about 10 N/kg. To calculate how much a bag of fruit with a mass of 2 kg would weigh on the Earth's surface:

$W = m \times g = 2 \times 10 = 20\,N$

4. Which quantities determine the weight of an object?

5. Explain what is meant by the 'mass' of an object.

6. Explain why the weight of an object can vary, but the mass always stays the same.

Acceleration in gravitational fields 》》》

The pulling force on an object in a gravitational field causes it to accelerate in the direction of the force. The stronger the field, the bigger the acceleration – they have the same numerical value. For example, on the Earth' surface the field strength of 10 N/kg causes an unsupported object to accelerate towards the Earth at 10 m/s². The acceleration depends on the gravitational field strength but not on weight or mass.

When investigating acceleration in the Earth's gravitational field, other factors such as air resistance can affect the results.

FIGURE 3.5.8b: All masses close to the Earth's surface are pulled by the gravitational field strength of 10 N/kg.

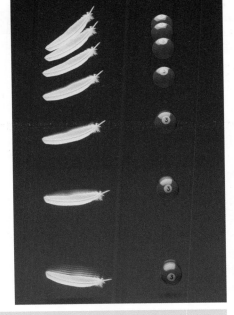

FIGURE 3.5.8c: Do different masses really fall at the same rate?

Did you know...?

The 'rule' about all objects falling at the same rate applies when there is no air resistance. Air resistance has varying effects on different masses and objects of different shapes.

Key vocabulary

gravitational field

gravitational field strength

weight

mass

7. Explain the relationship between gravity and weight.

8. Different masses fall towards the Earth at the same rate if air resistance is not a factor – explain why.

9. Design an activity to find out if air resistance affects the rate at which objects fall.

Applying ideas about gravitational fields

We are learning how to:

- Apply the concept of gravity causing weight to other situations.
- Explore the implications of varying gravitational field strength.

It is common to think of gravity on Earth as a very strong force, when in fact you easily overcome the force of gravity when you lift objects or make your whole body jump up into the air.

However, gravitational fields exist over huge distances and reach far into space.

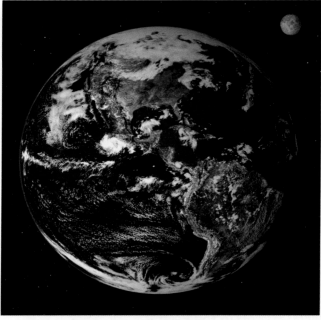

FIGURE 3.5.9a: Even weak gravitational fields reach far into space.

Gravity on a planet's surface

We know that a **gravitational field** becomes weaker the further away you travel from the object causing it. On the Earth's surface the gravitational field strength is about 10 N/kg. However, if you travel to a height of 2000 km above the Earth's surface the field strength is less than 6 N/kg.

The same applies to all bodies in space – the further away you are from them, the weaker their gravitational field.

1. Explain why you weigh less in space than on a planet's surface.

2. If you dropped two objects, one 1 m above the Earth and the other 1000 km above the Earth, how would their motion differ?

3. Suggest what gravitational fields you would experience exactly halfway between the Earth and the Moon.

Field strengths of planets and stars

The strength of the gravitational field of a star or a planet depends on its mass. The strength of the Sun's gravitational field on the surface of the Sun is about 270 N/kg – many times stronger than gravity on the Earth's surface.

If you compare the strength of the gravitational field on the surface of two planets of equal mass but different diameters, you would also find a difference. The planet with the smaller diameter would have a stronger field at its surface because the surface is closer to the centre of the field.

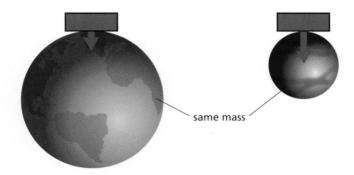

same mass

FIGURE 3.5.9b: The radius of a planet, as well as its mass, affects how strong the gravitational field is at its surface.

4. Explain how two planets of equal mass could have different diameters.

5. Draw a diagram to show the gravitational field lines around a planet. Use this to explain how an object's weight is different on a planet's surface compared to high above it.

Applying Newton's ideas >>>

Newton's theory of gravity has successfully explained many things we observe around us. Astronomers had observed the movement of the planet Uranus from when it was discovered in 1781. They then predicted the path of the Uranus orbit. However, Uranus did not quite follow the predicted path. Some suggested that there was an undiscovered planet, whose gravitational field was affecting the Uranus orbit. This turned out to be the case and led to the discovery of Neptune.

6. Explain what led astronomers to look for the planet Neptune.

7. Explain how making predictions based on scientific theories is an important aspect of scientists' work.

8. Imagine a newly discovered planet of similar mass to Earth. If your weight on the planet was lower than on Earth, what would this suggest about the planet's radius?

Did you know...?

The mass of a black hole and its gravitational field strength are so great that anything that gets too close cannot escape. Even beams of light are trapped.

FIGURE 3.5.9c: Stephen Hawking has done ground-breaking work to help us understand gravity and black holes.

Key vocabulary

gravitational field

Looking at motion in the Solar System

We are learning how to:

- Relate ideas about gravitational fields to the Sun–Earth–Moon system.
- Use these ideas to explain the position and motion of these bodies.

Ancient civilisations were just as fascinated by the stars and planets as we are today. They believed that everything rotated around the Earth. New observations and new theories helped scientists to understand the mysteries of how the planets move.

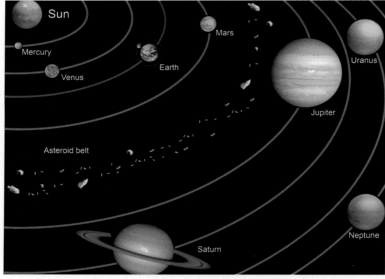

FIGURE 3.5.10a: The planets of the Solar System orbit the Sun. (Distances and planet sizes are not shown to scale.)

Motion of objects in the Solar System

The paths of the planets around the Sun – their **orbits** – are not quite circular. They follow the shape of an **ellipse**. An elliptical orbit means that a planet's distance from the Sun varies during its orbit.

The time taken for each planet to orbit the Sun differs. For example, the Earth takes 365.25 days. However, Saturn takes nearly 30 times as long.

There are also thousands of **asteroids** orbiting the Sun, mainly in a belt between Mars and Jupiter. Asteroids are lumps of rock smaller than planets.

1. Draw a diagram to compare the elliptical orbit of Mars around the Sun to that of the Earth's orbit.

2. How might an elliptical orbit affect the conditions on a planet?

3. Table 3.5.10 shows the names of the planets in the Solar System. Write them in order of increasing distance from the Sun.

> **Did you know...?**
>
> Pluto was originally thought of as a ninth planet in the Solar System, but it has been reclassified as a dwarf planet because it has a similar size to objects in the asteroid belt.

The effect of gravitational fields >>>

The Sun has the biggest mass in the Solar System and so has the strongest gravitational field. The gravitational attraction between the Sun, the planets and the moons provides the forces that keep them moving in regular orbits.

Table 3.5.10 shows the approximate number of moons orbiting each planet in the Solar System. Additional moons are regularly being discovered. The orbit of a moon is centred on its planet rather than the Sun, due to the planet's gravitational field.

TABLE 3.5.10: Moons observed in the Solar System

Planets in order of mass (smallest to largest)	Number of moons observed
Mercury	0
Mars	2
Venus	0
Earth	1
Uranus	27
Neptune	14
Saturn	62
Jupiter	66

4. How does the motion of a moon differ from that of a planet?

5. Look at Table 3.5.10. To what extent does the mass of a planet affect the number of moons it has? Suggest different factors which could affect the number of moons a planet has.

6. Suggest why the Sun has so many planets, with their moons, in orbit around it.

Forces, speed and orbits >>>>

If an object such as the Moon was stationary above the Earth, gravitational attraction would make it fall to Earth. If the object was travelling very fast away from the Earth, it would escape from the Earth's gravitational field. At a particular speed the object does neither – it falls on a curving path right around the Earth. The International Space Station follows such a path – a continuous free fall. Astronauts in the space station feel weightless because they are falling along with the space station.

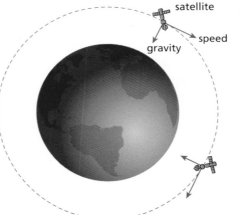

satellite

speed

gravity

A satellite placed in orbit is set in motion at the correct speed.

The force acting on it is gravity, which is pulling it towards the planet.

It stays in motion because its direction is always changing.

FIGURE 3.5.10b: How a gravitational field keeps objects in orbit.

7. What affects whether or not an object stays in orbit around a planet?

8. Suggest how the speed and height of a satellite orbiting the Earth might be different from the same satellite orbiting Saturn, if they were both to remain in orbit.

9. Some people have described Jupiter as a 'cosmic vacuum cleaner' because of the amount of space debris that hits it. Explain why this occurs and to what extent it *can* be compared to a vacuum cleaner.

Key vocabulary

orbit

ellipse

asteroid

Describing stars and galaxies

We are learning how to:

- Describe the characteristics of a star.
- Relate our Sun to other stars.
- Explain the concept of galaxies and the position of our galaxy compared to others.

Our Sun is the star that maintains the conditions that allow life to exist on Earth. It sits in a galaxy called the Milky Way. The Milky Way is one of over 170 billion galaxies in the Universe. Each galaxy contains a few billion stars.

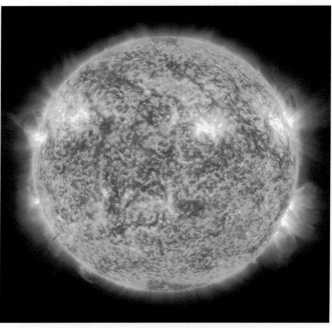

FIGURE 3.5.11a: The Sun – huge amounts of energy are released by nuclear fusion.

Characteristics of a star

A **star** forms when a huge cloud of matter (usually hydrogen) is pulled together by its own gravitational field. Eventually the temperature and pressure become so high that the hydrogen atoms join to make helium. This process, known as **nuclear fusion**, releases the huge amount of energy that makes a star shine so brightly.

Our Sun is quite a small star. However, it has a diameter 109 times that of the Earth and it contains 99.9% of the matter in the Solar System.

1. What are the main chemical elements in the Sun?

2. Describe where the Sun gets its energy from.

3. Thinking about energy, what is the main difference between a star and a planet?

Different types of stars

The size and age of a star determine its characteristics. Figure 3.5.11b shows two of the brightest stars in the night sky – Rigel and Betelgeuse. At about 57 times the diameter of the Sun, Rigel is a blue-white supergiant that shines with an intensity more than 50 000 times larger than the Sun. The extremely high rate at which it is fusing hydrogen accounts for its brilliance. Betelgeuse is a bigger, older star known as a **red giant**. It has run out of hydrogen so is now fusing helium atoms as its source of energy. Its average diameter is about 950 times that of the Sun.

> **Did you know...?**
>
> When the biggest stars in the Universe collapse and die, their cores contract so much that they reach an unimaginable density, and become a black hole.

When a star much larger than our Sun approaches the end of its life, its inner core can collapse to form a neutron star. A **neutron star** has a mass similar to that of the Sun, concentrated into a diameter of about 10 km.

4. Suggest what the surface gravity of a neutron star would be like.

5. Explain why stars do not have an infinite life span.

Stars and galaxies

With the naked eye it is only possible to see a tiny fraction of the stars. Even our closest stars, such as Proxima Centauri and Sirius A, are approximately 100 000 000 000 000 km away from the Earth. In scientific notation this is written as 10^{14} km.

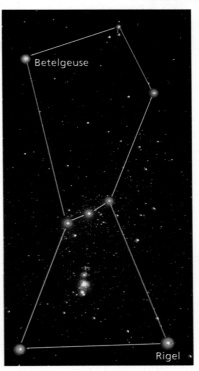

FIGURE 3.5.11b: Rigel and Betelgeuse are stars in the constellation of Orion.

FIGURE 3.5.11c: Andromeda galaxy – the bright haze consists of many distant stars.

Evidence about space is collected through telescopes and through analysis of the light that reaches the Earth. Scientists have shown that since the Universe was created in the Big Bang, it has been continually expanding. By analysing the light that arrives on Earth from distant **galaxies**, scientists are able to measure the rate of expansion.

6. Explain why scientific notation is sometimes used for writing numbers.

7. Explain the differences between these terms, including their order of size: star, Universe, planet, galaxy.

8. When the theory about the Universe expanding was first put forward, it was not accepted immediately. Suggest what may have led to it becoming more widely accepted.

Key vocabulary

star

nuclear fusion

red giant

neutron star

galaxy

Explaining the effects of the Earth's motion

We are learning how to:

- Describe variation in length of day, apparent position of the Sun and seasonal variations.
- Compare these with changes in the opposite hemisphere.
- Explain these changes with reference to the motion of the Earth.

The Earth's rotation defines day length. The time taken for the Earth to orbit the Sun defines the length of a year. Because the orbit takes 365.25 days, we have an 'extra' day every leap year. Without this the seasons would drift – after 730 years, midsummer would be in December.

the Earth spins around its axis every 24 hours

sunlight

this side of the Earth is facing towards the Sun – it is day here

this side of the Earth is facing away from the Sun – it is night here

FIGURE 3.5.12a: Day and night are caused by the Earth spinning on its axis.

Day and night

Look at Figure 3.5.12a. On the side of the Earth that is facing the Sun it is day; and on the opposite side it is night.

Figure 3.5.12b shows how day length varies throughout the year at two locations.

1. Look at Figure 3.5.12b. Compare the day length in the Arctic Circle and in northern France on:

   a) 21 December

   b) 21 June.

2. What is special about 21 March and 21 September?

3. How would the graph look different for locations in the southern hemisphere?

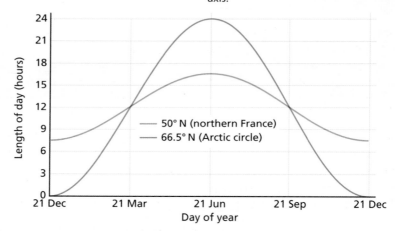

FIGURE 3.5.12b: Variation in day length

Tilt of the Earth's axis

The Earth's **axis of rotation** is tilted at 23°. Figure 3.5.12c shows this tilt and how the Earth orbits the Sun once a year. When the northern hemisphere is tilted away from the Sun, the daytimes are shorter. The Sun is low in the sky, even at midday and the amount of heat from the Sun is reduced – it is the **season** of winter. Six months later the Earth is on the other side of the Sun, which means that the northern hemisphere is now angled towards the Sun – it is summer.

4. Explain why the daytimes are longer than the night-times during summer.

5. At what times of the year are daytimes and night-times of equal length? Explain why this happens.

6. Explain the changes in seasons and day length a country on the equator experiences.

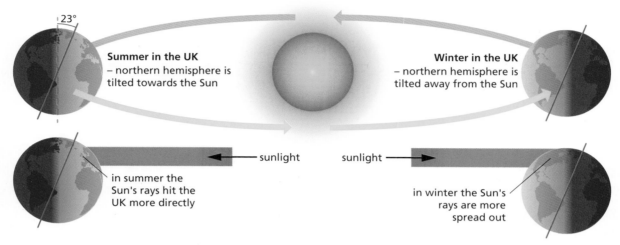

Summer in the UK – northern hemisphere is tilted towards the Sun

Winter in the UK – northern hemisphere is tilted away from the Sun

sunlight

sunlight

in summer the Sun's rays hit the UK more directly

in winter the Sun's rays are more spread out

FIGURE 3.5.12c: The seasons are caused by the Earth's tilt.

Implications of the Earth's tilt

If the tilt angle of the Earth's axis were zero, we would not experience seasons as we currently do. There would be only small annual variations because of the Earth's slightly elliptical orbit meaning that the Earth is closer to the Sun at some times than at others.

If the Earth's axis was tilted more than its current 23°, it would make the seasonal variations more extreme. At places where the Sun is directly overhead, the amount of energy reaching that place is at a maximum. Whereas if the Sun's rays meet a place at an angle, the available energy is spread out over a larger area.

7. At midsummer on Earth, the Sun never sets at the poles – explain why. Draw diagrams to help.

8. Explain why plants grow less well in the winter than they do in the summer.

9. Mars is tilted more on its axis and has a much more elliptical orbit than the Earth. It rotates at about the same rate as the Earth, but takes twice as long to complete one orbit. From this information, suggest how Mars days, seasons and years might differ from those on Earth.

Did you know...?

The planet Uranus has a unique feature in the Solar System – its axis is tilted at 82°, meaning it rotates 'on its side' as it orbits the Sun. Its orbit takes 84 Earth years.

Key vocabulary

axis of rotation

season

Measuring distances in the Universe

We are learning how to:

- Recall that the light year is used to measure astronomical distances.
- Explain the limitation of units such as km in describing astronomical distances.
- Describe a technique for measuring the distance to distant objects.

The distance from the Earth to the Sun is about 150 million km or more than 3700 times the length of the Earth's equator. This distance is tiny compared to distances to other stars. Dealing with such vast distances is difficult, so a unit other than the kilometre is needed.

FIGURE 3.5.13a: The light from some of these stars has taken many millions of years to reach us.

Light years

When measuring distances across the Universe the unit often used is the **light year** (or ly for short). It gives more manageable numbers than using kilometres. The unit is defined by how far light will travel in a year. When travelling through a vacuum, light has a speed of just under 300 000 km/s. This means that in 1 year, light will travel 9 460 000 000 000 km through space – this is how many km there are in 1 ly.

1. What does the abbreviation 'km/s' mean?

2. What unit is often used to measure distances across the Universe?

3. Explain why distances across the Universe are not normally measured in kilometres.

Distances in the Universe

Measuring in light years still does not stop the distances involved being almost mind-numbing. Look at Table 3.5.13. Even when Pluto is at its closest to the Earth it is hundreds of times further away from us than the Sun. However, the distance to Pluto from the Earth is minuscule compared to distances to other stars.

Light from the far reaches of the Universe has taken 15 billion years to reach the Earth. This means that we are seeing those places as they were 15 billion years ago.

Did you know...?

As well as using light years to measure distance, astronomers use other units – the astronomical unit (AU), where 1 AU = the mean distance between the Earth and the Sun, and the parsec (pc), where 1 pc = 3.26 ly.

TABLE 3.5.13: Some approximate distances in the Universe

Examples in the Universe	Distance (ly)
Distance across the Milky Way galaxy	100 000
Earth to Sirius (one of our nearest stars)	8.6
Earth to the most distant point of the Universe	15 000 000 000
Earth to Pluto (at their closest)	0.000 44
Earth to the Sun	0.000 016
Earth to the Andromeda galaxy	2 500 000

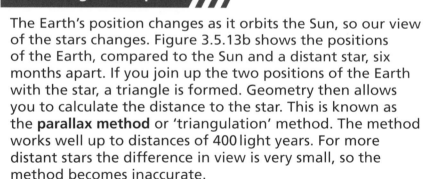

4. Explain why:

   a) the distance between Pluto and the Earth varies

   b) distances to the other bodies appear not to vary.

5. When you look at two stars that are different distances away, you are not seeing them at the same point in time – explain why.

Measuring techniques ⟫⟫

The Earth's position changes as it orbits the Sun, so our view of the stars changes. Figure 3.5.13b shows the positions of the Earth, compared to the Sun and a distant star, six months apart. If you join up the two positions of the Earth with the star, a triangle is formed. Geometry then allows you to calculate the distance to the star. This is known as the **parallax method** or 'triangulation' method. The method works well up to distances of 400 light years. For more distant stars the difference in view is very small, so the method becomes inaccurate.

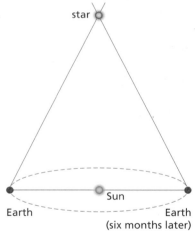

FIGURE 3.5.13b: The parallax method of determining the distance to a 'nearby' star

6. When using the parallax method, why are the positions of a star compared six months apart rather than after a shorter or longer period?

7. **a)** How many times further away is Sirius (our second nearest star) from the Earth than the Sun is from the Earth?

   b) If you made a scale model in which the distance from the Earth to the Sun was 1 mm, how far away would Sirius need to be in km?

Key vocabulary

light year (ly)

parallax method

Checking your progress

To make good progress in understanding science you need to focus on these ideas and skills.

- Collect data about distance travelled and time taken for types of movement or journeys.

- Present data you have collected or data you have been given as distance–time graphs.

- Construct distance–time graphs for complex journeys.

- Describe some features of distance–time graphs.

- Analyse distance–time graphs to describe an object's movement at different stages in a journey.

- Explain distance–time graphs for complex journeys, including where an object travels at different speeds and accelerates at different rates.

- Describe a situation where objects are travelling at different speeds.

- Apply the idea of relative speed to two objects moving in situations involving overtaking and collisions.

- Apply the concept of relative motion to several moving objects in a variety of situations.

- Identify the forces acting on an object and explain how they may cancel each other out so that a stationary object does not move.

- Explain how opposing forces may or may not be in equilibrium and the effect that this has on a stationary object.

- Explain how multiple forces may or may not be in equilibrium and identify the effect this has on an object.

- Identify the forces acting on an object moving at a constant speed and explain how they can cancel each other out so that there is no change in speed or direction.

- Explain how opposing forces may or may not be in equilibrium and the effect this has on an object's motion.

- For a moving object, explain how multiple forces can act and how they may or may not be in equilibrium; identify the effect this has on an object's motion.

Explain what causes an object to have weight.

Describe how gravity affects the weight of an object.

Explain the relationship between gravitational field and the weight of an object.

Describe how an object's weight can vary.

Predict how an object's weight would vary depending on its position in relation to large bodies such as planets.

Use the concept of gravitational field to explain various phenomena, including the orbits of planets around stars.

Describe the movement of the Sun, Earth and Moon in relation to each other.

Explain the effects of the relative motion of the Sun, Earth and Moon.

Explain the relative movement of the Sun, Earth and Moon using the idea of gravity.

Describe the differences between the Sun, other stars and galaxies.

Describe the relationship between the Sun, other stars and galaxies.

Relate ideas about the Sun, stars and galaxies to evidence visible from Earth.

Describe the effects that the tilt of the Earth's axis has on Earth.

Explain the causes of daily and seasonal changes.

Explain what would happen if the Earth's axis was tilted by a different amount.

Recognise the need for large units to measure distances in space.

Describe how light years can be used to measure distances.

Explain the implications of other stars and galaxies being many light years away from Earth.

Questions

Questions 1–7

See how well you have understood the ideas in the chapter.

1. Which one of these units is *not* used for speed? [1]

   a) km/h   **b)** m/s   **c)** ly   **d)** mph

2. Which one of these statements about the stars is true? [1]

   a) The Sun is at the centre of the Universe.   **b)** A star's energy comes from burning gas.
   c) There are nine stars in the Solar System.   **d)** Stars have large gravitational fields.

3. What does the strength of the gravitational field on the surface of a planet depend on? [1]

   a) the mass and radius of the planet   **b)** the mass of the planet and its distance to the Sun

   c) the shape and radius of the planet   **d)** the rotation speed of the planet

4. Which of these statements about forces and movement is *always* true? [1]

   a) A moving object will stop unless a force acts on it.
   b) A stationary object with forces acting on it will start to move.
   c) When all the forces acting on an object are in equilibrium, its position will not change.
   d) When all the forces acting on an object are in equilibrium, its speed and direction of movement will not change.

5. Which unit is used instead of km to measure distances in space? Explain why. [2]

6. Explain what causes day and night on Earth. [2]

7. Describe the changes in daytime length and temperature that countries like the UK experience from winter to summer. Explain what causes these changes. [4]

Questions 8–14

See how well you can apply the ideas in this chapter to new situations.

8. In which of these locations would the gravitational field be the strongest? [1]

   a) on the surface of a red giant star   **b)** on the Moon as it orbits the Earth
   c) at the edge of the Earth's atmosphere   **d)** on the Earth's surface

9. A van takes 1 hour to travel along a 60 km stretch of road. A car takes 45 minutes to do the same journey. Which of these statements is true about their relative speeds? [1]

   a) The van is 15 km/h faster.   **b)** The van is 15 km/h slower.

   c) The car is 20 km/h faster.   **d)** The car is 20 km/h slower.

10. Draw a diagram to show what would happen to a satellite if the Earth's gravity was suddenly turned off. [1]

11. Which of these statements would be true for a spacecraft leaving the Solar System in a straight line at a constant speed? [1]

    a) It would start to orbit the Sun.   **b)** The forces on it would not be in equilibrium.

    c) No stars would be visible.   **d)** No strong gravitational forces would be acting on it.

12. A child on a scooter is pushing herself along with a force of 100 N. Another child is helping to push the scooter along with a force of 70 N. Air resistance is 20 N and friction on the scooter's wheels is 140 N. What is the overall force on the scooter? What will happen to its motion? [2]

13. The Earth's axis is tilted at 23° to the Sun. Imagine a planet tilted twice as much and following the same orbit as the Earth. Explain what differences the northern hemisphere of that planet would experience. [2]

14. Draw a distance–time graph for two horses moving across a 500 m field. One horse trots steadily across the field in 4 minutes. The other accelerates to a gallop, stops for 1 minute to eat grass and then gallops the rest of the way, reaching the far side after 3 minutes. [4]

Questions 15–16

See how well you can understand and explain new ideas and evidence.

15. In Figure 3.5.15a, time-lapse photography is used to record the position of a ball at 1 second intervals.

start   1 m

FIGURE 3.5.15a: The position of a rolling ball at 1 second intervals

    a) Which of these statements best describes the motion of the ball? [1]

        i) The ball starts off slowly and gets faster and faster.

        ii) The furthest the ball travels in 1 second is 0.5 m.

        iii) The ball reaches its maximum speed after rolling down the first ramp.

        iv) The only force acting on the ball is friction.

    b) Complete the following sentence: If the same experiment was carried out in a vacuum, you would expect the ball to go only slightly further because... [1]

16. Scientists believe that there is a massive black hole at the centre of our galaxy, with a mass 30 billion times that of the Sun. Explain what evidence could suggest its existence. If a spacecraft set off in a straight line at a constant speed towards the black hole, what additional evidence would indicate the presence of the black hole? What challenges would the spacecraft face? [4]

Waves and Energy Transfer

Energy stores and transfers

An object stores energy depending on how high it has been raised. This is because it is affected by the Earth's gravitational force.

When elastic materials are stretched or squashed they have more energy stored in them.

Energy is transferred when changes happen, and this transfer can happen in many different ways. It may be transferred from place to place in a material or from one form of storage to another.

Fuels are energy stores

Fuels are energy stored chemically. They include wood, fossil fuels and hydrogen.

Fuels only burn if oxygen is present. The products of combustion also store energy, but less than that in the fuel and oxygen together.

When a fuel is burned in oxygen, energy is transferred to the surroundings and to the combustion products.

Sound waves

Energy is transferred by sound in the form of waves.

Sound waves are longitudinal waves transmitted by vibrating air particles.

They may be reflected by hard materials and absorbed by soft materials.

In this chapter you will find out

Energy transfers

- Conduction and radiation are important ways of moving energy from place to place.
- The quantity of energy transferred in a change can be measured.
- How quickly energy is transferred is important and this can also be measured.

Energy in the home

- Fuel bills show how much energy is used and its cost.
- Knowing the quantity of energy transferred is useful and can be calculated.
- Similarly, knowing the rate of energy transfer is also useful and can be calculated.

Water waves

- Waves in water are transverse waves that carry energy.
- Water waves, like sound waves, need a medium to travel through.
- Water waves can be reflected.

Light waves

- Light travels as transverse waves that carry energy.
- Light waves can travel through a vacuum.
- Light can be reflected, absorbed and refracted.
- White light can be split into a spectrum of colours.

Making waves

We are learning how to:

- Describe the movement of waves in water.
- Understand reflection of waves.
- Understand superposition of waves.

When you watch the waves at the seashore, it seems as if the water is coming towards you. However, watching boats and seabirds floating on the sea, you can see that they bob up and down as the waves pass by. We need to try to explain why something moving up and down seems to be carrying energy along.

FIGURE 3.6.2a: This boat bobs up and down as the waves pass by it.

Reflecting waves

You know that sound waves are reflected, or bounced back, by hard flat surfaces – this is what makes echoes. However, it is not just sound waves – all waves can undergo **reflection**.

The behaviour of waves in water can be explored using a water tank. If some single straight water ripples are generated in the tank, then blocking their path shows how the wave is reflected (Figure 3.6.2b). The wave is reflected by the barrier and the angle it is reflected at is the same as the angle it arrived at.

1. Explain what we mean when we say that light has been reflected.

2. What do you notice about the direction in which a wave hits a barrier and the direction in which it is reflected?

3. Suggest why a bumpy surface does not produce a reflected wave that is the same shape as the wave that arrived.

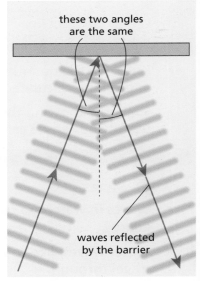

these two angles are the same

waves reflected by the barrier

FIGURE 3.6.2b: Ripples of water bounce off the barrier.

Ripples in a pond

Previously, we explored sound waves, which are **longitudinal waves**. A longitudinal wave moves backwards and forwards in the same direction that it is travelling in.

Water waves, however, are **transverse waves**. Unlike longitudinal waves, they move up and down rather than

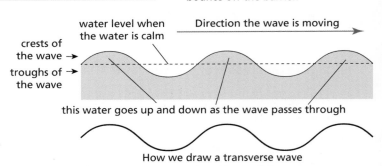

water level when the water is calm

Direction the wave is moving

crests of the wave →

troughs of → the wave

this water goes up and down as the wave passes through

How we draw a transverse wave

FIGURE 3.6.2c: Cross-sections through a ripple on water; volumes of water oscillate up and down as the wave passes.

backwards and forwards. Transverse means 'across' – the water is moving across the direction the wave is travelling in.

All waves **oscillate**, moving either up and down or forwards or backwards in a regular rhythm – rather like the rhythm of a swinging pendulum.

4. Describe the movement of water in a wave.

5. Describe the difference between a crest and a trough.

6. Explain the difference between a transverse wave and a longitudinal wave.

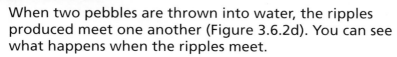
Superposition

When two pebbles are thrown into water, the ripples produced meet one another (Figure 3.6.2d). You can see what happens when the ripples meet.

When two waves from different starting places meet, they either combine to make a bigger wave or cancel each other out. This is called **superposition**.

If the crests coincide, the waves add together and make a bigger wave.

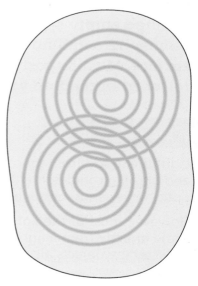

FIGURE 3.6.2d: The circles show the crests of the waves produced when two pebbles are thrown into water. They spread outwards.

FIGURE 3.6.2e: Superposition produces bigger waves.

If the crests of one wave coincide with the troughs of the other, the waves cancel out, resulting in no wave.

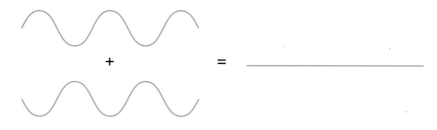

FIGURE 3.6.2f: Superposition can lead to waves cancelling one another out.

7. Describe the idea of superposition.

8. Explain the effect of combining two waves when the crests of one coincide with the troughs of the other.

Did you know...?

The largest water wave recorded was in Lituya Bay, Alaska in 1958. It was 524 metres high.

Key vocabulary

reflection

longitudinal wave

transverse wave

oscillate

superposition

Exploring light waves

We are learning how to:

- Describe light as travelling in waves.
- Understand the similarities and differences between water waves and light waves.
- Explain the frequency of a wave.

Light from the Sun travels 149 600 000 km through empty space before entering the Earth's atmosphere and finally reaching the Earth's surface. Most importantly, it transfers energy released in the Sun to Earth.

FIGURE 3.6.3a: Even on a cloudy day, light from the Sun still reaches Earth.

Sight and light

Light is emitted from sources such as the Sun, electric lamps and burning candles. It enters the eye (see Topic 6.5) and the optic nerve sends messages to the brain, which is how we see.

However, most of the light that enters the eye does not come directly from a light source. It is light that has been reflected by objects all around us.

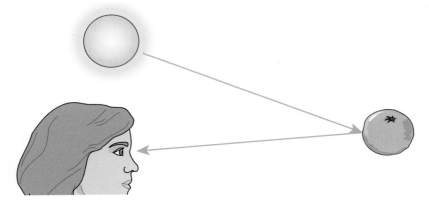

FIGURE 3.6.3b: Light from the Sun is reflected from the orange into the eye.

1. Describe, with the help of a sketch, how light from:

   a) a candle flame reaches the eye

   b) a person's face reaches another person's eye.

2. Explain why it is more difficult to see things at night.

Comparing water and light waves

Waves in water and sound waves are examples of mechanical waves. Mechanical waves need a medium (material), such as water or air, to travel through.

Light waves are examples of electromagnetic waves. Electromagnetic waves do not need a medium. They can travel through empty space (a vacuum). This is why light from the Sun can reach the Earth.

Waves in water and light waves are transverse waves – they oscillate up and down, forming **crests** and **troughs**.

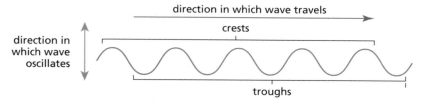

FIGURE 3.6.3c: Light is transverse waves that can travel through empty space.

3. Give two examples of mechanical waves.

4. Describe how the oscillation of a transverse wave differs from the direction that the wave travels.

5. Explain why an MP3 player will not make a noise in a vacuum.

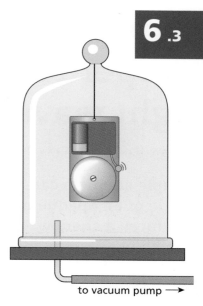

FIGURE 3.6.3d: When the air is sucked out of the jar, the bell cannot be heard, but it can be seen. This is because sound waves need a medium (air), but light waves do not.

Frequency and wavelength ▶▶▶

If water waves were being studied, the number of crests or troughs that pass a certain place every minute could be counted. From this the number per second could be calculated – this is the **frequency**, measured in **hertz (Hz)**. One hertz is the frequency of one wave per second.

The distance between the crests is the **wavelength**.

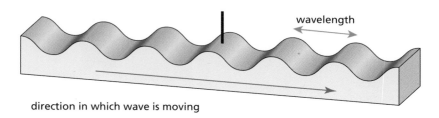

FIGURE 3.6.3e: The frequency is the number of crests that pass a fixed point every second. The distance between crests is the wavelength.

6. Explain what is meant by the frequency of a light wave.

7. The hertz is the unit of frequency. Explain what its value tells us about a wave.

8. If water waves are travelling at a steady speed, but their frequency is increased, what will have changed about their wavelength?

Did you know...?

The Sun is close enough to the Earth to provide enough energy to support life. However, the Earth is far enough away that it is not damaged by too much energy from the Sun.

Key vocabulary

crest

trough

frequency

hertz (Hz)

wavelength

Explaining properties of light waves

We are learning how to:

- Describe how light passes through different materials.
- Understand how light can be absorbed by materials.
- Explain the difference between diffuse scattering and specular reflection.

Simple sundials can be made easily. The pointer is made of an opaque material that blocks light and produces a shadow. The position of the shadow can be used to tell the time.

FIGURE 3.6.4a: A sundial

See-through?

Light passes through gases, some liquids and some solids. Materials that light waves can pass through freely are said to be **transparent**. They do not produce shadows.

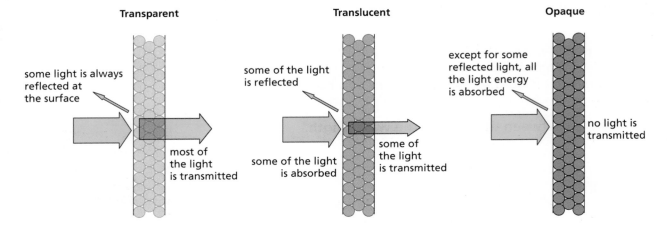

FIGURE 3.6.4b: This shows what happens to light when it falls on transparent, translucent and opaque materials.

Other materials cast shadows by either completely or partially blocking the passage of light. **Opaque** materials block the passage of light waves completely, producing a dark shadow, whereas **translucent** materials only allow some of the light to pass through, casting weak shadows.

1. Give three examples of transparent materials.
2. Compare the shadows produced by an opaque material and those by a translucent material.
3. Explain why an opaque object casts a shadow.

FIGURE 3.6.4c: Frosted glass provides some privacy because it does not allow all the light to pass through it.

When light hits a surface or a boundary, some or all of it is reflected – it bounces back in a direction away from the surface. The reflection produced by a flat, smooth surface is called **specular reflection**. All the light is reflected in the same direction. It allows us to see an **image**.

A rough reflective surface bounces light back in many directions. We can think of the surface as being a mixture of small flat surfaces at different angles. The effect is called diffuse reflection, or **diffuse scattering**.

FIGURE 3.6.4d: The result of specular reflection in a calm lake

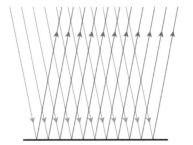 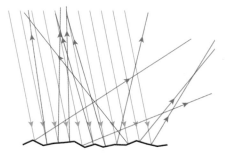

FIGURE 3.6.4e: The diagram on the left shows specular reflection. The one on the right shows diffuse reflection.

4. Describe the difference between specular reflection and diffuse reflection.

5. Explain why diffuse scattering happens on rough surfaces.

6. Explain why reflections in lakes or ponds cannot be seen if the water is choppy.

Absorption of light ▶▶▶

Translucent and opaque materials **absorb** some or all of the light that falls on them. The energy of the light waves is transferred to the particles of the material.

Transparent materials do not absorb light. The light passes straight through and comes out on the opposite side, where it is transmitted.

All surfaces reflect some of the light that falls on them – that is how we see them.

7. Describe what happens when light waves strike a block of ice.

8. Explain what happens when light waves strike a flat steel panel.

> **Did you know…?**
>
> You can see through a piece of frosted glass (make it 'see-through') simply by putting a piece of clear sticky tape on it.

Key vocabulary

transparent

opaque

translucent

specular reflection

image

diffuse scattering

absorb

Using the ray model

We are learning how to:

- Describe the ray model of light.
- Explain how the direction of light rays can be changed.
- Explain how a pinhole camera and the eye work.

If you look at a swimming pool from above, it looks shallower than it really is. If a spoon is placed at an angle in a glass of water, it appears to have bent or broken at the water surface. Both of these effects are caused by refraction. To explain refraction, and reflection, we need to use the ray model.

Explaining reflection

Light travels as waves, but a **ray model** allows us to show clearly in a diagram the direction of light and how it can change its direction when it meets a surface.

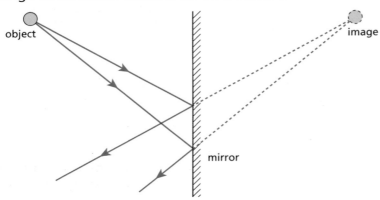

FIGURE 3.6.5a: Refraction causes the spoon to look as if it has broken into two parts.

FIGURE 3.6.5b: The solid lines represent light rays. The dashed lines show where the light rays appear to be coming from – the image. This is the same distance from the mirror as from the object to the mirror.

1. Describe what Figure 3.6.5b shows.

2. Describe how the ray diagram showing image formation in a mirror needs to be changed if the object is:

   a) further away   **b)** closer

FIGURE 3.6.5c: The specular reflection of light from a mirror allows you to see an image.

Refraction

Light travels through transparent materials, such as glass and air. However, its speed depends on the density of the material. The denser the transparent material, the slower light travels through it. Glass is denser than air, so light travels through it slower than it travels through air.

When the light slows down, the wavelength of its waves becomes shorter. Each of the crests catches up with the one in front. If the light then emerges into a less-dense medium it will speed up again. This effect is called **refraction**, and can cause the direction of the light to change.

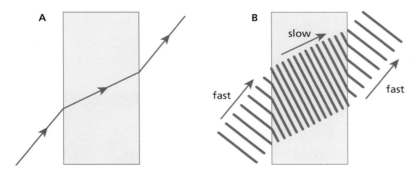

FIGURE 3.6.5d: A: ray model to show refraction of light; B: the wavelength shortens in a denser material.

3. Describe what happens to light waves when they travel into a dense material.

4. Sketch a diagram to suggest what would happen if a light ray was to hit a glass rod as shown in Figure 3.6.5e.

FIGURE 3.6.5e: A light ray hitting a glass rod – what happens?

The human eye >>>>

Light enters an eye through the **cornea** and then travels through the **lens**. These both refract light rays, focusing them on a common point. An image forms on the **retina**. The optic nerve sends information to the brain, which interprets it.

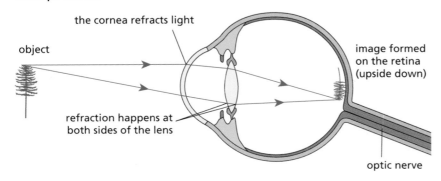

FIGURE 3.6.5f: How the eye works

5. Name the parts of an eye that refract light.

6. Explain what the lens does to the rays of light.

7. Explain why the image formed on the retina is upside down.

Did you know...?

You can make a working pinhole camera from a cardboard box, greaseproof paper and sticky tape using nothing more than a pin and a pair of scissors.

Key vocabulary

ray model

refraction

cornea

lens

retina

Understanding energy transfer by light

We are learning how to:

- Describe light as a way of transferring energy.
- Give examples of chemical and electrical effects when materials absorb light.
- Explain changes that happen when materials absorb light.

Curtains, carpets and other fabrics are often affected by strong sunlight. Colours fade and fabrics do not look as bright as when they were new. The sunlight is causing chemical changes to the pigments used to put colour into the fabrics.

Light carries energy

Light waves carry energy and transfer it from place to place. They may come from a light source, such as the Sun, flames and electric lamps, or the light waves may be reflected from objects. The waves travel in straight lines until they are reflected, refracted or absorbed by a material.

When light is absorbed, there is **energy transfer** to the particles that make up the material. Sometimes this leads to chemical reactions or to a flow of electric current.

1. Describe the difference between a source of light, such as a bulb, and reflected light, such as from a mirror.

2. Describe what happens when a material absorbs energy carried by light.

3. Name two possible changes that might happen when a material absorbs light.

FIGURE 3.6.6a: Some coloured fabrics fade in sunlight.

Photosynthesis and photovoltaic cells

Energy absorbed from light can be put to good use. In **photosynthesis**, energy carried by sunlight is transferred to chlorophyll in the cells of green leaves. The transferred energy is involved in a chemical change that produces glucose in plant leaves. The other product is oxygen.

carbon dioxide + water ➔ glucose + oxygen

Scientists have also developed ways of harnessing energy from absorbed light. Some manufactured materials absorb light and produce an electric current. An example

> **Did you know...?**
>
> Before digital cameras, images were captured on photographic film. The film had a surface made from compounds that changed colour when exposed to light.

is highly purified silicon. Such materials are used to make photovoltaic (PV) cells. These have a number of applications, such as powering calculators.

A PV material absorbs sunlight, which releases electrons from the material's particles. This is called the **photovoltaic effect**. The movement of the freed electrons results in an electric current (a flow of electrons). So a PV cell is similar to the cells in a battery, except that electrons are freed by sunlight rather than by a chemical change.

FIGURE 3.6.6b: Solar panels consist of banks of PV cells.

4. Explain what is meant by the 'photovoltaic effect'.

5. Give an example of a material that exhibits the photovoltaic effect.

6. Explain why a solar panel consists of large numbers of PV cells.

Photochemical smog ⟩⟩⟩

Absorbing energy from light can also cause problems. Photochemical smog forms when pollutants in the atmosphere react in the presence of sunlight (see Figure 3.4.3b in Topic 4.3). One of the initial **photochemical reactions** is the breaking down of nitrogen dioxide to give nitrogen monoxide, as shown in Figure 3.6.6c.

7. Describe what can happen to air pollution on a sunny day.

8. Explain what can happen when nitrogen dioxide particles absorb sunlight.

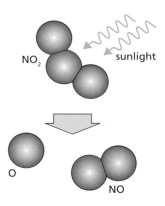

FIGURE 3.6.6c: Energy absorbed from sunlight makes nitrogen dioxide molecules vibrate faster and split into an oxygen atom and a nitrogen monoxide molecule.

Key vocabulary

energy transfer

photosynthesis

photovoltaic effect

photochemical reaction

Exploring coloured light

We are learning how to:

- Describe how a spectrum can be produced from white light.
- Compare the properties of light of different frequencies.
- Explain how light of different wavelengths can be split and recombined.

Some days it can be raining and, at the same time, the Sun can be shining. This is when a rainbow can often be seen. To make a rainbow, sunlight and droplets of water are needed.

Spectrum from white light

Sunlight is made up of light waves of different **wavelengths**. The range of wavelengths that the human eye can detect as different colours is called the visible **spectrum**. Seen together they make what is called white light. This white light can be split up to produce the colours of the spectrum. For example, if sunlight is shone through a prism (triangular-shaped block of glass), it is refracted into different colours.

1. Describe the shape of a prism.

2. Describe the spectrum obtained when white light passes through a prism.

3. Which colours appear at each edge of a rainbow?

FIGURE 3.6.7a: A prism produces a spectrum from white light.

Different wavelengths

Light waves travel at the same speed in the same medium. The longer the wavelength, the fewer the crests that pass a fixed point every second and, therefore, the lower the **frequency**.

FIGURE 3.6.7b: In the visible spectrum, waves of red light have the longest wavelengths and waves of violet light, the shortest.

When a light wave passes into and out of a glass prism, the wave is refracted. The shorter its wavelength, the more it is refracted – so violet light is refracted more than red light. The 'white light' is split up and spreads out to form a spectrum.

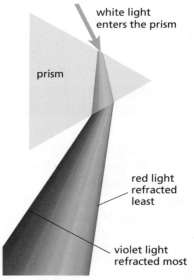

white light enters the prism

prism

red light refracted least

violet light refracted most

FIGURE 3.6.7c: The white light is split up by refraction.

Waves with different wavelengths can be combined – this is additive colour mixing. It is different to mixing paints. Mixing red, blue and green light produces white light. Mixing red, blue and green paint produces muddy brown paint.

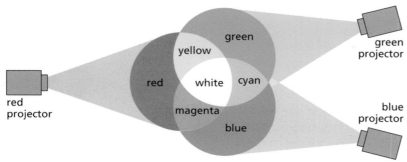

FIGURE 3.6.7d: Recombining waves to make white light

4. Explain the relationship between the wavelength and the frequency of a wave.

5. Which has the longest wavelength – red light or blue light?

6. Explain why white light spreads out to produce a visible spectrum when it passes through a prism.

Frequency and behaviour »»

Some materials are coloured, but can still be seen through, such as coloured plastic sheets and solutions of food dyes. They only absorb light waves of certain frequencies. The light that passes through consists of light with frequencies that were not absorbed.

Some opaque materials are coloured. This is because light waves of certain frequencies are absorbed by the material, but the light with other frequencies is reflected.

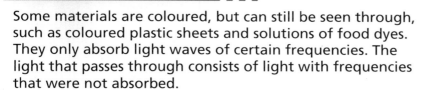
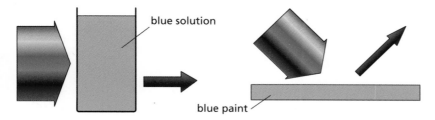

FIGURE 3.6.7e: A blue solution absorbs wavelengths of light other than blue. Only blue light passes through. Blue paint absorbs wavelengths of light other than blue. Blue light is reflected. No light passes through.

7. Explain why a solution of red food colouring is red, but also transparent.

8. Explain why green paint appears green.

Did you know...?

Light with frequencies lower and higher than those at the extremes of the visible spectrum cannot be seen by the human eye. Infrared radiation has frequencies lower than that of red light. Ultraviolet radiation has frequencies higher than that of violet light.

Key vocabulary

wavelength

spectrum

frequency

Applying key ideas

You have now met a number of important ideas in this chapter. This activity gives an opportunity for you to apply them, just as scientists do. Read the text and study the diagrams first, then have a go at the tasks. The first few are fairly easy – then they become a bit more challenging.

Rainbows

Imagine that the Sun is shining and, at the same time, it is raining. If you were to look in the direction of the Sun (not straight at it – that could harm your eyes) you would just see rain and sunshine. However, if you were to turn round so that the Sun was behind you, the chances are that you would see a rainbow. Sometimes you might even see a double rainbow.

If it is sunny, but not raining, you can still make a rainbow. You need a hose pipe or some other way of producing a spray of water. Turn the water on, adjust the hose to produce a fine spray and direct it upwards and away from you. You may need to play around a little to find the ideal direction of the spray to produce the clearest rainbow.

Rain consists of very small droplets of water. Each behaves in a similar way to a prism – it splits white light into a continuous spectrum, from red to violet. The combined effect of all the water droplets is to produce a rainbow.

In Figure 3.6.8a, the ray diagram shows what happens to sunlight when it meets a raindrop. A beam of light meets the surface of the raindrop and starts to pass through. It is split into a spectrum, which reflects back from the inside of the raindrop before passing out and back into the air. It is impossible to represent a continuous spectrum using a ray diagram, so the two lines shown represent the extreme ends of the spectrum – red and violet.

A double rainbow has two bows – an inner one and an outer one (this is sometimes called a secondary rainbow). The inner bow is produced just as for a single rainbow. Formation of the outer bow, however, involves an extra change within the raindrop.

In Figure 3.6.8c, the ray diagram shows how the outer bow of a double rainbow (a secondary rainbow) forms. The process is similar to the inner-bow formation except that light reflects back twice on the inside of the raindrop before passing out into the air.

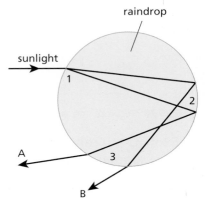

FIGURE 3.6.8a: Sunlight entering and leaving a raindrop to form a rainbow.

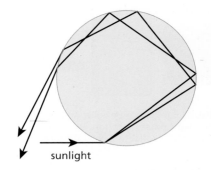

FIGURE 3.6.8b: A double rainbow

FIGURE 3.6.8c: Sunlight entering and leaving a raindrop to form a secondary rainbow.

Task 1: Making a rainbow

Read the text and describe the conditions needed for a rainbow to be formed.

Task 2: Colours of the rainbow

Look at Figure 3.6.8a. Describe what happens to rays of light when they:

a) pass from the air into a raindrop (point 1 on the ray diagram)

b) reach the far side of the raindrop (point 2 on the ray diagram)

c) pass from the raindrop back into the air (point 3 on the ray diagram).

You should use the words 'refraction' and 'reflection' in your answer.

Identify the colours of light waves A and B emerging from the raindrop.

Task 3: Explaining direction changes

Use what you have learned about the properties of light to explain what happens to sunlight in a raindrop from when it enters until when it has passed out again.

Task 4: Double rainbows

Describe the difference between the colours of the inner bow and the colours of the outer bow.

Look at Figures 3.6.8b and 3.6.8c. Explain the formation of a secondary rainbow.

Task 5: CDs, DVDs and rainbows

If you move a CD or DVD in the light, you will find positions in which you can see the colours of a rainbow. The discs have a thin layer of transparent material on top of a material that has a highly reflective surface. Using your knowledge of refraction and reflection, draw a ray diagram to explain how the colours form.

Understanding energy transfer and change

We are learning how to:

- Describe the ways in which energy is stored.
- Describe the ways that energy can be transferred from one store to another.
- Explain that any change – physical or chemical – results in a transfer of energy.

All changes, chemical and physical, involve transfer of energy. But which comes first – the change or the energy transfer? Energy transfers do not make things happen. Energy is transferred when a change happens.

Storing energy

Energy is stored in several ways – we could say that there are different types of **energy store**.

- All materials store energy because of their warmth (thermal store) and the interactions between their particles (chemical store).
- All objects store energy when they are pulled by gravity (gravitational store), when they are moving (kinetic store) and when they are stretched or squashed (elastic store).
- Magnetic materials store energy (magnetic store) because of the attraction of unlike poles and the repulsion of like poles.

Later in your science work you will also learn about electrical charge stores (capacitors) and nuclear stores.

FIGURE 3.6.9a: Apples on a tree store energy in many ways. One is gravitational. When an apple is ripe, its stem breaks. Energy is transferred as the apple falls.

1. Identify three ways in which an apple on a tree stores energy.

2. Identify one way in which an apple on a tree does not store energy.

3. Name six ways in which energy is stored.

Types of energy transfer

When change happens, there is **energy transfer** from one store to another.

The transfer can happen in a number of ways. For example it could be done electrically when energy is transferred by electric current, or it could be done by heating when energy is transferred by thermal conduction through a material or between two touching materials. It could be done mechanically, when energy is transferred by a moving object or material – for example by releasing a stretched spring or rubber band. It could be transferred by radiation – when energy is transferred by light waves for example.

4. Name four ways in which energy is transferred.

5. Describe how energy is transferred when a metal rod is heated at one end.

6. Explain how sound waves transfer energy mechanically.

Explaining change and energy transfer

Transferring energy does not 'make things happen'. Energy is transferred because a change takes place. The change might be chemical or physical.

When a fuel burns in oxygen, energy stored in the reactants is transferred to energy stored in the products (often carbon dioxide and water). When the products cannot store all the energy released, the excess is transferred to the surroundings, which warms them.

When a battery-powered electric car moves, energy stored chemically in the battery is transferred to an electric motor by an electric current. The motor transfers energy mechanically, which makes the car move. Moving parts cause friction and some of the energy is transferred by heating, which warms the surroundings.

FIGURE 3.6.9b: When a guitar string is plucked, energy stored elastically in the stretched string is transferred to air particles, which then move faster and store the transferred energy kinetically.

Did you know...?

When a candle burns, 40 per cent of its stored energy is transferred by radiation (light) and 60 per cent is transferred by heating the surroundings.

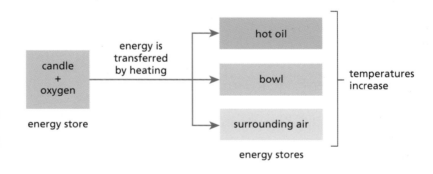

FIGURE 3.6.9c: Energy is stored in the candle and oxygen in the air. When these burn, this stored energy is transferred and stored in the hot oil, bowl and surroundings.

7. Describe how energy is transferred when an electric lamp (light bulb) is switched on.

8. Explain why it is not correct to say that energy is needed to cause a change.

Key vocabulary

energy store

energy transfer

Explaining thermal conduction and radiation

We are learning how to:

- Describe the warming and cooling of objects.
- Explain the relationship between energy transfer and temperature change.
- Compare the transfer of energy by thermal conduction and by radiation.

If you want to keep a drink hot or cold you can use an insulated flask or a vacuum flask (often called a thermos flask), which is more efficient but more expensive. What are the differences between the two? Which one would be the best value for money?

Cooling and warming >>

The warmer something is, the higher its **temperature**. Monitoring temperature changes is a useful way to measure how quickly energy is being transferred. The rate of cooling of a material may be investigated by measuring how its temperature changes over time and plotting a graph of temperature against time. This is often called a cooling curve.

1. Describe the relationship between how hot something is and its temperature.

2. Look at the graph in Figure 3.6.10b. Describe what is happening.

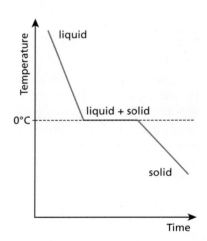

FIGURE 3.6.10a: An insulated flask is useful for slowing down temperature changes.

Energy transfer and temperature change >>>

Energy will transfer from a warm object (higher temperature) to a colder one (lower temperature).

If you pour hot water into a cold saucepan, the temperature of the water decreases and the temperature of the saucepan increases. Energy is transferred from the water to the saucepan.

If nothing else interfered, the temperature of the water and the saucepan would become the same. However, the saucepan is standing on something and is surrounded by air. Energy is transferred to its surroundings until the saucepan and the surroundings, including the water, reach the same temperature. We say that **thermal equilibrium** has been reached.

FIGURE 3.6.10b: A cooling curve for a test tube of water put in a mixture of ice and salt and cooled to −20 °C.

Materials that transfer energy well (quickly) are called **thermal conductors**. Materials that do not are called **thermal insulators**.

3. Describe what happens to the temperature of cold water if it is put into a hot metal can.

4. Describe the direction of energy transfer when a metal worker plunges a red hot piece of metal into cold water.

5. Think about the situation shown in Figure 3.6.10c and try to explain the meaning of 'open system'.

Conduction and radiation

Energy is transferred through a material, or through two materials that are touching, by thermal conduction. This is the method of energy transfer in a solid. If a solid is heated, energy is transferred to its particles. They vibrate faster and transfer energy as they continually collide with their neighbours. Some materials are not as good as others at transferring the energy from particle to particle.

FIGURE 3.6.10c: The water, saucepan and surroundings are an 'open system'. Energy transfers happen in all parts of it.

Did you know...?

Double glazing works because a gas is sandwiched between two panels of glass. Originally it was air, but nowadays argon is often used because it is a better insulator than air.

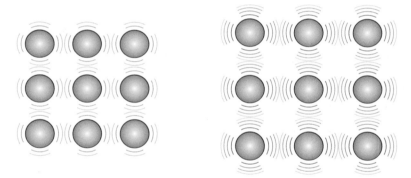

FIGURE 3.6.10d: The hotter a solid, the more its particles vibrate and collide.

Energy may also be transferred by radiation, such as light waves. As we have seen, light waves have a range of frequencies and wavelengths. **Infrared radiation** has frequencies lower than that of red light and cannot be seen by the eye. However, it transfers energy by heating – the infrared waves are emitted and absorbed. A hot object in a cool room will emit more radiation than it absorbs. It cools down until thermal equilibrium is reached.

6. Describe the difference between a conductor and an insulator.

7. Explain why gases are poor thermal conductors.

8. Explain what happens to the particles of a solid when it is heated.

Key vocabulary

temperature

thermal equilibrium

thermal conductor

thermal insulator

infrared radiation

Understanding energy transfer by fuels and food

We are learning how to:

- Describe the use of fuels in the home.
- Explain that foods are energy stores and that the amount stored can be measured.
- Explain that energy is not a material and can be neither created nor destroyed.

Natural gas and electricity are used in homes to supply energy. Our bodies, too, need supplies of energy. But is energy for the body the same as energy for the home?

Fuels and energy in the home

The National Grid supplies homes in the UK with electricity and with gas. Many homes use both, but some do not use gas – they may use oil, coal or wood. Energy stores that undergo combustion (burning) to provide us with energy by heating are called **fuels**.

FIGURE 3.6.11a: Gas pipelines and electricity cables supply us with energy.

FIGURE 3.6.11b: The use of electricity and gas is metered.

The amount of electricity used in a home is measured in a unit called **kilowatt-hours (kWh)** by an electricity meter. Gas is also metered and the amount used is measured in cubic metres.

1. Name four fuels that might be used in homes.

2. Name the instrument used to measure how much electricity is used in a home.

3. In a home, what units are used for the amounts of the following?

   a) electricity

   b) gas

> **Did you know...?**
>
> Conservation of energy and conservation of mass are fundamental laws of physics. However, energy can be converted into mass and vice versa. When 25 kWh of energy are transferred to any object its mass increases by 0.000 001 g. This is summarised by Einstein's famous equation $E = mc^2$, where E = energy, m = mass and c = the speed of light.

Food and energy

Food is fuel for our bodies. Energy stored in food is often called its 'energy content', sometimes measured in **calories** – 1000 joules (J) = 240 calories [1000 J is 1 kilojoule (kJ)]. During digestion food is changed into chemicals that store energy in the body's cells.

Metabolism is the name given to the chemical reactions that happen in the body. They enable growth and reproduction, responses to the environment and keeping healthy. All rely on energy being transferred from chemical stores in the body's cells which, in turn, depends on the food eaten.

4. Explain how the body builds up stores of energy.

5. Explain why information about energy stored in food is useful.

6. Calculate the energy content of 100 g of the food product shown in Figure 3.6.11c.

Conservation of energy

Whenever change happens, energy is transferred. However, no energy is ever 'lost' or 'used up'. The quantity of energy stored before the change is the same as the quantity stored after the change. This fundamental law of physics is called the **Law of Conservation of Energy**.

For example, when a fuel burns in air, energy stored in the fuel and in oxygen is transferred to the surroundings, which warm up. The energy stored in the products of combustion and the warmer surroundings equals the energy stored in the fuel and oxygen.

Similarly, warming a room with an electric heater causes a change that results in energy being transferred to the surroundings (air, walls, ceiling, furniture and so on). The total amount of energy remains the same, even though it is more spread out.

When we eat food, changes happen. Energy stored in food is transferred to energy stored in our bodies. This stored energy is transferred further during metabolism. However, whenever these changes happen, energy is not used up but is simply transferred to different places.

7. Give two other examples of changes taking place that involve energy being transferred and explain where you think the energy has been transferred to.

8. Describe, in your own words, the Law of Conservation of Energy.

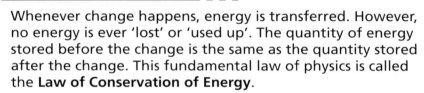

Nutrition Facts

Serving Size 5 oz. (144g)
Servings Per Container 4

Amount Per Serving		
Calories 310	**Calories** from Fat 100	
		% Daily Value*
Total Fat 15g		**21%**
Saturated Fat 2.6g		**17%**
Trans Fat 1g		
Cholesterol 118mg		**39%**
Sodium 560mg		**28%**
Total Carbohydrate 12g		**4%**
Dietary Fibre 1g		**4%**
Sugars 1g		
Protein 24g		

Vitamin A 1%	•	Vitamin C 2%
Calcium 2%	•	**Iron** 5%

*Percent Daily Values are based on a 2,000 calorie diet. Your daily values may be higher or lower depending on your calorie needs:

	Calories	2,000	2,500
Total Fat	Less Than	65g	80g
Saturated Fat	Less Than	20g	25g
Cholesterol	Less Than	300mg	300mg
Sodium	Less Than	2,400mg	2,400mg
Total Carbohydrate		300g	375g
Dietary Fibre		25g	30g

Calories per gram:
Fat 9 • Carbohydrate 4 • Protein 4

FIGURE 3.6.11c: Energy content is given as part of the nutritional data on a food label.

Key vocabulary

fuel

kilowatt-hour (kWh)

calorie

metabolism

Law of Conservation of Energy

Comparing rates of energy transfer

We are learning how to:

- Describe what is meant by 'rate of energy transfer'.
- Recall and use the correct units for rate of energy transfer.
- Calculate quantities of energy transferred when change happens.

Chinese food is often cooked in a wok. Using a frying pan instead never seems to produce the same flavours. The reason is speed of cooking – woks are thinner than frying pans (about one-third the thickness). Energy is transferred much more quickly through them and the food is cooked more quickly – essential to create that authentic Chinese taste. How do we measure how quickly energy is transferred?

FIGURE 3.6.12a: Warm clothes slow the rate of energy transfer from the children's bodies to the cold air, helping to keep them warm.

Rates of energy transfers

When materials change, energy is transferred from one energy store to another. How quickly this happens is called the rate of energy transfer, or **power**:

$$\text{power (rate of energy transfer)} = \frac{\text{quantity of energy transferred}}{\text{time taken for the transfer}}$$

If the change can be controlled, so can the rate at which energy is transferred. For example, to make a lamp transfer energy more quickly it would need a more powerful light bulb.

1. Describe what is meant by rate of energy transfer.

2. Explain how rate of change and rate of energy transfer are linked.

3. Give an example of how controlling the rate of change is important.

Comparing rates of energy transfer

Power is a measure of how quickly energy is transferred. It is measured in **watts** (W), 1 W = 1 J/s. A thousand watts is a **kilowatt** (kW). The power rating of electrical appliances varies. For example, microwave ovens vary from 600 W to 1000 W; toasters vary from 800 W to 1500 W.

Microwave oven, 1000 W (1 kW)

Laptop computer, 20 W

Toaster, 1200 W (1.2 kW)

Electric kettle, 2000 W (2 kW)

6.12

Electric oven, 2150 W (2.15 kW)

FIGURE 3.6.12b: Some typical power ratings

4. What is the rate of energy transfer in joules per second for a 20 W laptop?

5. Based on Figure 3.6.12b, put the following in order from lowest to highest power: electric oven, microwave oven, toaster.

6. Calculate how many laptop computers could be run by the power needed for a 2150 W electric oven.

Quantities of energy transferred ⟫⟫

When a change happens and energy is transferred, the quantity of energy transferred can be calculated in joules (J) and kilojoules (kJ) using:

energy transferred = power × time

- A 20 W laptop computer transfers 20 J/s.
  So if it is used for one hour (1 × 60 × 60 = 360 s), it transfers 20 × 360 = 7200 J = 7.2 kJ.

- A 2.15 kW electric oven transfers 2.15 kJ of energy per second.
  So if it is used for one hour (1 × 60 × 60 = 360 s), it transfers 2.15 × 1000 × 360 = 774 000 J = 774 kJ.

7. How much energy is transferred when a 1.2 kW toaster runs for three minutes?

8. Calculate the energy transferred when one store transfers energy to another store by heating it for five minutes at a rate of 15 J/s.

9. a) Calculate the energy transferred when a 10 W bulb is left on for three days.

   b) Calculate the energy saved if the same light bulb is turned off every day for eight hours.

> **Did you know...?**
>
> The unit of energy, the joule, is named after James Joule, a Salford brewer who discovered the link between heat and work. He spent part of his honeymoon in Switzerland making measurements to show that the water at the bottom of a waterfall was slightly warmer than the water at the top.

Key vocabulary

power

watt

kilowatt

Looking at the cost of energy use in the home

We are learning how to:

- Describe the information a typical fuel bill provides.
- Explain and use the units used on a fuel bill.
- Explain how the cost of energy used can be calculated.

When you look at your gas or electricity bill there are two charges. One is for the amount used, and the other is a fixed charge. Why do energy providers make a fixed charge on top of the cost of the electricity or gas used?

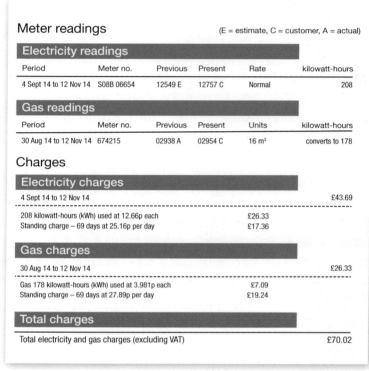

Meter readings (E = estimate, C = customer, A = actual)

Electricity readings

Period	Meter no.	Previous	Present	Rate	kilowatt-hours
4 Sept 14 to 12 Nov 14	S08B 06654	12549 E	12757 C	Normal	208

Gas readings

Period	Meter no.	Previous	Present	Units	kilowatt-hours
30 Aug 14 to 12 Nov 14	674215	02938 A	02954 C	16 m³	converts to 178

Charges

Electricity charges

4 Sept 14 to 12 Nov 14	£43.69
208 kilowatt-hours (kWh) used at 12.66p each	£26.33
Standing charge – 69 days at 25.16p per day	£17.36

Gas charges

30 Aug 14 to 12 Nov 14	£26.33
Gas 178 kilowatt-hours (kWh) used at 3.981p each	£7.09
Standing charge – 69 days at 27.89p per day	£19.24

Total charges

Total electricity and gas charges (excluding VAT)	£70.02

FIGURE 3.6.13a: This energy bill shows the quantities and charges for electricity and gas used in a home.

Fuel bills

Electricity and gas for the home is bought from energy suppliers. Users receive energy bills that show:

- the 'standing charge' – a fixed amount regardless of how much energy is used
- the price of each unit of energy and the number of units used.

Each **unit of electricity** is 1 kWh = 3 600 000 J or 3600 kJ.

A typical home might use several hundred **kilowatt-hours (kWh)** of energy every month (see Figure 3.6.13a) – in other words, hundreds of millions of joules.

1. Describe how energy use in a home is measured.

2. The energy content of a food can be measured in joules. Why do electricity meters not use joules?

3. What are the standing charges shown in the energy bill in Figure 3.6.13a for the following?

   a) electricity   **b)** gas

4. Explain the difference between a standing charge and the cost of energy used. (Hint: As well as the fuel used, what else needs to be paid for?)

Did you know...?

In 2013, the average household cost of electricity and gas was £1400. About half of this is for heating the home. Double glazing can reduce heating bills, but it is expensive to install. It has been estimated that it can take 80 years before the savings are more than the cost of the double glazing.

Power of domestic appliances »»

Remember that the rate at which energy is transferred is called power, measured in watts (W) – 1 watt = 1 joule per second (1 W = 1 J/s). Electrical appliances have a power rating, usually shown on the label.

The amount of energy used by an appliance is calculated by multiplying its power by the time for which it was used (see Topic 6.12). Electricity supply companies use the electricity unit kilowatt-hour (kWh), so we need to use hours, not seconds, in the calculation. An appliance with a power rating of 500 W running for five hours transfers 0.5 × 5 = 2.5 kWh.

Choosing an electrical appliance with the optimum power rating for the intended purpose is important. A more powerful electric kettle will use more energy per second but it will take less time to do the job.

FIGURE 3.6.13b: The power rating of the electric fan heater is shown on the label. It is 2000 W.

> 5. Which transfers energy faster – a 1600 W hair dryer or a 120 W computer?
>
> 6. Explain the difference between 'energy' and 'power'.

Calculating the cost of energy used »»»

The quantity of electricity used in a home is shown on an electricity meter in kilowatt-hours (kWh). The quantity of gas is shown on a gas meter in cubic metres (m^3). This will probably be converted into kilowatt-hours (kWh) on an energy bill.

The typical price of 1 kWh of electricity is about 13p, and the typical price of 1 kWh of gas is about 4p. If you used 900 kWh of electricity and 700 kWh of gas, the cost would be:

electricity: 900 × 13 = 11 700 p = £117.00

gas: 700 × 4 = 2800 p = £28.00

So the total energy cost = £117.00 + £28.00 = £145.00

FIGURE 3.6.13c: The cost of 1 kWh of energy from electricity is more than three times that of 1 kWh of energy from gas.

> 7. a) 4.2 J of energy must be transferred to raise the temperature of 1 cm^3 of water by 1 °C. How much energy is needed to raise the temperature of 1 litre of water from 20 °C to 100 °C?
>
>   b) Convert this to kilowatt-hours and calculate the cost of electricity needed to heat this water, if 1 kWh costs 13p.
>
> 8. Calculate the annual cost of energy for a home that uses, on average, 700 kWh of electricity (at 13p per kWh) and 700 kWh of gas (at 4p per kWh) each month.

Key vocabulary

unit of electricity

kilowatt-hour (kWh)

Check your progress

To make good progress in understanding science you need to focus on these ideas and skills.

Recognise that energy may be transferred by different types of waves, and know the difference between longitudinal and transverse waves.

Explain wave oscillation, the reflection and superposition of waves, and the terms frequency and wavelength.

Compare the properties of sound waves, waves in water and light waves.

Recognise that light can be reflected by some materials and absorbed by others.

Explain how some materials absorb energy, and the differences between transparent, translucent and opaque materials.

Use diagrams to explain the difference between diffuse and specular reflection.

Describe the ray model of light, using the idea that light travels in straight lines.

Explain the difference between reflection and refraction, and describe what happens when light waves are refracted.

Use ray diagrams to explain how a pinhole camera and the eye work.

Recognise that various effects can occur when materials absorb light, for example chemical reactions or a flow of electric current.

Explain how the transfer of energy carried by light happens during photosynthesis in plants and by electron release in photovoltaic cells.

Explain the formation of photochemical smog.

Describe the formation of a spectrum from white light.

Explain how white light can be split into a continuous spectrum of colours, called the visible spectrum.

Use the concepts of reflection and absorption of light to explain why some materials (transparent, translucent and opaque) are coloured.

Describe different ways in which energy can be stored and different ways in which energy can be transferred.

Explain that energy is transferred from one type of energy store to another when change happens, and understand that energy transfer does not cause change.

Explain that all changes, physical or chemical, result in a transfer of energy.

Describe the transfer of energy by heating and cooling.

Explain the relationship between energy transfer and temperature difference.

Compare the transfer of energy by conduction and by radiation.

Recall the units used to measure quantities of energy, including joules, calories and kilowatt hours.

Explain that energy can be neither created nor destroyed (the Law of Conservation of Energy).

Carry out calculations of quantities of stored and transferred energy.

Describe what is meant by rate of energy transfer.

Identify the rate at which electrical appliances transfer energy (their power rating), using the correct units (watts or kilowatts).

Compare rates of energy transferred when electrical appliances are used.

Explain the data given on an energy bill, including the units used for energy 'consumed' (transferred to appliances in the home) and the meaning of 'standing charge'.

Use the power rating of an appliance to calculate the amount of energy transferred.

Calculate the cost of energy used in different scenarios.

Questions

Questions 1–7

See how well you have understood the ideas in the chapter.

1. Which of the following describes what happens when a water wave hits a barrier? [1]

   a) it is absorbed   **b)** it is reflected   **c)** it is refracted   **d)** it passes through

2. Which of the following is true of light waves, but not of waves in water? [1]

   a) they travel through empty space   **b)** they are transverse waves

   c) they can be reflected   **d)** they are not longitudinal waves

3. Which of the pairs of waves in Figure 3.6.15a would cancel each other out? [1]

FIGURE 3.6.15a

4. In which of the following materials does light travel the fastest? [1]

   a) water   **b)** glass   **c)** air   **d)** transparent plastic

5. Describe two effects that may happen when materials absorb light. [2]

6. Give an example of two energy stores and describe how energy is transferred from one to the other. [2]

7. List the information found on an energy bill, including the units used. [4]

Questions 8–14

See how well you can apply the ideas in this chapter to new situations.

8. Imagine looking at a small object through a block of glass. Complete a copy of Figure 3.6.15b to show where the object appears to be (its image). [1]

FIGURE 3.6.15b

9. Think about what happens to sunlight when it passes through transparent materials, and then explain why we see different colours in stained glass windows. [1]

10. Explain why an electric kettle has a power rating of 2000 W, but a small TV has a power rating of 65 W. [1]

11. When the temperature of 1 cm³ of water increases by 1 °C, 4.2 J of energy are transferred. Calculate the energy transferred when 50 cm³ of water at 20 °C is heated to its boiling point. [1]

12. Describe the energy transfers that happen when an archer pulls back and then releases a bow to shoot an arrow. [2]

13. Figure 3.6.15c shows a graph of water temperature as the water cools in a beaker. Describe:

    a) what happens to the rate of energy transfer as the water cools.

    b) how the graph might be different if the water had been kept in an insulated flask. [2]

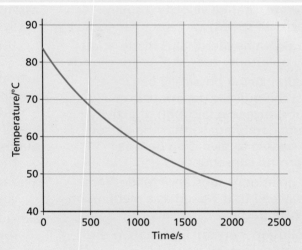

FIGURE 3.6.15c

14. A car covered in dirt and dust does not shine. Washing it and then polishing it makes it shine. Explain why. [4]

Questions 15–17

See how well you can understand and explain new ideas and evidence.

15. Explain why the presence of chlorophyll in leaves makes them green. [1]

16. Describe and explain what you would see if transparent red sticky tape were put on a piece of frosted glass. [1]

17. Nutritional information about food products is shown on their labels. It includes 'energy', which means energy stored. Table 3.6.15 shows some information about different types of milk.

    What does this tell you about the differences between whole, semi-skimmed and skimmed milk? [4]

TABLE 3.6.15

		Amounts in 100 cm³ of milk		
	Unit	Whole (full cream)	Semi-skimmed	Skimmed
energy stored	kilojoule (kJ)	282	201	148
protein	gram (g)	3.4	3.6	3.6
carbohydrate	gram (g)	4.7	4.8	4.9
fat	gram (g)	4.0	1.8	0.3

Glossary

absorb take in or soak up, for example energy from sound

accelerate change velocity (usually increase speed)

acid rain rainwater that is made acidic by pollutant gases, e.g. sulfur dioxide

addiction being physically or psychologically dependent on a substance (e.g. alcohol) or activity (e.g. gambling) so that the person is unable to give it up despite harmful consequences

agar gelatinous substance made from seaweed that is used as a medium on which bacteria can grow

air pollution harmful materials in the Earth's atmosphere

air resistance frictional resistance when something moves through the air

alcohol a legal, depressant drug made from fermented fruit or vegetables

alcoholic (noun) a person physically addicted to alcohol

alcoholism the condition of being addicted to alcohol

amino acid a small molecule from which proteins are built

amorphous a non-crystalline solid, lacks a specific shape or pattern in the structure

antibiotic a drug that kills bacteria, e.g. by disrupting its cell wall

antibody a molecule made by the immune system that recognises microbes and helps get rid of them

anticline an upfold in the Earth's crust

antiseptic a solution that destroys microbes and that is safe to use on the skin

asexual reproduction reproduction without sex, involving one parent, e.g. taking cuttings of plants

asteroid a small object in an orbit in the Solar System

asteroid belt the region of the Solar System located roughly between the orbits of Mars and Jupiter where many asteroids orbit

astronomical unit (AU) the mean distance between the Earth and the Sun (149 597 870 700 metres, or almost 92.956 million miles)

atmosphere the mixture of gases around the Earth

average speed speed calculated over the complete distance travelled

axis of rotation the centre around which something rotates

bacteria (singular: bacterium) simple unicellular (single-celled) organisms, some of which can cause illness

balanced forces forces on an object that act in opposite directions and are equal in size

base an oxide of a metal

Big Bang the theoretical beginning of the Universe, when energy and matter expanded outwards from a point

binder a substance used to make other substances stick together

biodiversity the range of different organisms within an ecosystem

biotechnology the use of living organisms to make useful products

black hole a point in space where gravity is so strong that even light cannot get out

blast furnace a furnace used for smelting, to extract metal from its ore (usually iron)

bond-breaking overcoming the force of attraction between molecules – requires energy

bond-making molecules are brought together by the force of attraction – energy is given out

calorie a unit of energy often used instead of the joule to show the energy in food

cancer an illness caused by cells growing out of control to make lumps of cells which can invade normal healthy areas of the body

cannabis an illegal depressant drug, harvested from the cannabis plant

carbon cycle the way in which carbon atoms pass between living organisms and their environment

carbon fibre an extremely strong and light reinforced polymer containing carbon fibres

carbon footprint the total amount of greenhouse gases emitted as a direct or indirect result of an individual or group

catalyst a substance that speeds up a chemical reaction

catalytic converter a system that converts pollutant gases into harmless ones using a catalyst

cellulose a large carbohydrate molecule contained in the walls of plant cells

ceramic an inorganic, non-metallic solid prepared by heating and then cooling substances such as clay

cermet a composite material composed of ceramic and metal materials

CFCs chlorofluorocarbons (containing hydrogen carbon, chlorine, fluorine) – chemicals that used to be present in refrigerators and aerosols but have been phased out due to the damage they do to the ozone layer

chitin a tough, protective substance made from glucose

chromosome a piece of DNA that contains genes

class A drug a type of illegal drug considered to be extremely harmful – including heroin, ecstasy and cocaine

classification the way that scientists group organisms, for example into a genus or species

climate change a significant and lasting change in weather patterns over time

clone a living thing that is genetically identical to its parent

cocaine an illegal, class A drug that acts as a stimulant

coke a fuel with a high carbon content and some impurities

colony a visible cluster of bacteria growing on the surface of a solid medium such as agar

combustion a reaction of fuels with oxygen that produces heat

composite a material made up of different parts

concrete a composite material made of water, coarse granular material and a binder material

conjoined twins twins that are physically joined at birth, sometimes sharing organs or limbs

constant speed speed that stays the same, with no acceleration or deceleration

continental drift slow movement of continents (land masses) relative to each other

continuous variation variation that is distributed along a continuum, rather than in discrete (separate) categories, e.g. weight and height

convection current the movement of hot material upwards and the cooler material downwards

cornea the transparent, front layer of the eye that covers the pupil and iris

correlation how well sets of data are linked; high correlation shows that there is a strong link between two sets of data

crest the point on a wave that exhibits the maximum amount of positive or upward displacement from the rest position

cross-link a bond that links one polymer chain to another

crust the rocky outer layer of the Earth

crystalline resembling crystals in terms of distinct pattern in structure or in transparency

decomposer an organism that breaks down dead plant or animal tissue

deposition the geological process by which sediments, soil and rocks are added to a landform or land mass

depressant a drug that slows down the body systems such as heart rate and breathing rate, e.g. alcohol and cannabis

desertification land degradation in which land becomes increasingly dry and loses wildlife and vegetation due to a water shortage

diffuse scattering reflections of waves (such as light) not in an ordered, uniform way

discontinuous variation variation that is distributed in discrete (separate) categories, for example, eye colour, left or right handedness

disinfectant a solution that destroys microbes, used on surfaces such as worktops and floors

displacement reaction a chemical reaction in which one substance takes the place of another in a compound

distance–time graph a graph showing the relationship between distance and time

DNA deoxyribonucleic acid – the molecule in the nucleus of cells that carries genetic information

DNA profile an analysis of a person's DNA to show the sequence of bases

double helix the structure of the DNA molecule, like a twisted ladder

down-cycle loss of viability or value in a product as it is recycled

earthenware general term for pottery that is not a specific type, e.g. porcelain or stoneware

ecosystem a community of organisms along with the non-living components (such as air, water, soil)

ecstasy an illegal, class A drug that is a stimulant

electrolysis a chemical process that involves using electricity

ellipse a regular oval shape

elliptical orbit an orbit tracing a regular oval shape

endangered species a species that is so few in number that the species could become extinct

endothermic the term for a chemical reaction in which energy is taken in, causing a cooling of the surroundings

energy store a source of energy that can be utilised later

energy transfer the passing on of energy from one energy store to another energy store

enzyme a biological catalyst – a substance that speeds up chemical reactions in the body

equilibrium a state of rest or balance due to opposite forces being equal

erosion the wearing away of rock or other surfaces such as soil

evolution the change in a species over a long period of time

exothermic term for a chemical reaction in which energy is given out, causing a warming of the surroundings

extinction the process of a species dying out

extrusive the way that igneous rocks are formed at the surface of the Earth when hot magma is thrown from inside the Earth and then cools

fibreglass a lightweight, strong, robust material made from a plastic matrix reinforced with glass fibres

field an area in which an object experiences a force, e.g. due to charge, gravity or magnetism

fissure a fine, long crack in the Earth's surface

forensic science the scientific method of collecting and examining scientific information about events in the past

fossil the preserved remains of a living thing that lived millions of years ago

fossil fuel coal, natural gas and crude oil that were formed from the compressed remains of plants and other organisms that died millions of years ago

free fall the motion of a body when gravity is the only force acting upon it

freeze–thaw a process that weathers rocks – water seeps into tiny cracks in rock, the water then freezes and expands as it forms ice, which causes the rock to crack further and pieces may break off

frequency the number of waves passing a set point, or emitted by a source, in a second

friction a force that opposes movement

fuel a material that is burned for the purpose of generating heat

fungi (singular: fungus) the largest of the micro-organisms, e.g. yeast and moulds

galaxy a group of billions of stars

gene a section of DNA that controls an inherited feature

gene bank a store of genetic material (such as seeds) that can be used in the future to grow more organisms

genetic caused by genes, inherited

genetic disorder a disorder caused by a fault in one or more genes

glass an amorphous solid material containing silicon dioxide and sodium oxide

global warming gradual increase in the average temperature of the Earth's atmosphere and oceans

glucose a simple sugar molecule containing carbon, hydrogen and oxygen

gravitational field region where a mass experiences an attractive force because of the presence of another mass

gravitational field strength the gravitational force per unit mass at a particular point; measured in newtons per kilogram, N/kg

gravity force that pulls masses towards one another

greenhouse effect the trapping of the Sun's infrared radiation by the Earth's atmosphere

greenhouse gas any gas in the atmosphere, such as carbon dioxide, that reduces heat transfer away from the Earth

haemoglobin the chemical in red blood cells that carries oxygen

hallucinogen a drug that causes the user to see things that do not exist, e.g. psilocybin in magic mushrooms

heroin an illegal, highly addictive class A drug

hertz (Hz) the unit of frequency (1 Hz = 1 wave per second))

HIV (human immunodeficiency virus) a virus most commonly spread by unprotected sex and sharing infected needles; it causes AIDS (acquired immunodeficiency disease)

hydrocarbon a compound, such as is in many fuels, that contains only carbon and hydrogen

hypothesis an idea that explains a set of facts or observations, and is the basis for possible experiments

identical twins twins that developed from a single egg and share the same genetic information

igneous type of rock formed from the solidification of magma

illegal against the law

image picture of an object that we see in a mirror or through a lens or system of lenses

immune system the parts of our bodies that fight disease caused by pathogens such as viruses and bacteria, including the white blood cells

impurity substance inside a liquid, gas or solid, which differs from the chemical composition of the material or compound

inbreeding breeding (mating) with close relatives

infectious disease a disease that is caused by pathogens (such as bacteria and viruses) and can be spread from one person to another

influenza a disease caused by the influenza virus, causing symptoms such as aches and fever

infrared radiation a type of electromagnetic radiation given off by hot objects

inherit derive a feature or characteristic from parents

inherited a feature or characteristic that has been passed on genetically

inoculate introduce a substance, such as a vaccine, into the body to bring about an immune response

intrusive igneous rock formed from magma forced into older rocks within the Earth's crust

joule unit of energy

karyotype the number and appearance of the chromosomes in a cell nucleus

kilowatt unit of power equal to 1000 watts or joules per second

kilowatt-hour (kWh) the energy transferred in 1 hour by an electrical appliance with a power rating of 1 kW

landfill a site where rubbish or waste is dumped

lava molten rock (magma) from beneath the Earth's surface that has erupted from a volcano onto the Earth's surface

Law of Conservation of Energy energy cannot be created or destroyed, but it can be transferred from one type of energy store to another

leachate a solution resulting from leaching, such as waste liquid from mining

legalise change the rules so that an act or substance is no longer against the law

lens a piece of transparent material that refracts light passing through it to form an image; there is a lens in the eye, in a camera, in a microscope and in a telescope

light year the distance travelled by light in one year

lithosphere the rocky outer section of the Earth, consisting of the crust and upper part of the mantle

longitudinal wave a wave in which the oscillation is parallel to the direction of energy transfer

magma molten rock inside the Earth

mantle the semi-liquid layer of the Earth beneath the crust

mass the amount of matter in an object, measured in kilograms (kg)

mass extinction the extinction of a large number of species at the same time

matrix a substance in to which other materials are embedded

mean value an average of a set of data

memory cell a white blood cell that makes antibodies to fight infection caused by a pathogen; it can quickly fight the same pathogen if it should enter the body again

metabolism the chemical processes that occur within a living organism in order to maintain life

metal carbonate a metal compound which contains a combination of one carbon element and three oxygen elements in it

metamorphic a type of rock formed when other rocks are heated and put under a lot of pressure

metamorphose change from one type to another, such as a sedimentary rock becoming a metamorphic rock

micrometre unit of measurement (symbol μm) equivalent to 0.001 mm

mineral solid metallic or non-metallic substance found naturally in the Earth's crust

MMR a vaccine developed to provide children with resistance to the pathogens causing measles, mumps and rubella

monomer a small molecule that becomes chemically bonded to other monomers to form polymers

moon a large natural satellite that orbits a planet

MRSA methicillin-resistant *Staphylococcus aureus* – a bacterial infection that is resistant to many different antibiotics and so is difficult to treat

naked eye using only the eye to look rather than instruments such as a telescope or binoculars

native metals metals that occur naturally

natural selection process by which characteristics that can be passed on in genes become more common in a population over many generations if they help the organism survive

neutron star the product of the explosive transformation of a massive star

nicotine an addictive substance in cigarettes

non-contact force a force that exists between objects that are not touching

non-infectious disease a disease that cannot be passed from one person to another and is due to genetic factors or lifestyle, e.g. cancer and diabetes

non-renewable resource a resource that cannot be renewed in our lifetime, for example, coal, oil and gas

northern hemisphere the half of the planet that is north of the equator

nuclear fusion nuclear reaction in which two small atomic nuclei combine to make a larger nucleus, with a large amount of energy released

nuclear transfer a form of cloning where the genetic material is removed from an unfertilised egg and is replaced with the nucleus from the organism to be cloned

opaque cannot be seen through, not transparent

optic nerve the nerve connecting the eye and the brain

orbit the near-circular path of an astronomical body around a larger body

ore rock from which metal is extracted

organism a living thing

oscillate move back and forth in a regular rhythm

oxidation chemical reaction that increases the amount of oxygen in a compound

ozone layer a layer of gases found high up in the atmosphere that absorbs ultraviolet rays from the Sun

painkiller a drug that suppresses parts of the brain that allow us to feel pain, e.g. paracetamol

parallax method a method of measuring distance to an object, such as a nearby star, by triangulation

parsec (pc) an astronomical unit of distance

passive smoking the inhalation of smoke (second hand smoke) from other smokers

pathogen a disease-causing organism

phagocyte a type of white blood cell that ingests and digests harmful particles such as bacteria

photochemical reaction a chemical reaction initiated by the absorption of energy in the form of light

photosynthesis the process carried out by green plants, in which sunlight, carbon dioxide and water are used to produce glucose and oxygen

photovoltaic effect the process in which two dissimilar materials in close contact produce an electrical voltage when exposed to light or other radiant energy

phytoplankton microscopic plant life, often forming the basis of aquatic food chains

planet a large sphere of rock or gas orbiting a star

pollutant a harmful substance in the environment

polymer a large molecule made up of a very long chain of smaller molecules

polythene polyethylene, the most common plastic, which is used for carrier bags

porcelain a ceramic material made by heating materials, usually including clay, in a kiln to temperatures between 1200 °C and 1400 °C

power amount of energy that something transfers each second, measured in watts

prescription drug a drug prescribed by a medical doctor for medical purposes, such as antibiotics

producer component of a food web or chain that produces its own food (typically a green plant)

protein a large molecule made of one or more chains of amino acids

PVC a type of polymer (short for polyvinylchloride)

range in a series of data, the spread from the lowest number to the highest number

rate a measure of speed or the number of times something happens in a set amount of time

rate of reaction a measure of the speed of a reaction, for example the number of molecules of product produced over a set time

ray model a simple diagrammatic model used to show how light behaves as it reflects off a mirror or passes through lenses

reactivity how vigorously an element reacts in a chemical reaction

reactivity series the ordering of metals by reactivity, with the most reactive at the top

reclamation returning something (e.g. waste land) to a former, better state

recreational drug a drug used for pleasure

recrystallise metamorphic process where grains of atoms or molecules of rock are packed closer together under intense heat or pressure

recycling the process of changing waste materials into something useful

red giant an old star that has expanded greatly and appears red

reducing agent an element or compound that loses (or 'donates') an electron to another substance in a reaction

reduction chemical process that reduces the amount of oxygen in a compound

reflection when a wave, such as sound or light, bounces off a surface

refract change the direction of a wave such as light

refraction a change in the direction of a wave such as light, caused when it enters a material of a different density

refractory ceramics ceramic materials that are able to retain their strength at high temperatures

rehabilitation period during which a person is helped back to health after illness or addiction

reinforcement material included in a composite material for strength

relative motion the motion of an object with regard to some other moving object

relative speed the calculation of the speed of an object with regard to some other moving object

renewable resource a resource that will not run out, for example, solar energy and wind energy

resistance (genetic) an inherited feature of an organism that suppresses the growth or development of a pathogen

respiration the process in living things in which oxygen is used to release the energy from food

retina the back layer of the eye, containing the receptor cells

rock cycle the relationships between different types of rock and the processes that occur to change these over long periods of time

scattergraph a graph of plotted points to show the relationship between two sets of data

scientific notation a way of writing very large (or very small) numbers that makes them easier to deal with in calculations, e.g. 600 000 000 = 6.0 × 10^8 in scientific notation

season a division of the year, marked by changes in weather, ecology and hours of daylight; summer, autumn, winter and spring

sedimentary a new rock formed by compressing small fragments of rock, e.g. sandstone

selective breeding mating of two individuals chosen because of their characteristics, to produce offspring with a combination of desired characteristics

side effect an effect of a drug that is not the main purpose of using the drug, e.g. antibiotics may have a side effect of diarrhoea

smallpox an infectious disease caused by a virus and against which the first vaccine was developed

smelting a method of extracting a metal from its ore

smog fog mixed with pollutant gases

solar panel a series of solar photovoltaic cells that capture the Sun's energy and convert the sunlight into electricity

southern hemisphere the half of the planet that is south of the equator

species group of organisms that can interbreed and produce fertile offspring

spectrum an infinite range of values within a set range

specular reflection mirror-like reflection from a smooth surface, angle of incidence is equal to the angle of reflection

speed formula $speed = \dfrac{distance}{time\ taken}$

star massive, luminous sphere of plasma held together by its own gravity

stationary still, not moving

sterile technique a method used to keep equipment as free from microbes as possible; also known as 'aseptic technique'

stimulant a drug that causes an increase in body systems such as heart rate and breathing rate, e.g. ecstasy and nicotine

stoneware a type of ceramic made from non-refractory clay

subsidence the motion of a surface (usually the Earth) as it shifts downwards

superbug bacteria that are resistant to many different types of bacteria, making them difficult to treat

superposition the overlapping of waves to give a combined effect

sustainable using a resource or process in such a way that it will be available to future generations

symptom a change in the body or mind that indicates that a disease

syncline bowl-shaped layer of rock, where the rock has been forced downwards

synthetic made by a chemical process, not naturally occurring

tar the chemical in cigarettes that causes lung disease

tectonic plate a section of the Earth's crust that slowly moves relative to other plates

temperature the measurement of how hot or cold an object is, usually measured in degrees Celsius (°C)

thermal conduction the transfer of energy by the vibration and collisions of particles of a material, from regions at a high temperature to regions at a low temperature

thermal conductor a material that allows energy to pass through it quickly by the process of thermal conduction

thermal decomposition a chemical change caused by heating when one substance is changed into at least two new substances

thermal equilibrium the point where two systems that were at different temperatures reach the same constant temperature

thermal insulator a material that does not allow energy to pass through it quickly by the process of thermal conduction

time-lapse sequence a series of images are recorded and then played back at a higher frequency

trait a characteristic

translucent a material that lets some but not all light pass through

transparent a material that allows light to pass through

transverse wave a wave in which the oscillations are at right angles to the direction of energy transfer

trisomy a chromosomal disorder characterised by an extra chromosome, e.g. Down's syndrome

trough the opposite of a crest, the minimum or lowest point in a cycle

unbalanced forces opposite forces acting on an object that are not equal

unit of alcohol one unit of alcohol is 10 ml of pure alcohol

unit of electricity one unit of electricity is exactly equal to 1000 watts of power used for 1 hour

upfold a dome-shaped layer of rock that has been pushed upwards

uplift upwards movement of the Earth's surface in response to natural processes such as earthquakes

upthrust a force acting in an upward direction, e.g. on an object in water

vaccination medical procedure, usually by injection, that provides immunity to a particular disease

vaccine weakened form of micro-organisms that are given to bring about immunity to a particular disease

vacuum a space where there are no particles of matter

variation the range of characteristics across individuals of the same group

virus the smallest type of micro-organism; a virus can only replicate inside other living cells

viscous thick (liquid), slow-flowing, glutinous

watt unit of power, or rate of transfer of energy, equal to a joule per second

wavelength the distance along a wave from one point to the next point where the wave motion begins to repeat itself, e.g. crest to crest

weathered rocks, soils and minerals that have been changed over time by factors such as wind and rain

weathering the breaking down of rocks, soil and minerals

weight force of gravity acting on an object

white blood cell cells in the blood that help to fight disease, for example by producing antibodies

wind erosion the breaking down of rocks caused by wind beating against them

withdrawal ceasing to take drugs

yield the amount of useful product, sometimes expressed as a percentage of the total possible amount of product

Index

Index

Acknowledgements

The publishers wish to thank the following for permission to reproduce photographs. Every effort has been made to trace copyright holders and to obtain their permission for the use of copyright materials. The publishers will gladly receive any information enabling them to rectify any error or omission at the first opportunity.

(t = top, c = centre, b = bottom, r = right, l = left)

Cover image © Riyazi/Shutterstock

pp 8-9 Jolanta Wojcicka/Shutterstock, p 8 (t) Khoroshunova Olga/Shutterstock, p 8 (tc) Chris Humphries/Shutterstock, p 8 (bc) Innerspace Imaging/Science Photo Library, p 8 (b) Eye of Science/Science Photo Library, p 9 (t) Sue McDonald/Shutterstock, p 9 (tc) Catmando/Shutterstock, p 9 (bc) Benjamin Albiach Galan/Shutterstock, p 9 (b) Gelpi JM/Shutterstock, p 10 (t) Bartosz Budrewicz/Shutterstock, p 10 (tc) Sue Green/Shutterstock, p 10 (c) Eduard Kyslynskyy/Shutterstock, p 10 (bc) Robynrg/Shutterstock, p 10 (b) John Wollwerth/Shutterstock, p 11 (t) Ian Rentoul/Shutterstock, p 11 (b) Ewan Chesser/Shutterstock, p 13 (t) Menno Schaefer/Shutterstock, p 13 (b) Constant/Shutterstock, p 14 Karen McGaul/Shutterstock, p 15 (t) WaveBreakMedia/Shutterstock, p 15 (b) AFP/Getty Images, p 16 (t) Ludovikus/Shutterstock, p 16 (b) Eduard Kyslynskyy/Shutterstock, p 17 (t) Niels Quist/Shutterstock, p 17 (c) JamesChen/Shutterstock, p 17 (b) BMJ/Shutterstock, p 18 Hemis/Alamy, p 19 (t) Nicku/Shutterstock, p 19 (b) Universal Images Group/Getty Images, p 20 (tl) Foaloce/Shutterstock, p 20 (tc) AnetaPics/Shutterstock, p 20 (tr) Daz Brown Photography/Shutterstock, p 20 (bl) EvaStudio/Shutterstock, p 20 (br) Waldemar Dabrowski/Shutterstock, p 23 (t) T-Design/Shutterstock, p 23 (bl) Lakomanrus/Shutterstock, p 23 (br) Hulton Archive/Getty Images, p 24 Patricia Chumillas/Shutterstock, p 25 (t) Benjamin Albiach Galan/Shutterstock, p 25 (b) Science Photo Library, p 26 Natalia Paklina/Shutterstock, p 27 (t) Pablo Paul/Alamy, p 27 (b) Matej Kastelic/Shutterstock, p 29 (t) Universal Images Group/Getty Images, p 29 (b) BSIP SA/Alamy, p 30 Nemeziya/Shutterstock, p 31 Getty Images, p 32 (t) North Wind Picture Archives/Alamy, p 32 (b) Wildlife GmbH/Alamy, p 33 (t) Frans Lanting, Mint Images/Science Photo Library, p 33 (b) MasPix/Alamy, p 38 (t) Nerthuz/Shutterstock, p 38 (tc) Aleksandr Petrunovskyi/Shutterstock, p 38 (b) PHOTOTAKE Inc./Alamy, p 39 (t) Photographee.eu/Shutterstock, p 39 (tc) Asier Romero/Shutterstock, p 39 (bc) Lenetstan/Shutterstock, p 39 (b) Suzanne Porter/Alamy, p 38-39 Hybrid Medical Animation/Science Photo Library, p 40 Mikfoto/Shutterstock, p 41 Peeravit/Shutterstock, p 42 (t) Danie Nel/Shutterstock, p 43 (t) Anneka/Shutterstock, p 43 (c) Simon Fraser/Science Photo Library, p 44 (t) Hamik/Shutterstock, p 44 (b) Anton Albert/Shutterstock, p 45 Sunabesyou/Shutterstock, p 46 (t) MedusArt/Shutterstock, p 46 (bl) Alik Mulikov/Shutterstock, p 46 (bc) Rangizzz/Shutterstock, p 46 (br) Bashutskyy/Shutterstock, p 48 (b) Diverse Images/UIG/Getty Images, p 49 Photographee.eu/Shutterstock, p 50 (t) Gserban/Shutterstock, p 50 (tc) Imagedb.com/Shutterstock, p 50 (bc) Kontur-Vid/Shutterstock, p 50 (b) Eric Gevaert/Shutterstock, p 51 (t) Pascal Goet Gheluck/Science Photo Library, p 51 (b) Ed Kashi/VII/Corbis, p 52 (t) ZStock/Shutterstock, p 52 (b) ToskanaINC/Shutterstock, p 54 Pavla/Shutterstock, p 55 Dmitrijs Bindemanis/Shutterstock, p 56 Science Photo Library, p 57 (r) Schankz/Shutterstock, p 57 (l) Sciepro/Science Photo Library, p 59 (t) French School/Getty Images, p 59 (b) Berents/Shutterstock, p 60 (t) PHOTOTAKE Inc./Alamy, p 60 (b) Galyna Andrushko/Shutterstock, p 61 (t) Wacpan/Shutterstock, p 61 (b) Anyaivanova/Shutterstock, p 62 (t) Voyagerix/Shutterstock, p 62 (b) Image Point Fr/Shutterstock, p 63 Scott Camazine/Alamy, p 64 Medical-on-Line/Alamy, p 65 (t) Image Point Fr/Shutterstock, p 65 (b) Lowell Georgia/Science Photo Library, p 69 Lune4/Shutterstock, pp 70-71 Lee Prince/Shutterstock, p 70 (t) Ludinko/Shutterstock, p 70 (c) Phil Degginger/Alamy, p 70 (b) Bogumil/Shutterstock, p 71 (t) Papa1266/Shutterstock, p 71 (tc) SciencePhotos/Alamy, p 71 (bc) Barbara Eads/Shutterstock, p 71 (b) NASA/Science Photo Library, p 72 (tl) Papa1266/Shutterstock, p 72 (tc) Jiri Vaclavek/Shutterstock, p 72 (tr) Jiri Vaclavek/Shutterstock, p 72 (bl) Dorling Kindersley/UIG/Science Photo Library, p 72 (bc) Dorling Kindersley/UIG/Science Photo Library, p 72 (br) Dorling Kindersley/UIG/Science Photo Library, p 74 (t) Phil Degginger/Alamy, p 74 (c) Andrew Lambert Photography/Science Photo Library, p 74 (b) KariDesign/Shutterstock, p 76 (l) SciencePhotos/Alamy, p 76 (r) SciencePhotos/Alamy, p 77 Andrew Lambert Photography/Science Photo Library, p 78 (t) Kilukilu/Shutterstock, p 78 (b) Richard Peterson/Shutterstock, p 79 Jan Lipina/Shutterstock, p 80 (t) Jiri Vaclavek/Shutterstock, p 80 (c) Martyn F. Chillmaid/Science Photo Library, p 80 (b) Zelenskaya/Shutterstock, p 82 (t) Rangizzz/Shutterstock, p 82 (b) Ashley Cooper/Visuals Unlimited, Inc./Getty Images, p 83 (t) Prill/Shutterstock, p 83 (b) Awe Inspiring Images/Shutterstock, p 84 (t) Sanit Fuangnakhon/Shutterstock, p 84 (tc) Valentin Agapov/Shutterstock, p 84 (bc) Chaiya/Shutterstock, p 84 (b) Siwasasil/Shutterstock, p 86 (l) Bluesnote/Shutterstock, p 86 (c) Barbara Eads/Shutterstock, p 86 (r) Paul Mayall/Alamy, p 88 (t) Igor Zh./Shutterstock, p 88 (b) Charles D. Winters/Science Photo Library, p 90 Martyn F. Chillmaid/Science Photo Library, p 92 Steve Gorton/Getty Images, p 93 Terry Smith/Rex Features, p 94 (t) JPC-PROD/Shutterstock, p 94 (tc) RCB Shooter/Shutterstock, p 94 (bc) Wasanajai/Shutterstock, p 94 (b) Surakit/Shutterstock, p 96 ChainFoto25/Shutterstock, p 98 BJonesPhotography/Shutterstock, p 99 KPG_Payless/Shutterstock, p 100 (t) John Copland/Shutterstock, p 100 (b) Prill/Shutterstock, p 102 Arina P Habich/Shutterstock, p 103 (t) Lichtmeister/Shutterstock, p 103 (b) David Acosta Allely/Shutterstock, pp 108-109 Mark Garlick/Science Photo Library, p 108 (t) Kativ/iStock, p 108 (tc) Huyangshu/Shutterstock, p 108 (bc) Huguette Roe/Shutterstock, p 108 (b) Alice-Photo/Shutterstock, p 109 (t) Paolo Bona/Shutterstock, p 109 (tc) Guentermanaus/Shutterstock, p 109 (bc) Joy Brown/Shutterstock, p 109 (b) Chris Moody/Shutterstock, p 110 Mark Garlick/Science Photo Library, p 111 Stocktrek Images, Inc./Alamy, p 112 Age Fotostock/Alamy, p 113 (t) Hung Chung Chih/Shutterstock, p 113 (b) V.Schlichting/Shutterstock, p 115 FloridaStock/Shutterstock, p 116 FLPA/Alamy, p 118 M. Pellinni/Shutterstock, p 119 (t) Andrey Shchekalev/Shutterstock, p 119 (t) Wildnerdpix/Shutterstock, p 119 (b) Guentermanaus/Shutterstock, p 120 Huguette Roe/Shutterstock, p 121 Jim West/Alamy, p 126 Orhan Cam/Shutterstock, p 127 (tl) Twonix Studio/Shutterstock, p 127 (tr) Stocktrek Images/Getty Images, p 127 (bl) Siim Sepp/Shutterstock, p 127 (br) Gyvafoto/Shutterstock, p 128 (t) Leene/Shutterstock, p 128 (b) Pasieka/Science Photo Library, p 129 Peter Hulla/Shutterstock, p 130 (t) Ivan Varyukhin/Shutterstock, p 130 (b) Ollie Taylor/Shutterstock, p 131 (t) Lisa S./Shutterstock, p 131 (tc) Sigur/Shutterstock, p 131 (bc) Bortel Pavel-Pavelmidi/Shutterstock, p 131 (b) LesPalenik/Shutterstock, p 133 (t) Pitamaha/Shutterstock, p 133 (b) AFP/Getty Images, p 136 Kevin Schafer/Getty Images, p 137 (t) Smit/Shutterstock, p 137 (b) Elena Yakusheva/Shutterstock, pp 138-139 Standret/Shutterstock, p 138 (t) Mark Owen/Shutterstock, p 138 (tc) Dudarev Mikhail/Shutterstock, p 138 (bc) 2happy/Shutterstock, p 138 (b) Triff/Shutterstock, p 139 (t) Feoktistoff/Shutterstock, p 139 (tc) Stuart G Porter/Shutterstock, p 139 (bc) Keith Publicover/Shutterstock, p 139 (b) FlyingLife/Shutterstock, p 140 Jacek Chabraszewski/Shutterstock, p 142 Stocker1970/Shutterstock, p 143 Juan J. Jimenez/Shutterstock, p 144 Christian Mueller/Shutterstock, p 145 (t) Dmitrydesign/Shutterstock, p 145 (b) Marigo20/Shutterstock, p 146 GIPhotostock/Science Photo Library, p 147 (t) OJO Images Ltd/Alamy, p 147 (b) Justin Kase Zfivez/Alamy, p 148 (t) Mark Owen/Shutterstock, p 148 (b) Ortodox/Shutterstock, p 149 fStop Images – Caspar Benson/Getty Images, p 150 (t) i4lcocl2/Shutterstock, p 150 (b) Bloomberg/Getty Images, p 152 (t) Adrian Hughes/Shutterstock, p 152 (b) Gordon Bell/Shutterstock, p 153 (r) Dorling Kindersley/Getty Images, p 153 (l) Erich Schrempp/Science Photo Library, p 154 NASA, p 155 David Fowler/Shutterstock, p 156 (t) Ktynzq/Shutterstock, p 156 (b) Walter Myers/Science Photo Library, p 158 Triff/Shutterstock, p 159 (l) Mironov/Shutterstock, p 159 (r) Yuriy Kulik/Shutterstock, p 162 Majusko95/Shutterstock, pp 168-169 Luis Abrantes/Shutterstock, p 168 (t) Maxisport/Shutterstock, p 168 (c) Gadag/Shutterstock, p 168 (b) Ron Ellis/Shutterstock, p 169 (t) Cebas/Shutterstock, p 169 (tc) Stephen Mulcahey/Shutterstock, p 169 (bc) Shaun Dodds/Shutterstock, p 169 (b) BJonesPhotography/Shutterstock, p 170 Maria Dryfhout/Shutterstock, p 172 ImagePost/Shutterstock, p 174 (t) Alex Hubenov/Shutterstock, p 174 (b) Auremar/Shutterstock, p 175 Sergey Krasnoshchokov/Shutterstock, p 176 (t) Kukhmar/Shutterstock, p 176 (b) Rob Bayer/Shutterstock, p 178 Martyn F. Chillmaid/Science Photo Library, p 179 Thomas Klee/Shutterstock, p 180 GIPhotoStock/Alamy, p 182 Asaf Eliason/Shutterstock, p 184 Catalin Petolea/Shutterstock, p 185 (t) Edyta Pawlowska/Shutterstock, p 185 (b) Africa Studio/Shutterstock, p 186 Imagedb.com/Shutterstock, p 187 Ffolas/Shutterstock, p 188 (t) Eugene Chernetsov/Shutterstock, p 188 (bl) FedericoFoto/Shutterstock, p 188 (br) DVPhotos/Shutterstock, p 189 Shelby Allison/Shutterstock, p 190 David Hanlon/Shutterstock, p 191 (l) You Can More/Shutterstock, p 191 (cl) Hurst Photo/Shutterstock, p 191 (cr) Sutsaiy/Shutterstock, p 191 (r) Jiang Hongyan/Shutterstock, p 191 (b) PPArt/Shutterstock, p 193 (t) Sheila Terry/Science Photo Library, p 193 (c) Deyan Georgiev/Shutterstock, p 193 (b) SGM/Shutterstock.